THE ETHNIC PROJECT

Stanford Studies in
COMPARATIVE RACE AND ETHNICITY

THE ETHNIC PROJECT

Transforming Racial Fiction

into Ethnic Factions

Vilna Bashi Treitler

Stanford University Press

Stanford, California

Stanford University Press
Stanford, California

Printed in the United States of America on acid-free, archival-quality paper.

Library of Congress Cataloging-in-Publication Data

Bashi Treitler, Vilna, author.
  The ethnic project : transforming racial fiction into ethnic factions / Vilna Bashi
Treitler.
      pages cm--(Stanford studies in comparative race and ethnicity)
  Includes bibliographical references and index.
  ISBN 978-0-8047-5771-3 (cloth : alk. paper)--
  ISBN 978-0-8047-5772-0 (pbk. : alk. paper)
   1. Ethnicity--United States--History. 2. Racism--United States--History. 3. Race
--Social aspects--United States--History. 4. United States--Ethnic relations--
History. I. Title. II. Series: Stanford studies in comparative race and ethnicity.
  E184.A1B273 2013
  305.800973--dc23   2013017962

ISBN 978-0-8047-8728-4 (electronic)

Typeset by Bruce Lundquist in 10.5/15 Adobe Garamond

People are history: Their experiences, feelings, adjustments, imaginings, hopes, uncertainties, dreams, fears, regrets, tragedies, and triumphs compose our past. . . . Our parents and grandparents . . . are worthy of scholarly attention: they have been actors in history, making choices as they left their homelands and settled in America. They helped to transform their adopted country, and in turn, were themselves changed as they became Americans.

Ronald Takaki, *A Larger Memory:*
A History of Our Diversity, with Voices

TABLE OF CONTENTS

ACKNOWLEDGMENTS

"Well, if race isn't biological, then what is it?" Students would ask this question over the many years that I have worked to teach them that race is socially constructed. And I always thought it was wholly insufficient to tell students that race isn't real, but racism is. Surely, as analysts of our social world, we sociologists could come up with something more theoretically sophisticated than simply saying to our students that race is no more than the trope that allows racism to happen. I am especially grateful to those undergraduate students who journeyed with me in the classroom as I moved toward a more complex and satisfying answer to the question, for that journey led me to writing this book.

With my graduate students, I explored and taught them what I call "race theory"—works of writers who had grappled with questions about where race comes from, what it accomplishes, or whether it had structure. I developed a course that I called "Comparative Racial Structures," where I taught (and learned) that what we know about race is best understood in a comparative context, because its transparent and "unreal" nature makes it inordinately difficult to put a finger on race when you're standing right in the midst of it. The lessons I learned from bringing comparative material together for my students are the subject of chapter 2. The ideas behind subsequent chapters of this book were also developed from my experience in teaching students. As I was teaching a course titled "Minority Groups in American Society," I noted that there were similarities among the stories of ethnic and racial conflict that students learned about in the assigned texts. I wondered if they saw them as well, and began to offer an optional paper assignment—if the students caught these similarities, they could ace the paper, and opt out of the final exam. A number of them did, and so I knew I was onto something. This idea became *The Ethnic Project*. I take this opportunity to thank those hardworking undergraduate and graduate students for helping me learn from them even while I was teaching. I give special thanks to three inordinately inspiring young women, Devon Chiapetta, Camille Voitot, and Melody Mills.

I also thank all the scholars who labor to study and write on ethnic history and racial theory. To them I am indebted because it is from these secondary sources that I've learned enough to write theory and historical case studies of my own.

I must acknowledge, too, the memory of Gaunzie Jembere. She was my beloved third-grade teacher at P.S. 156 in Queens, and I was just one of the many little children of color who were lucky enough to learn from her. I name her here because I suppose that she must have been the first to show me that race was a social construction. She taught me that no matter how closed it might have appeared when I was away from her classroom, the world was actually wide open—even to me, a little black girl who at that time knew no one who had even been to college. I think it's no coincidence that her class was the last time I was in a regular classroom; afterward, I was in gifted classes, and later, I skipped two years of high school and earned more degrees than anybody really needs.

I give special thanks to all my writing support systems. These include members of the Writers of Color women's writing group (especially Judith Corbett Carter, Kelly Josephs, Natasha Gordon-Chipembere, and you too, Tzarina Prater, even though you're now far away) who met with me Fridays at the Graduate Center in Midtown Manhattan. Judith and I agree—it is amazing to have a space in the middle of the best city in the world, just for us, full of support and magic. I thank Kristy Wilkerson Johnson for her superior editorial help and extreme generosity. A special flourish is owed to scholar-friends Daphne Lamothe, Kesha Moore, and Manuela Boatcă, who are mistaken in thinking they get more from my friendship with them than I do. I am also grateful to Eduardo Bonilla Silva and Stephen Steinberg who reviewed the proposal for and manuscript of this book and offered advice and words of encouragement. I thank my mother, Vilna Simmons Welch, for constantly wishing that she could help me get this book done. I am overwhelmingly grateful for my children, Jannik and Ariel, for being the glowing, spinning planets in my universe, happily being there for me whenever I got up from the keyboard and more than occasionally pulling me away from it.

Finally, there are not enough words of gratitude in the English language to properly thank my husband Christian. He believed so strongly in this project that he never tired of saying, "Vilna, you've got to write that book!" He also read chapters as soon as they left the printer and then asked all the tough questions that sent me back to my desk; cooked slammin' meals day in, day out, so I would have more time to write; and cared for our boys while teaching them to stay out of the office when "Mama's working." He even has an extensive personal library on Native American nations (including many first prints) from which I borrowed to write ethnic histories. He's a partner with whom my most frequent arguments are about who'll do the dishes (because we always want to save the other from the work!) and who's smarter (because we each believe the other to be). As tough as it was to write this book, it is even more difficult to adequately describe the meaning he has to my work and in my life.

THE ETHNIC PROJECT

BRER THULDY'S STATUE
LIBERTY FRIGHTENIN DE WORLD.
To be stuck up on Bedbug's Island - Jarsey Flats, opposit de United States.

(Only Authorized. Edition.)

Brer Thuldy's Statue, lithograph published by Currier & Ives (1884). Caption: "Liberty frightenin de world: To be stuck up on Bedbug's Island–Jarsey Flats, opposit de United States." Only authorized ed. Source: Museum of the City of New York/Art Resource, NY.

RACISM AND ETHNIC MYTHS

Racial beliefs and practices harm large segments of our population. Yet few of us see society's current state as unnatural or unjust; most deny that race or other structural forces limit the life chances of individuals and groups. We do not believe that our attitudes or actions are based on racial considerations. Instead, race has become commonsense: accepted but barely noticed, there though not important, an established fact that we lack the responsibility, let alone the power, to change. The color line has come to seem a fiction, so little do we apprehend its daily mayhem.

Ian F. Haney López, *Racism on Trial*

The United States has a fabled history of immigration, culturally signified in the sonnet by Emma Lazarus, who implores foreign nations to send "your tired, your poor, / your huddled masses yearning to breathe free, / the wretched refuse of your teeming shore. / Send these, the homeless, tempest-tossed to me, / I lift my lamp beside the golden door!" in a "world-wide welcome" to them all.[1] The sonnet is inscribed on the interior of the pedestal of the "Mother of Exiles" (as the verse names the Statue of Liberty). This iconic sonnet encapsulates the mythos that the United States is a nation built on the labor of immigrants and still welcomes immigrants from around the world. Histories that look at the travails of nonwhites since the inception of the first Thirteen Colonies and on until today could testify that the reality has never quite lived up to the words that Lazarus issued from the Statue of Liberty's "silent lips." Those histories, instead, read as a complex contest for resources, one that was from the beginning contextualized in a language that demarked the deserving from the undeserving, arranging the humans involved into unequal ethnic groups.

The American polity is legendarily characterized as a "melting pot," a nation brought together under Lady Liberty's torch of enlightenment and crown of seven spires (representing the seven continents and seven seas),[2] welcoming the world's "tired" and "poor" who are willing to work or "pull themselves up by their bootstraps."[3] Although people from all over the world have come and still come to "America" (read "the United States") to restructure their lives, they are not all seen as equally endowed with the ability to fit in or become American. For example, the American Protestant Association (APA1) was formed in fearful response to the spread of Catholicism, which they believed was "subversive of civil and religious liberty," in 1842 in Philadelphia, the "City of Brotherly Love." The American Protective Association (APA2, formed in 1887 with an identical agenda) never saw any of its favored legislation passed but claimed two million members in 1895. Members of APA1 were encouraged to swear that they would denounce the Catholic Church, never join a workers' strike with a Catholic, and never knowingly allow a Catholic to join the association; APA2 sought to ban Catholics from elected office, remove Catholic teachers from schools, and make speaking English a prerequisite for citizenship.[4] These sentiments about who made appropriate compatriots were far from isolated. At around the same time, the U.S. government instituted the first of many laws declaring populations inappropriate for immigration, naming the Chinese as the first ethnic/national-origin group to be so deemed. Still, Catholics kept coming, as did the Chinese and other previously undesirable migrants, even though they received unequal welcomes and were not equally considered real "Americans."

But that does not mean that each group would prefer and eagerly adopt the unhyphenated version of the term "(ethnic)-American" in lieu of their other ethnic options, for many are quite fond of and embrace their separate ethnic identities. Well, that is true to a point. We have known for some time that people will change ethnic identifiers as they pick and choose among possible ancestries in order to portray themselves in the most positive light. Mary Waters (1990), in her book *Ethnic Options*, explains how people decide which ethnicities to choose, preferring, for example, to say they are "part-French" but failing to acknowledge that they're also part-Polish.

How do some ethnicities become more desirable and others less so? How were all these ethnic groups incorporated into the American polity and how do we develop legend and lore about who is better than whom? Despite the inequality that persists among ethnic groups in the United States, ethnic conflict is minimal compared to many other parts of the world. How has incorporation occurred with so little ethnic conflict? And what does the process of ethnic group inclusion and the differential outcomes tell us about how our society is organized? Is there a way to explain differences in outcomes that can be reasonably applied to several cases?

Two interrelated histories can provide answers to these questions. The first is a demographic record of the lands that comprise the United States of America, one that involves encounters with people who were living their lives when they were "discovered" by Europeans who chose conquest over community along with voluntary and forced migrations. A chronicle of the inclusion or incorporation of these disparate peoples, the circumstances that brought them here, and what happened to them afterward is helpful in interpreting the commonalities and differences among groups of various ethnicities. The second history explains how these people from the Americas and lands farther away were drawn together into an economically and socially stratified American society. These joint histories frame the ways various groups were differentially integrated into American society. But if incorporation has happened for nearly all groups in U.S. history, why is ethnicity still relevant? My answer is that these histories describe the racial and economic interactions that have kept ethnic, racial, gender, and class divisions alive, allowing them to persist even beyond the births and deaths of generations of now-homegrown "Americans" who remain ethnicized.

We have mostly folkloric histories about who got here and when, and why some succeed and others do not, all retold as if people used only their will and wits to make a living and create a legacy. In these histories we find that some ethnic groups have been able to achieve a kind of racial uplift and have the rest of society think of them with a much-improved racial status. Perhaps the catchy title of Noel Ignatiev's *How the Irish Became White* makes Irish American history the best-known example of racial uplift for persons who were first considered black-equivalents but have since become whitened, but there are other relevant histories (e.g., those of the Chinese and Mexicans). Some achieve true or pseudo-whiteness, and some do not. For example, the Chinese were once so hated that we started closing our borders against them using our first immigration laws; now, Americans of means seek out Chinese children to adopt and love them as their own. Many who we now think of as racially worthy (the Irish, Greeks, Japanese, Chinese, etc.) have started at the racial hierarchy's "bottom" and moved "up" over time. What accounts for the success of those who become our ethnic heroes by reaching status positions higher than the positions they had when first incorporated, while others remain in low status positions and become our ethnic villains? Which groups rise so high as to reach the hierarchy's very top category and become white, and how did they accomplish it? Which ones have not, and why? Physical difference/similarity alone cannot be responsible, because former nonwhite groups (like the Irish and Polish) were also once believed to be wholly racially different in appearance from "white," and some (perhaps the Chinese) seem unable to achieve total whiteness but have achieved mobility nonetheless. What explains this?

ETHNIC PROJECTS

In specific historical moments various outsider groups undertook concerted social action (namely, an "ethnic project") to foster a perception of themselves as "different" from the bottom and "similar" to the top of that racial hierarchy. Ethnic groups are variously successful at this enterprise. Ethnic projects succeed to the degree that the dominant population accepts that the new group is culturally or racially different enough from the hierarchical bottom to merit a recognizable "ethnicity," which itself references the dominant society's use of different racial overtones. If one's project is successful, it provides group members some relief from the pejorative labels, damning prejudices, and exclusionary practices that had originally plagued the group.

Although many ethnic groups have made attempts to achieve "racial uplift" in this way, only a few have been successful. The theory of the ethnic project can be summarized as follows. An ethnic group begins as a collection of a significant number of "outsiders" who poorly fit into the racial frame that is operative at the time of their insertion into their geographic communities. As "strangers," members of the group are first identified as equivalent to the "bottom of the barrel," racially speaking. The European colonizers of North America are the exception: they created the system of racial domination and put themselves at the top; they neither experienced incorporation, nor can they be considered a minority group; and only racial subordinates require incorporation as minority groups.[5] Most ethnic groups incorporated into the United States since the colonial era are looked down upon at the time of incorporation and given very low racial status—this we call "racialization."[6] For example, those nations that occupied the North American landmass before European conquest (variously grouped as a single ethnicity called "Native Americans" or "First Nations") were branded as savages, albeit sometimes "noble" ones. The savage ideation remained, even after some groups (namely the Cherokee and the Choctaw, among others) adapted the ways of transplanted Europeans, giving up their indigenous lifestyles in a futile attempt to preserve their existence and save their own lives. The Europeans who proselytized about the ways of "civilization," and who promised to spare cultural adapters, instead betrayed them. They did the same to those Native American nations who were less culturally malleable. In not so different fashion, albeit with different outcomes, Greek and Polish immigrants were seen as the worst kinds of brutes, uneducable but useful because of their ability to labor at "what would kill a white man."[7]

Ethnic project theory argues that many racialized groups (some immigrant, some native-born) launch similar campaigns for "racial uplift," but specific factors account for a group's success or failure in these efforts. A group's success is predicated on its ability to benefit from the marginalization initially designed to segregate the group and deny its members access to the socioeconomic opportunities and rewards that those at the top of the racial hierarchy are routinely granted.[8] That is, groups that succeed take the racial structure as a given and primarily work to change only their place in it.

Ethnoracial groups hopeful for ethnic project success undertook some subset of activities intended to foster relationships separate from and possibly superior to ethnic nonwhite others. In some cases groups used their workplace and neighborhood relationships with African Americans to show those deemed to be "white" that they were not themselves also "black." They proved themselves to be nonblack by ostracizing and in some cases brutalizing their black neighbors, friends, spouses, children, and coworkers. They separated themselves from supposed racial inferiors by self-segregating their residences, workplaces, and sites of leisure. Many took the added step of forbidding intermarriage between themselves and (only) racial inferiors. They chose to protect and maintain their racial superiority by enforcing a racial labeling that was intended to make the aforementioned racialized/racializing segregation commonsensical. Occupations, neighborhoods, and activities were labeled according to the racial hierarchy—as "white," "civilized," or "cultured" as opposed to "black," "savage," "heathen," or "street." Chinese immigrants in the Mississippi Delta, Mexicans in Texas, and the Irish in the Northeastern United States all had lived among and intermarried with African Americans, yet to achieve racial uplift they decided to segregate themselves residentially, occupationally, and romantically from the "blacks" with whom they had been formerly conjoined and compared.

In their quest for increased racial status, ethnic groups with successful strategies did not threaten to bring down the racial status quo. Successful groups only sought to raise their own status within the hierarchy and did not question the legitimacy of racialized thinking or human hierarchies. For example, Mississippi's Chinese chose to open retail stores and become economic middlemen, refusing to sharecrop any longer alongside African Americans. But neither did they argue against the existence of the sharecropping system, the unfair advantage whites took, or the maltreatment of blacks who were left with sharecropping as their only employment alternative. In similar fashion, the Irish said that they would no longer work with blacks because Irishmen now "did white men's work." In sum, racial status-seekers appeal to the hierarchy's racial superiors regarding their group's racial worth, and they often offer justifications regarding the worthlessness of racial inferiors. Even ethnic groups who have attained "whiteness" and wished to secure their position regularly reassert their superiority. Only Native Americans and African Americans made appeals to the equality of men and women of all races, yet in choosing this (failing) universal human rights strategy to combat racial enmity, they were certainly unrewarded.

Of course, not everyone in a group automatically agreed to compliance. Thus, ethnicized seekers of higher status would commonly institute mechanisms of punishment for those within their own group who would ignore the incipient or ongoing ethnic project and instead trespass over hierarchically lower color lines—through varied attempts to inappropriately fraternize or cooperate with racial "others." For example, Mississippi Delta Chinese would ostracize those in their group who would not break off romantic liaisons with African American mates, spouses, or co-parents. Similar actions took place among Mexican and Irish intermarried groupings. White women who refused to leave the Native American families they joined often were labeled kidnap victims, bringing to their new families violence from white families of origin who wanted their kin "back home."

Unsuccessful ethnic projects, though they may have done many or all of these same things, are characterized by the fact that they have not, to date, gained high racial status for their group. The reason some have not triumphed is that their ethnic project efforts actually threaten the racial status quo. In their endeavors to raise their status, groups who pose a threat to the racial hierarchy itself must fail if those who dominate the racial system are to retain their power.

HOW AN ETHNIC GROUP
COMES TO BE RECOGNIZED AS SUCH

The basis for all these projects is ethnoracial mythmaking, which creates an ethnic group and racial lore to characterize the group. For such mythmaking to succeed, there needs to be a demographically significant subpopulation that is large and sociologically significant enough to require the group to be identified by a name, a creation story that explains how they got here, and a justification for their place in the society into which they are incorporated. This process of mythmaking has several steps that can be identified for the purposes of making it recognizable. Not all steps are required, nor is there a singular sequence to them.

First, societal recognition is available only to those groups that are socially significant enough to count. The history of the United States is in large part a history of the *demography* that recounts how the population of this nation became the admixture it is today. This population includes three categories: (1) persons present on this land well before the current nation was even a thought, for whom the land offered food to eat and a place to call home; (2) persons who arrived voluntarily to labor and find their way in a new land; and (3) persons forced to migrate here, whether pushed from their own lands by violence and hardship or forced by contract or enslavement to provide labor on this land in exchange for survival. Chronicling the demography of a nation is not a mere counting exercise. We must know who someone is in order to count them, tally their characteristics and historical events, and tell their story. This in turn requires decision making about which of their characteristics are salient. Which characteristics and events "count," and how do we weigh them to decide what makes up a group and what facts are relevant to their history?

Another step is *naming*. We believe ethnicity to be created by a group's own process of cultural production, but the truth is that not all groups get to name themselves. Think of American "Indians," or immigrant "West Indians," so named because of Columbus's geography errors. Neither group named themselves, nor do they have the power to erase the mistakes. This is why I describe this ethnic creation process as one that takes place in the context of *racialization*. Ethnic projects are not merely about the creation of an ethnic identity, for many of these groups are not actually embracing the ethnicity they have chosen but rather one that was imposed on them. Think of the ways we create amalgamations of many so-called American Indian nations, or of West Indian/black Caribbean persons from islands so multitudinous and varied that they speak different languages and emerged from different colonial histories. Persons in dominant races who never cared what those people called themselves long ago snatched from them their original names and applied names that fit the dominant way of thinking.

A third step: *characterization*. This is where one might recognize such myths as those meant to convince that upward mobility may be achieved by hard work and moral righteousness (a.k.a. the "bootstrap" or "model minority" myths) or that some groups are more prone to drunkenness or criminal activity. It is characterizations of this kind (lodged against "savages" and "heathens") that created races in North America.[9]

Counting, naming, and characterizing groups are all steps in the process that sociologists call *incorporation*. Are groups welcomed, embraced, accepted, included, integrated, blended, or assimilated? Tolerated or ignored? Marginalized, segregated, rejected, "rehabilitated," ostracized, or annihilated? By whom are they embraced, tolerated, or rejected? What power does the dominant element have to disseminate and popularize their assessments? How much control, agency, and responsive power does the subordinate group have? Thus, two histories are relevant and conjoined: the history of the lives of those in the group; and the history of their absorption, offering perhaps related, perhaps different stories of the systematic ways generations of "these people" are incorporated into a social order.

Together in the United States, these demographic and social incorporation histories describe a register of interactions that have created and kept alive ethnic and racial (and related gender and class) divisions among us, allowing them to persist through the births, lives, and deaths of generations of home-grown but still ethnicized and racialized "Americans." Even as we presume to blend subsequent waves of offspring and foreign-born newcomers into this na-tion, we continually recreate an economically and socially stratified society of subgroups—some of which we create out of whole cloth when no such group "existed" before. Why are people in the United States the "Americans" when the Americas cover two continents? Why do only some of those in the United States actually get to embrace the "American" moniker? There were people who lived on land in Arizona and Texas even before Arizona and Texas existed, and now that these states exist, why do we call the people who have never moved "Mexicans" instead of "United Statesians"? What are "Indians"? What are "Afro-Americans"? How did such stratifications come to be?

RACISM BEGETS ETHNIC MYTHS, ETHNIC MYTHS BEGET ETHNIC PROJECTS

Sociological theory about ethnicity suggests that group members who share culture and heritage form their own ethnicities and assert their own ethnic identities. By contrast, the theory says, racial groups are formed when outsiders decide what characteristics define each group and who is in it. But the reality of ethnic group formation in North America is that ethnic groups are formed in a racial context, meaning that the group itself does not always have control over how they are read by those in the larger society. The history of the United States of America is full of moments of creating and applying ethnic labels to groups of people who had different characterizations for themselves than the ones the larger society is encouraged to believe, and it is the racially dominant group that controls the ethnoracial landscape.[10] They project ethnic and racial rationales in order to protect their high-status position in the racial status quo. Newcomer ethnicities become salient when a significant number of "outsiders" (persons who don't fit well into the racial frame operative at the time) join their geographic communities. It is as "strangers" that they are first identified as hav-ing a status equivalent to the "bottom of the barrel," racially speaking. Many ethnic groups we now think of as white have started at the bottom and then moved "up" the racial hierarchy.

Once created, ethnic groups may either embrace their new assignment, effectively creating an identity that they're willing to embrace, or they may actively struggle against the characterization imposed upon them by society's majority. Once they choose a form of (in)action, they have at hand a number of tools to use to invoke new characterizations of their ethnic identity. These actions form the basis of an ethnic project.

All ethnic groups are initially racialized. Perhaps this is why we confuse and conflate race and ethnicity—for in the long view, both race and ethnicity involve identity creation in the context of racialization. But one can at the same time be a racial object and hold one or more ethnic identities. Indeed, one might fail to name an ethnicity for oneself, but no one in the United States is allowed to be without a race.[11] Since racialization cannot be avoided one (or one's group) must engage it. In their responses to ethnoracialization—a process that has most new ethnic groups enter at the bottom of the racial hierarchy—a group likely chooses to recreate their ethnicity in a way that can serve as a counterweight to the severely limiting racial characterizations they are assigned.

I have argued elsewhere (and will restate in the following chapter) that ethnicity can even be read as a type of racial marker, a placeholder in the ordered listing of racial categories that comprise the racial hierarchy of the United States.[12] In the United States today, the inequality among ethnic groups is congruent with the way North Americans structure their *racial* hierarchy. The history of most ethnic groups is truly a tale of their racial inclusion. Newcomers to the United States are labeled so that groups of outsiders can be aware—and also beware. The ethnic lore about these groups is based on a racialized fiction about their origins, prospects, culture, and physical appearance that indicates their status position.

Normally, upon first encounters, new groups find themselves at the bottom of the racial hierarchy. Even those who were successful in their ethnic projects were racially denigrated in the first instance. Indeed, their ethnic label becomes nearly synonymous with the bottom of the racial hierarchy, of late identified as "black," where the position of privilege is fixed as "white." However, I argue that while the commonly known and broad racial categories (like "white" and "black") are fixed, ethnicity itself is far more flexible. Some groups have been able, in certain circumstances, to manipulate this flexibility enough to change the racial connotation of their ethnic label. They do so by controlling their economic and social position; undertaking ethnic "marketing" campaigns to change the public image their ethnic labels connote; and creating a new ethnic identity for themselves, which also creates distance from the bottom of the racial hierarchy.

While many ethnic groups have made attempts to achieve "racial uplift" in this way, only a few (like the Irish, Chinese, Jews, and Italians) have been successful. Ethnic projects succeed to the degree that the dominant population accepts that the new group is culturally or racially different enough from the hierarchical bottom to merit a recognizable "ethnicity," which itself references the dominant society's use of different racial overtones. If one's project is successful, it provides group members some relief from the pejorative labels, damning prejudices, and exclusionary practices that had originally plagued the group.

By contrast, some groups have a more uneven record of achieving racial uplift, while others altogether fail. A group's failure to achieve uplift may be traced to several factors. Foremost among these are efforts to dismantle the racial status quo, the launch of campaigns to appeal to the wrongheadedness of human hierarchies, and the failure to use the tools of racial denigration against ethnic others in order to look superior by contrast and in this way increase one's own group status. Ironically, what I am suggesting is that even something as "radical" as the public embrace of our common humanity apparently is a tool far too weak to dismantle the racial order—at least that is what the test of history has found. There seems to be no way out of this conundrum: one may become a racializer, even a racist, and be rewarded for it; but a group that both embraces human difference and equally values all human beings will likely be punished for such progressive and enlightened thinking—particularly if they broadcast these ideas while holding a position at the racial nadir.

Racialized societies are inherently hierarchical—the *purpose of race* is to assign differential value to human lives. Human differences exist without race, but race or racial thinking is surely required in order to put a worth on human differences. Where hierarchies exist (racial or otherwise) the higher strata are the most desirable. Groups in hierarchical societies naturally would seek to ascend the hierarchy and attain more desirable positions to improve their social, economic, and political positions, while those already at the top work to maintain their positions. Relatively powerless newcomers to hierarchical systems like these are incorporated into the lower strata, at least until they figure out how the system works and form their own responses to their incorporation. Then they too vie for increased status, jostling for higher positions against others already ranked in the hierarchy. This is the crux of a group's ethnic project.

Ethnicity and race are not wholly distinct, but neither are they interchangeable. While the differences between these systems are elaborated upon in the next chapters, it is useful to make one important distinction here: race is an *ascribed* set of character traits with which individuals and groups are *labeled* by others. Thus ethnicity is understood to be most often *asserted*, or *claimed*, by the individual or group in question. Racial assignment in the United States is pro forma. Confirming this is the frequently posed but rather insensitive question, "What are you?" or worse, "No, but where are you *really* from?" These questions are lodged repeatedly at only a few people who are expected to assist the inquirer in assigning the racially ambiguous or "foreign-looking" respondent to the appropriate box. The sociological realm has treated racialization as a top-down process that almost seems to be some amorphous entity (called "society" by many who otherwise grasp for a better term). But society is comprised of real persons, and the ones racialized are just as real. One theoretical group racializes, the others receive and perhaps resist racialization. But racialization is neither silently nor inconsequentially imposed.

Ethnic group responses to being racialized stand on two presumptions: first, *racialization* by definition requires downgrading the status of some in order to uplift others; and, second, the response to being the target of downgraded racialization is to seek higher status. Those painted with a racial brush do not just stand there and silently allow it to occur—they act, and such actions may be mapped on a sociohistorical timeline. Perhaps we give so much credit to the overwhelming power of race that—except for large-scale movements like the abolitionist movement, or the civil rights movement—we downplay the less successful actions undertaken by groups who resist racialization. Perhaps because we have had little public recognition of alternative theories, we have put far too much store in social myths like "assimilation," "pulling oneself up by the bootstraps," and other ethnicity-focused folkloric variants of Horatio Alger tales. Horatio Alger was a late-nineteenth-century novelist who actually wrote about those who were down-and-out and then rescued by wealthy patrons. Yet he was largely redrawn as a figure who penned tales about heroes that overcame obstacles, corrected their impulses, and, by the end of his stories, are on the road to success because of their moral righteousness. The message, then, is that whatever the obstacles, the individual can triumph by living an exemplary life. Alger's stories appeared at the peak of European immigration, and the immigrant represented the historical enactment of an Alger story. Social scientists projected the Alger viewpoint, which became a precursor for scientific tales about how assimilation occurs. Thus ethnic groups have been deemed either ethnic heroes or ethnic villains.[13]

This theory about the importance of ethnic projects in reifying race is not at all meant to downplay the importance of structural forms of racism and unequal opportunity that have aided in generating and sustaining inequality in the United States among racial and ethnic groups. The proportion of blame to be attributed to structural and institutional forces behind perpetuated inequality can hardly be underestimated. But this book argues that what we call "institutional racism" is not the only culprit in perpetuating racial inequality, and we individually and within our social (ethnic) groups contribute to the perpetuation of racial falsehoods. These racial fictions do not persist because we are all members of hate groups. Our racial mythology would have died long ago if regular folk had no role in buying into racial systems and perpetuating them. While I am not saying that racialization is a process completely within the control of an ethnic group, neither would I say that we have no agency in or ability to respond to the way racialization occurs in our society. This theory of the ethnic project, and the empirical investigation supporting it presented here, are meant not to erase the importance of social structure in the human hierarchies we create out of race and ethnicity but only to rebalance the scales by allowing a focus on what we collectively do to reify these systems. That is, every day we perform and remake (or socially construct) our races and ethnicities and act on behalf of our own ethnoracial group or are perceived by others to have done so. Inequality among races and ethnicities is to some degree directly attributable to actors who struggle for higher ethnoracial status.

Sociologists have a role in obscuring the ways ethnic thinking promotes racial hierarchy, and some actively contribute to the racialization process. That is, a problematic ideation exists in much of the work by sociologists on the mobility of groups of individuals that see themselves as ethnically related to one another, especially when sociologists explain ethnic group upward mobility as resulting from the strivers' ethnic culture. Sociologists similarly use cultural arguments (oftentimes mixed in with references to structural obstacles, but reliant upon culturally based reasoning nonetheless) to explain why ethnic groups who are at the bottom of the socioeconomic hierarchy stay there. The inclination to write this way is iconic in the landmark writings of Nathan Glazer, Daniel Patrick Moynihan, and Norman Podhoretz, but may also be found in the works of contemporary writers. Followers in this classic tradition include Dinesh D'Souza, Thomas Sowell, William Julius Wilson, Alejandro Portes, and Jennifer Lee. As Toni Morrison explained in her 1973 *Time* magazine article titled "On the Backs of Blacks," "In race talk the move into mainstream America always means buying into the notion of American blacks as the real aliens. Whatever the ethnicity or nationality of the immigrant, his nemesis is understood to be African Americans."[14] She notes that every immigrant group to enter the United States steps on the backs of African Americans in order to rise above them. A study of the ethnohistorical record shows her to be correct—antiblackness appears to be a necessity under the U.S. racial regime. The only way to change this is to change the regime. Surely change is possible, but it requires withdrawing from the game of ethnic "king of the hill"—the contest where groups threaten and withdraw from one another in order to better compete for status superior to the others in the game. Unfortunately, the prognosis found in the histories presented in this book is that for the United States, the game is built into the nation's political and cultural DNA, and it seems ineradicable and therefore unending. The real regime-changer we need—a multiethnic coalition standing up for equal consideration for all humans—seems by contrast to be a progressive's pipe dream.

We make ethnic lore to explain to one another the characteristics of any group of people, be they Irish, or Latina, or Terrorists,[15] but we struggle to describe a group without reference to where they fit in the socioeconomic or politicultural hierarchy. This understanding of how they "fit in" is the key to their racialization. What we know about ethnic groups—all that we've ever known about them—is what we know about them *racially*. In the United States, what we know and report about any given ethnic group has much to do with how we talk about that ethnic group's racialization process—namely, ethnic myths are in large part, if not strictly, racializing myths. We create these myths about ethnic groups themselves but also about who "we" are (as Americans, as a society, as a "norm" against which others are measured). Moreover, ethnic groups' identities are formed in concert and conversation with the racial views about the group. The ethnic groups themselves read the racial writing about them and rethink who they are by reflecting on the racialization they are currently experiencing and that which they experienced in the past.

Each ethnic group has the power to respond to their racialization. Indeed, the cases presented here will show that ethnic groups do respond, launching repeated and reiterative campaigns to educate and reeducate the racializing masses about who they really are, with the intent to improve their reputations and increase their racial status. We have tended to read these variously as identity movements, but they might also be read as active responses to their racialization. I use these pages to reinterpret ethnic history in light of the racial developments occurring during the time of their incorporation. In sum, ethnic groups are organic—who comprises the group, how group members see themselves, and how others perceive them are all fluid, not fixed, characteristics. Ethnic assertions, choices, and group (not personal) identities, then, might be thought of as small-scale character campaigns. These campaigns are carried out by persons aligned with ethnic groups who openly, publicly proclaim their pride in being part of them.

Understanding ethnoracial lore in this way allows me to do a couple of things: to see race where others have not seen it before, even as they may have talked about race but not used the label; and to see the social *agency* (the dynamic power social groups have and use to draw their images on the society's canvas) where others have seen a more passive "identity" politics. External processes are taking shape in places sociologists have understood as more internalized (except when such processes have become so extreme as to cause them to be labeled identity *movements*). The ethnic group identity call and response—again, an iterative process that can be historically traced and compared to the group formation process and identity responses of others—is what I call an "ethnic project." The chapters that follow engage the ethnic histories of Irish, Italian, Jewish, Chinese, Mexican, Afro-Caribbean, Cherokee, Choctaw, Nez Percé, and African American ethnic groups to show how ethnic projects (or campaigns for increased racial status) were waged and how their efforts were variously rewarded as groups were racially reevaluated, or not. In the end, racial uplift does indeed come on the backs of African Americans, who are throughout American history largely denigrated by the other ethnic groups. Reading the historical record here, one might say that whitening is exactly rooted in behavior that distances from and denigrates African Americans. (Note that here I do not mean "blacks," but I specifically mean the ethnic group we constantly reinvent using ever-evolving racializing constructs—like the racial segregation of workplaces, occupations, and domiciles—and rules of hypodescent in the face of hundreds of years of admixture.)

We need look no further than at our own actions to understand our continued failure to undermine the rigid racial hierarchy that plagues the United States of America. We reshape and reembrace the fallacy of race because it benefits most of us to do so. Play the ethnoracial game well and your group can rise in status, although it requires publicly denigrating others that the group decides are beneath them. But questioning the rules of the game, or the value and logic of playing it, leads to punishment.

We no longer need to question why this illogical social construction won't just die and go away. For it to die we have to learn to stop using the tools of race as we play ethnic "king of the hill" with our identities, cultures, and origins. We even play the ethnic project with the "Mother of Exiles," the Statue of Liberty that towers in the Hudson River between New Jersey and New York City. The idea of the statue was first developed in the mind of its true creator, the French scholar and activist Edouard Laboulaye. Laboulaye was chairman of the French Anti-Slavery Society, an organization devoted to celebrating freedom of slaves where they have been liberated, and promoting freedom in the nations where human enslavement still existed. The organization provided food and clothing for freed slaves in the United States, and the women's division of the Anti-Slavery Society (headed by Laboulaye's wife) raised funds and made the clothes donated to the former slaves. It was in 1865, the year the United States ended its reign over the trade in human bodies from the African continent, that Laboulaye thought of and proposed the idea of the gift of this statue to the United States.[16] He hoped to have the project done in the ten years that remained between 1866 and the United States' centennial celebrations, seemingly intending to conjoin black freedom with freedom and independence for the United States. The linking of these ideas is the topic of the political cartoon reprinted at the start of this chapter; its creator, Thomas Worth, posits that the statue is "Frightenin De World," and notes that in its recognition for black freedom will stand "opposit de United States" [sic] instead of within it. That Liberty is a Lady meant to welcome freedom for *black* men, women, and children is a bit of history that is lost to the average tourist who visits the statue's site. Americans are taught that Liberty welcomes the immigrant, the "ethnic" one might say, and not that she welcomes to the fold the free black offspring of former slaves over whose graves she watches.[17] We are not taught that Laboulaye's antislavery ideas led to Lady Liberty's creation; instead the statue's meaning is refashioned to support myths about our love of immigrants of all ethnicities. Did we not construct an ethnic project for her, raising her status by changing the lore about her formerly black origins and meaning, whitening her, too, so that she may welcome those ethnic groups we also see as formerly black and now also whitened?

Looking Backward, cartoon by Joseph Keppler, published in *Puck* magazine (1893). Caption (missing from image): "They would close to the new-comer the bridge that carried them and their fathers over." Source: Art Resource, NY.

CHAPTER 2

HOW ETHNIC AND RACIAL STRUCTURES OPERATE

If you want to understand how race works in American politics and society, you would do well to attend to ethnicity.

Victoria Hattam, *In the Shadow of Race*

There is not a country in world history in which racism has been more important, for so long a time, as the United States. . . . If racism can't be shown to be natural, then it is the result of certain conditions, and we are impelled to eliminate those conditions.

Howard Zinn, *A People's History of the United States*

THE ETYMOLOGY OF ETHNICITY

Surely, for as long as humans have been on the planet, we have formed family-like groups, created culture, honored our ancestry, named ourselves and our lands, and taught our names and cultural practices to our descendants. But I would hesitate before I call this "ethnicity," for the etymology of the terms "ethnic" and "ethnicity" hardly reflects such benign ideas about human constellations of heritage and identity.

The use of the word "ethnic" as a noun may be traced back to the fourteenth century, and its use as an adjective goes back to the fifteenth century.[1] In the *Merriam-Webster Dictionary* the first definition of "ethnic" is "heathen," which is linked to the Greek *ethnikos* (meaning "heathen") and the Latin *ethnicus* (meaning "heathen" or "pagan"). In Middle English the word "ethnic" denoted persons outside of the Judeo-Christian family of faiths. The word is also traced back to the Greek word *ethnos*, meaning "nation." The related term "ethnology" traces back to 1828 and refers to the anthropological discipline focused upon dividing humans into races and tracing their origins, cultures, relations, and characteristics. When the adjective "ethnical" emerged in the English language, it was born in the era of social Darwinism. This idea applied to human groups Charles Darwin's evolutionary theories about how the better-adapting species within a genus will thrive over successive generations.[2] "Ethnical" was probably most famously used in 1877 in ethnologist Lewis H. Morgan's book *Ancient Society,* where he identified "savagery," "barbarism," and "civilization," the three sequential "ethnical periods" of human development. *The Dictionary of Races or Peoples* published in 1911 by the U.S. Immigration Commission was likely the first to call cultural differences "ethnical."[3] The term "ethnicity" came into more common usage shortly after the end of World War II, but it wasn't until well after 1960 that the word could be found in U.S. English dictionaries.[4] It came into widespread use among anthropologists after 1971 in a departure from the use of the term "tribe."[5] References to "ethnicity" sprung into our collective and public consciousness in the 1970s post–civil rights era, as groups vying for public recognition jumped on the ethnic bandwagon. Seeing the success won by African Americans in forcing recognition of their group as deserving of equal treatment and even respect, other ethnic groups similarly vied for political and civil recognition. Social movements for Chicanos, Asians, Puerto Ricans, and Native Americans, as well as for white ethnic groups like Jews, Italians, Poles, and the Irish, followed.[6]

Thus the idea of ethnicity has perhaps always been tainted with notions of hierarchy, even if today in North American English we use the term to simply describe one's culture and heritage. The most useful definition of "ethnicity" that conforms to our contemporary and more benign use of the term is arguably Richard Schermerhorn's. He describes an ethnic group as "a collectivity within a larger society having real or putative common ancestry, memories of a shared historical past, and a cultural focus on one or more symbolic elements defined as the epitome of their peoplehood."[7] Examples of these symbolic elements are kinship patterns, geographic concentration, religious affiliation, language, and physical differences. If one knows about an ethnic group's ancestry and cultural symbols, one is knowledgeable about what markers connote their ethnicity. If I asked you to identify a group of people and told you that they are presumed to be dark in skin tone; were largely concentrated in the Southern United States prior to 1970; believe their people descend from persons who traveled from the African Continent involuntarily even if, more often than not, they cannot pinpoint the national origin of their ancestors with any certainty; identify in great numbers with the Baptist faith; founded the music tradition known as "jazz" and are known for "soul music" and "soul food"; and that other Americans tend not to intermarry with them, your mind would conjure up the ethnic group "African Americans."

Schermerhorn adds that ethnic groups are "self-conscious"; they see themselves as distinct. Someone born in the mainland United States of Puerto Rican parents might call himself "Puerto Rican," even if he does not "look" Puerto Rican and even if he has never been to Puerto Rico.[8] Ethnicity is the internal assertion of one's membership—that is, the members of an ethnic group have decided for themselves that they belong to that group. But there are instances when race trumps ethnicity. Contemporary thought seems to have forgotten the race-tinged etymology of ethnicity or Schermerhorn's admonition that cultural difference is not what makes us aware of ethnic groups, but that subjugation is at play in society's consciousness about any group within it.[9]

Perhaps an analogy would be useful here. Think of a racial paradigm as a chest of drawers, and think of ethnicities as the contents of the drawers. Generally a chest of drawers has a fairly rigid structure, but it is not made of stone, and its design can differ according to the woodworkers who designed and constructed it. There are many different kinds of chests of drawers, and one might think of these different kinds of chests as different kinds of racial paradigms operative in different times and places. Perhaps some chests have drawers that might be wholly removed. If you think of racial categories as the drawers themselves, then it is fitting to see the removal of the U.S. Census category "mulatto" as analogous to the removal of a drawer, but said removal does little to change the integrity of the chest, or racial paradigm, as a whole. Other sorts of chests are possible, too. Imagine a chest where not all the drawers are the same size; for instance, the top drawers have space for fewer groups (say, ethnic groups considered racially white); and the bottom drawers are larger and contain many more groups (of nonwhites). Or, perhaps, you might imagine a chest with drawers grouped together in clusters, with a set of top, middle, and bottom drawers. In this chest, both the drawers themselves and the clusters of drawers are hierarchically arranged. The "best whites" get the topmost drawer; lesser whites get the lower, white drawers; and all white drawers are above the drawers that hold yellow, brown, and black races.

Racialization is the idea that people and the groups to which they are considered to belong are judged according to the prevailing racial theories at the time of the judgment, and in ways that envelop them in a racial dialogue, ignoring preexisting divisions that may have preceded their racial incorporation.[10] The racialization process assigns a group to a particular drawer, which is normally the bottom drawer for newcomer groups, as Joseph Keppler's political cartoon *Looking Backward* (shown at the start of the chapter) illustrates. It shows former immigrants who have "made it" now barring newcomers thought to be beneath them in social standing. In other words, those ethnic groups who have reached the upper drawers bar from acceptance newcomers believed to be beneath them in stature, a belief reinforced by the very existence of the racial hierarchy that gives these gatekeepers the high perch from which they may look down upon others. It does not seem to matter that the achievers have similar origins; they now have status high enough to reinforce and even manipulate the system to their benefit while using it to denigrate others, and this is precisely what they do.

Still, in modern parlance we like to think that in the "postracial age," we have come to understand ethnic groups as not inherently different in human value, but instead only culturally or phenotypically different from one another. But we may become cognizant of the hierarchies we create among ethnicities when we compare across ethnicities in different racial drawers—for example, in comparing Mexicans to Irish, or African Americans to Italians. Ethnicities comprise the organizing system for people inside the drawers. You might think of your own chest of drawers as simply a way to hold your clothes, but there is a structure to it that makes sense to you. Putting socks together with jeans and T-shirts mixed in with underpants, well that is just crazy talk! Ethnic systems in racialized societies operate the same way, and ethnic groups in these systems band together to move themselves into the top drawers and keep the other groups beneath them, for there certainly cannot be room in the top drawer for all. The ethnic project is the plan for taking one's group to a higher level.

Ethnic projects perpetuate racism because in this system groups tend to be concerned only with raising their own status, questioning neither that people are organized in hierarchically organized drawers nor that the chest of drawers exists at all; worse, there seems little immediate reward to an individual ethnic group to make efforts to dismantle the chest itself. Instead, the quest for higher status reinforces acceptance of the drawer system, for groups' efforts are put only toward protesting their position and reaping the immediate rewards thereof.

UNDERSTANDING RACE AS A SOCIAL STRUCTURE

Sociologists say race is "socially constructed." This means two things: first, that we have constructed race out of whole cloth, or made it up; and second, that once we have made it, race becomes a free-standing social structure that shapes human interaction. Humans have indeed made up race, for there is no such thing if by that we mean a vector of characteristics that definitively mark all the members of one such grouping to the exclusion of all other humans. There are people of the "black race" that have dark skin, but some "blacks" look almost "white"; at the same time, some people with very dark skin, like South Asians, would not everywhere be considered "black." Most people with blue eyes are thought to be "white," but there are others not considered "white" who also have blue eyes. There are whites with kinky hair, and blacks with curly, wavy, or straight hair. With each example we discover that there is no single defining characteristic that marks any one group exclusively as a race that is not shared by persons outside of that racial group. Exclusive racial categories simply do not exist. If races cannot be exclusive, to hold onto the idea of race we must force differences to appear where they cannot logically be sustained.

Neither is it possible that an individual's genetic or biological makeup makes them identifiably one race and not another. There is no blood or organ test that will definitively assign a person to one race and no other. There is no gene that one would share only with the members of one's "race" and not with the members of any other "race"; nor is there one genetic trait that can concretely identify one's race. There is no way to concretely and uniquely establish in which race an individual must be placed, so to hold onto the idea of race we must then fabricate ideologies about who belongs where.

Belief in the ability to scientifically categorize humans follows a belief in positivism, which itself is only a belief that knowledge comes from scientific methods empirically applied to human behavior. (No such "belief" can be proven to be true, no matter how doggedly we behave as if it is so.) Race is socially constructed, as are many human phenomena, like sex or national identity. We mistakenly think of these things as "natural" and therefore "real" simply because they are believed to be set at the time of one's birth and unchanging. But neither of these things is set in stone, for humans are not so scientifically classifiable. While we behave as if nationality and the citizenship it confers are meaningful, these identifiers are linked to a given human being at birth solely because we give significance to where one's mother happened to be when one left the womb. (If one was dropped elsewhere on the planet, one's personal identification with a different nation could happen just as easily.) Similarly, the line between the sexes is often blurrier than we are led to believe. Even if genital criteria are the only factor in how people fit into unique sexual boxes, even those criteria are not always clear. Surely we know acquiring gender is a far more complicated process than having one's genitalia labeled. Race is an even more slippery concept than sexual categories. While national borders exist, and sexual categories useful for human reproduction exist, racial categories are completely inconsistent social fabrications. Neither the racial categories within which one can be placed nor the criteria with which one can be racially typed are consistent. No racial category is truly exclusive. Not only is this true of a single nation's ideology of race, but race is defined inconsistently across the globe. Salient racial categories differ among nations: for example, a census in Rio de Janeiro lists far more categories than one in Los Angeles. People may easily change categories simply by crossing a border: someone considered "black" in New York City might not be so in San Juan.

When we say that race is a social structure, we mean it is a set of superstitions and folk beliefs that we shored up with ideologies and pseudoscientific methods. We then distributed those beliefs around the world. Since scientists are humans like the rest of us, they fall prey to ideologies too, so there are social and natural scientists who still debate the verity of race, express belief in races, or devote their careers to searching for the evidence of the existence of race.[11] The overwhelming preponderance of evidence asserts that racial differences among humans are specious, fallacious, even entirely made up.

Still, we have much to learn from studying how and why we humans persist in differentiating ourselves from one another.[12] Some social scientists believe that by continuing to write about and research racial issues we merely perpetuate the collective myth, thereby giving strength to the fallacious arguments about the existence of racial difference.[13] The persistence of racial thinking means that race is a factor that continues to divide us. Ignoring race in order to hasten its "declining significance" is equivalent to living with its evils while hoping it goes away on its own. Those like Thomas Sowell, William Julius Wilson, and Dinesh D'Souza, who made careers of declaring the subject of race invalid, miss the mark by throwing out the realities of racism along with the validity of race.[14] Racism cannot survive without a system in which racial differentiation and hierarchy exist. The categories remain with us because they tell us to whom racism should be applied.

Other scholars believe that even if we cannot truly study "race"—since it does not exist—we should study *racism,* the systematic ways we reward and punish those of different "races." Racism shapes the life chances of the group so raced. It may be a matter of life and death to decide who has the propensity or even the right to work, eat, and live well and with what degree of freedom. It may be easier to study racism than anything else related to race, for the inequality that results can readily be measured, and said measures can be used as tools to point to racism and thereby combat it. Perhaps in the very long run, antiracist measures will aid the quest to eliminate altogether the idea of race, but completely ridding us of racial thinking is not the immediate goal. The important question is less whether race is real or fantasy, or whether racism is lessening in importance or only changing its face; let us focus instead on what ways we make race a reality, and work to discard the tools continually used to reconstruct it.[15] We do not have to live with racial thinking—we invented it and we can discard the invention. Racial ideology did not always exist; it emerged only in the sixteenth century when racial fictions were dispersed by those who sought to justify their perceived right to dominate over others that they, in some cases, had not even ever encountered face to face. Racial folklore was certainly not prevalent until colonialism in the nineteenth century; by then, the widespread distribution of these falsehoods (now conjoined with pseudoscience and politico-economic domination that "proved" them "valid") gave the ideas a reliability that they did not previously have. Thus, in the span of only about 150 years, local ideas of racial folk wisdom became part of our collective racial worldview.[16] As Audrey Smedley explains, while humans have a long history of making derogatory and even animalistic statements about other human groups, these ideas are not identical to the kind of institutionalized and systematic concept that race has become.

"Race" is a knowledge system, a way of knowing, perceiving, and interpreting the world and the human beings that walk upon it. Every culture has its own ways of perceiving the world in terms that simultaneously draw from cultural-historical experiences of difference and reflect contemporary social values, relationships, and conditions. Because the ideology of race has a unique birth and history in the United States of America, the American way of seeing humans as racial subjects has unique significance.[17] But each population constructs race in its own way.

When Stephen Steinberg writes that ethnoracial myths are socially constructed, he means that "they arise in specific times and places, in response to identifiable circumstances and needs, and they are passed on through processes that are readily observed."[18] Racial ideas may be made up out of whole cloth, but they are also based in social, political, or economic necessities. Socially constructed matter can be deconstructed, in a sense, by tracing the components that arise, identifying the times in which they emerge, detailing what needs and circumstances they fill, and demonstrating the processes through which they are passed on. Let's look at a racial example. There was a time in the United States when those we call "black" could not legally marry each other in many states, let alone marry those who we call "white." Black people were forbidden to marry because (at the time) they were presumed to be chattel with no right to self-determination. When black people were allowed to marry, they were forbidden to marry whites because the "races" were presumed to be as different from one another as animal species, and therefore they should not "mix." However, now everyone has the right to marry whomever they wish (if they are heterosexual). The racial rules about marriage change because racial processes change, and racial processes change because races are differently constructed according to the time and place.

Social constructs like race, then, can be traced through history to determine how they serve particular political ends and are carried out through specific means. By chronicling how human beings developed a specific construct over time and applied it differently in different places, one can understand how that social construct served as an entire social system. Race is both systematic (affecting not just one part of society, but the entire society) and structural (relating to the arrangements among the elements that make up the complex whole of society).

RACIAL PARADIGMS

As already noted, we like to think that races are "natural." Perhaps this is because one sees variation in the human species, and this variation makes one think race is obvious. But in an average human's lifetime, he or she samples not the whole of the species but only a few different parts of the human distribution. If one walks from the northernmost part of the globe to the southernmost, one could see the gradation of change in the spectrum of human difference. If instead one relies just on one's eyes, even in a global city, those humans that come into view don't seem to be organized in a spectrum but instead seem to cluster in types. Perhaps it is part of being human to fear human difference, but I do not believe this to be at all true. For example, we may cite many instances of legal and extralegal action to prevent miscegenation, or sexual relations and reproduction across races, but few that were designed to enforce cross-race liaisons. Laws must be enacted to legislate against what people actually will do! Those legislators felt the need to make laws because they wanted to stop actions that were taking place, that is, they thought that if people are naturally drawn to others across the color line, they must legislate against these tendencies. If people naturally feared difference, no such legislation would be needed!

Difference is only what we make of it. We use phenotypes to judge who is in what race, but we only see some of the differences among humans. We make nothing of the difference between those with long second toes and those whose big toe is longer; we don't push into a different subspecies those who can curl their tongues. The logic on which we hang the racial meaning of the differences among us become part of the racial paradigm, and the meaning of these differences is human-made, not made by nature or abstract social forces. Racial commonsense is more than just a motley collection of myths; it is systematic, and has a structure to it, just like the system of gender inequality between men and women, or the structure of unequal nations. A structure based on racial thinking is a racial paradigm.

A paradigm is a widespread way of thinking supported by authorities with vested interests in ensuring that the belief system perpetuates. Paradigms tell us what's relevant, what we know, and what still needs to be investigated.[19] Race is such a paradigm. It is predicated on early ideas about the natural state of white superiority and nonwhite degradation, along with the hope that scientific methods can be used to "prove" these so-called truths.[20] From these efforts, the human race acquired things like demography, statistics, and anthropology, all developed to monitor human development and search out the origins and future of the species. But we also gained eugenics, anthropometry, and standardized testing of intelligence and other properties, which promote ways of valuing humanity according to preconceived biases.[21]

The language and theory of racial paradigms are tools used to illustrate that racial systems are built by human beings, who propagate and profligate racial social constructions. These constructions, then, are not built by an entity so abstract as "society" through some mysterious and invisible process, nor are they simply built by particularly racist individuals with strong racial prejudices. A systematic public relations campaign waged by some human beings against other human beings, and in defense of their own racializing perspectives, is what keeps our racial constructions alive and well.

Race has become a worldview, an idea formed in North America and transported across the globe, but there are also systemic local variants with which we all must contend. A singular racial system might be called a *racial paradigm*. The term "racial paradigm" is a shorthand way to refer to the mechanisms people employ to racially organize themselves and the people they consider to be their racial subordinates. Racial paradigms organize the way in which "race" works in any given geographic space or historical moment. Racial paradigms have two basic components: *racial categories and hierarchies,* and *racial politicultures.* Racial categories are used to label persons, assigning them to various racial groups in order to group together certain individuals and segregate them from others. The categories are ranked in a hierarchy that stratifies racial categories according to the share of privileges and demerits accorded a given group. Racial politicultures encompass the de jure and de facto rules that determine who gets into which category. They also govern the monitoring of the boundaries of racial categories, determine how the boundaries between categories are monitored, and delimit the sanctions for crossing boundaries. Thus, in general, these politicultures provide the means for transmitting racial commonsense among the people living within a particular racial system.

I will take in turn each component of the racial paradigm and explain in greater detail how it operates. As you will note, the examples I employ in my explanations in this chapter are largely comparative. Using comparisons highlights the idea that racial paradigms are flexible. While it may seem to us today that we know who is who and what a label like "black" really means, the comparative method shows us very clearly that meanings continually change and are perpetually contested. The comparative method also demonstrates the socially constructed nature of race. If we construct race one way here, and another country does it differently there, or if we do it one way now and did it another way fifty years ago, then how "scientific" or "God-given" can our racial differences really be? Understanding the way racial paradigms work is important to keep in mind as you read the ethnic histories in later chapters. These categories, hierarchies, and politicultures are fought over, not set in stone, and the components of racial paradigms change as the result of the struggles around them. Once racial paradigms are understood to be firm but permeable social structures that stand separate from ethnicities, it will be easier to grasp the theory and history of how ethnic groups struggle for increased racial status by learning about and then manipulating the racial paradigms of the day.

Racial paradigms differ across historical time and geographic space. For example, we might say that the U.S. racial paradigm is one where the categories vary in name and number over the longue durée but where the basic hierarchy, a binary, is relatively constant and marked by a color line between white and nonwhite. The politiculture of this paradigm is such that the color line is constantly policed, marked by formal legal structures and informal patterns of social interaction (by individuals and institutions) that reinforce or contest that particular hierarchical distinction. Although Brazil may have many more categories (numbering up to 200 perhaps), the Brazilian system could have a similar binary hierarchy very much like that of the United States. Yet, the Brazilian politiculture is quite different from that in the United States. For one, Brazilian society has been described as a racial democracy, which suggests that racism is not a problem of great social significance there. While a great deal of scholarship and some political activism may contest this vision of Brazilian society, this contestation has to contend with the strength of a politiculture that largely blinds itself to categories and hierarchies. This politiculture is exemplified by a historical moment during which racial categories and their demographic size have gone uncounted, when the Brazilian government did not allow the enumeration of the population by racial category. We might make a further comparison to South Africa, which has fewer categories than either the United States or Brazil and is organized in a tripartite (not binary) hierarchy that also might be said to focus on the line between white and nonwhite. The paradigm is in flux, historically speaking, after having been reinforced by the politiculture of the former apartheid regime. While the political structure of apartheid has been dismantled, the culture of apartheid and its socioeconomic reflection have not yet been erased from the paradigm's operative pattern. As a last example, think of the paradigm that covers the Caribbean. Although the Caribbean islands have categories and a hierarchy similar to those in the United States, the politiculture is so different that black migrants from the Caribbean islands come to the United States and say, "We don't have that [way of racial thinking] back home!"[22] They must acquire a new knowledge that informs them that racial denigration applies not only to the stereotypical "lazy" African Americans in the United States who Caribbean people are told are perpetually on welfare and constantly commit crimes; the term "black" in the United States includes them too! Moreover, they learn that being black in the United States is a serious business that forces you to succumb or stand up to discrimination and inequality; in the Caribbean blackness is present, but not imbued with the same meaning.

Another advantage of paradigmatic language is that it allows one to see how racial paradigms change. Racial systems are constant only in theory, as can be seen from any cross-paradigm comparison (i.e., across different places or different times). The very nature of a paradigm is constructionist, because the people living in a particular time and place construct the racial system under which they live.

A third advantage that follows from this type of language is that it allows us to see social agency. If a paradigm changes, it is because someone changes it. Persons living in the paradigm are the ones who reconstruct it by manipulating the paradigms of their forebears, who in turn inherited the paradigms of their ancestors. As the materials of the paradigm (the categories, hierarchy, politiculture) are adapted to changing social, political, and economic challenges, so are the means by which people succumb to, reinforce, or contest the system.

Anti- or proracial social movements illustrate just one type of agency in a racial system, and ethnic projects exemplify another.

From the foregoing, we can infer two salient facts about racial paradigms. First, racial paradigms are made up of the categories, hierarchies, and politicultures that assign members of a society to certain groups and segregate them from other groups. Second, racial paradigms are dynamic rather than static, only jaggedly comparative rather than uniform, and socially constructed rather than natural or given. Racial paradigms and their components can be best examined by the use of qualitative and quantitative methods that refrain from essentialist notions (e.g., using race as a variable like height, or income) but instead query the ways racial systems and their component parts transform or remain consistent through varied social or demographic conditions or across time and space. Race (like class, gender, and other hierarchical social structures) must be constantly constructed in order to be usefully applied to persons who are assigned, however sloppily, to fill its categories and forced, however unequally, to contend with the confines or privileges accorded to each rank. Because categories and processes of assignment are both continually and locally constructed—that is, because they are continually being changed to fit ever-evolving notions of what "race" and its categories mean—it is useful to employ a comparative historical analysis to explain the components of racial paradigms. This analysis can show what race is and how it works.

RACIAL CATEGORIES AND RACIAL HIERARCHIES

Real racial difference may not exist, but phenotypic differences do. Perhaps we still use the term "race" because we consider it to be shorthand for "genetic variation."[23] Racial labeling is mainly associated with the phenotype of the racial object—one person looks at another and decides their racial type. The significance of this labeling is great because the racial object is inserted into a racial hierarchy the instant they are labeled, and society's rewards and demerits are accorded by race.

Racial categories are nonepithetic labels that reference either color or culture groupings meant to encompass the range of racial human nature. (Epithetic labels derive from popular sentiment around a given category at the time the epithet is created but are not racial categories themselves.) Each racial paradigm uses an established, albeit contested, set of categories. Men and women create these categories by law, practice, and societal consensus. One should not be surprised to see different sets of racial categories in use when one compares two different historical periods or any two geographic regions. Laws and practices in a single place change over time, and laws and practices differ from place to place; consensus has to be repeatedly regained since none lasts forever. Think about race in North America, Latin America, and Asia, for example. The English long ago chose a system of exclusive groups—rigid, unequal, and ordered—and this rigidity was later reflected in the racial systems it gave birth to in the United States, South Africa, and Australia. But even those single-source systems vary. South Africa has four categories (black, white, colored, and Asian).[24] The United States has about five categories (white, Asian, Hispanic, black, and the catchall "other"). Australia has a wholly different five (white, ethnic-looking [a special category for the not-so-white], Asian, Indian, and black).[25] By contrast, Brazil is said to have up to 200 categories based on skin shade; and Brazil's categories are far less rigid than the English-based system (e.g., one is able to "whiten" oneself with money and upward mobility).[26] Finally, note that in Japan, the Japanese and Koreans are seen as separate races that differ by "blood," whereas in the United States, Japanese and Korean people are grouped together racially.[27] All of this variation should be evidence enough to prove that racial categories and hierarchies are human inventions, not scientific fact.

The story of Johann Blumenbach (1752–1840) and his faculty adviser, naturalist Carolus Linnaeus (1707–1778), provides an interesting example of how literally I mean it when I say racial categories are a purely a-scientific human invention. Linnaeus, a naturalist whose career was to classify species of animals and plants, created from thin air a four-category taxonomy of human races: *Americanus* (for Natives to the Americas), *Europaeus* (Europeans), *Asiaticus* (Asians), and *Afer* (referring to Africans). Blumenbach's lifework began with his dissertation. He studied Linnaeus's work, and also the skull of a woman from the Caucasus Mountain region that he had obtained. Seeing that her skull was white, he presumed further that one's skin color matched one's skull color, that is, that nonwhite people must have nonwhite skulls. He also applied color theory to suggest that one begins with white and adds color to make other colors, but one cannot mix colors and obtain white. With all this information, Blumenbach was then assured that the original man must be white, and fashioned a hierarchy of races that specified descent with the melding of color theory (for which he had to invent a new race, the "Malay," to stand as the middle-tone brown race between "Caucasian" and "Ethiopian").[28] We remember Blumenbach not for the antiracist stances he had at the start of his career, but instead for his 1776 invention of the category "Caucasian" (a word still in wide use today) and his crowning as the first scientist to build a pyramid of racial categories, suggesting an evolutionary and hierarchical relationship among them that put Caucasians at the top.[29] This is just an example of how categories appear or disappear when existing racial schemes are refined. We may find other examples in the terms "mulatto," "quadroon," or "octoroon," designating fractions of whiteness in a racially black person. These terms were once widely used in the United States and have long since fallen out of favor.

Hierarchical positions relating to specific categories must be learned, and when changed, relearned. As suggested, immigrants have a difficult time with this. Clara Rodriguez has published much work on the ways that newcomers to the mainland United States from Puerto Rico have had to adapt to their new racial ascriptions. "White" Puerto Ricans are privy to a wholly different life than are "black" ones in the United States, whereas their lives were not so rigidly segregated in Puerto Rico. Similarly, Americans of European descent are taught, as children and later as adults, to accept their membership among "whites."[30] In the United States, the boundaries of the category "black" have changed quite significantly since the idea came to be—for example, it took much contestation before the now-ubiquitous rule of hypodescent (or "one-drop rule") reached a nationwide understanding.[31]

Categorization is ubiquitous, and in racialized societies no one is allowed to be without a race. The exception that proves the rule are persons racially ambiguous. They are continually asked more and more forceful versions of variously insulting questions such as "What are you?" or "But where are you *really* from?" because—as strange as it sounds—prolonged interaction with someone racially unidentifiable can bring the average North American some discomfort. North Americans, despite our belief that the United States is built on immigration and welcomes everyone, must be able to put each person in a racial box.

Just as North Americans have a long history of racial categorization, there is a long history of resistance to categorization. Racial categories and the struggles against being categorized are integral to ethnic projects. In later chapters I offer examples to show how the Irish in the Northeastern United States convinced themselves and other whites to accept the Irish as white, along with similar struggles for the American Jewish population.[32] But each of these groups has also been assigned a racial category—and at one time or another, each of the groups named in these examples have been called "black." That only one such group is still called "black" might be taken as evidence that ethnic projects are operative in the racial paradigm. More recently one might observe the successful petition by mixed-race persons for recognition that resulted in changes to the U.S. Census, which in 2000 offered more than one choice of racial category; and changes to the 2001 Census in England and Wales, which added a mixed-race category (in a departure from "pure" races). Now, it is possible that Hispanics/Latinos in the United States will get their own racial category in the U.S. Census, even though this group is said to comprise many races; persons from the Middle East may also get their own category. Meanwhile, the category "Negro" may disappear even though there are Americans who still use the term to identify themselves. It is clear that the struggles for categorical change are far from over.[33]

Racial categories relate to one another in a hierarchical fashion. Indeed, this hierarchy is the main purpose of the racial system, which is designed to make effectual prevailing theories about how unequal human beings are. The hierarchical feature of race is what allows persons designated as "white" to use their political and economic power to hoard privileges for themselves.[34] Without this inequality, race is a useless concept.

One might think that merely ridding ourselves of racial categories could solve the race problem. Indeed, many scholars have called for us to stop using race and racial categories altogether in the hope that disuse of the categories means we will also refrain from oppressing one another racially or perhaps cease obfuscating the real problem (which some argue is class-based inequality).[35] Underlying this call for the disuse of racial categories, perhaps, is the assumption that race functions primarily by use of those categories. But the simple disuse of racial categories can neither eliminate the racial hierarchy nor the impact that thinking hierarchically has on our society and economy. Race persists because it is expedient for those who are in the categories at the top of the racial hierarchy to maintain the use of racial categories in that hierarchical fashion.[36] Further, once categories are made, it may be almost impossible to unmake them in our thinking. We may decide to refrain from using racial categories, but "colorblindness" and "anti-racist beliefs" are hardly conceptual siblings, as scholars and pundits debating the existence of "colorblind racism" point out to us.[37] Why won't colorblindness work to eradicate race? Pretending that racial categories don't exist will not level the racial "playing field," and it will likely have the opposite effect—making it impossible to devise remedies for past race-based injustices and inequities. This is because race (as a system) is far greater than the mere categories and rankings we use to refer to the participants ensnared in that system.

RACIAL POLITICULTURES

Beyond racial categories and hierarchies, racial systems have rules for determining how humans establish racial assignments and deciding on how membership in a given category has socioeconomic effects on group members' lives. Racial dominants make these rules, which are both legal and extralegal processes to confer benefits and demerits among the subgroups within categories (ethnic groups, kinship groups, lineages and family names, neighborhoods and communities, etc.). These rules also specify the proper comportment of persons within a category and dictate the mores of interracial interactions.[38] They also change over time in contested ways,[39] and sometimes these changes may be signified as racial progress. These rules, regulations, mores, laws, and dictates are what I term the *racial politiculture*. Racial politicultures are marked by the use of *racial enforcement, racial sanctions*, and *racial commonsense*.

Racial enforcement centers on the ways we reinforce categories and police the boundaries among them. The body of legal scholarship on critical race theory probably is the greatest store of academic writings on racial enforcement. For example, Cheryl Harris explains that Homer Plessy and the train porters orchestrated Plessy's arrest in order to protest the spreading cancer of Jim Crow; it had to be orchestrated because Plessy looked white and only qualified as black because of the one-drop rule.[40] These men set out to prove the idiocy of the legislated denigration of blacks by forcing the racist rules of Jim Crow to be enforced on a white-looking black man. When Plessy lost his case, it was clear that the rigid lines drawn between black and white were to be rigidly enforced, even if they were nonsensical. (According to the ruling, as a black man Plessy was required to ride in the Jim Crow car like anyone else, but if Plessy was truly a white man he could not really be harmed by this rule because he could always appeal to the courts for redress, as all white men could.) Ian F. Haney Lopez's writings provide two other examples with the cases *Takao Ozawa v. the United States* and *United States v. Bhagat Singh Thind.*[41] The *Ozawa* and *Thind* cases were decided within months of each other. Ozawa, a Japanese man, sued, saying that he spoke no Japanese, was a Christian, educated himself and his children in the best schools, owned property, and was an upstanding member of society; therefore he was as white as anyone and should be accepted as such and allowed citizenship. The courts ruled that whites were Caucasians so he didn't qualify. Thind then sued, saying that his lineage was clearly from the region and peoples identified as Caucasian, and as a Caucasian by blood he would be as white as anyone and should be allowed citizenship. Thind was denied, with the ruling stating that white men knew what other white men looked like and that Thind didn't look the part, so he didn't qualify. Two contradictory Supreme Court rulings show how racial enforcement legally, albeit nonsensically, was reserved for whites, even as the Supreme Court of the United States could not agree on who was white. These cases, along with that of Homer Plessy, show that racial enforcement has little to do with the logic or nonsense of categories (i.e., we will legislate racial privilege and its opposite, whether or not we can get the categories straight).

Racial enforcement is made by racial states wherein race is used as a political tool by groups vying for political power, and they are the basis for coalition making or exclusion from the political process.[42] Think of antimiscegenation laws as one example. The word "miscegenation" in American English designates romantic relationships between whites and people of other race. Its root *"mis-"* signifies wrongdoing. Societies normally don't legislate that the marriage-eligible are required to choose someone from outside of one's clan or nation (indeed, the normal case of forcing someone to do this is to forge political alliances). Laws are made so that one does not marry one's own sibling or first cousin, but not many racialized societies make laws mandating that one must marry outside of one's own clan. Perhaps this is because when confronted with difference, men and women generally say "yum" not "yuck." Antimixing advocates must have their preferences mirrored in legislation precisely because when difference appears the natural tendency is to mix!

Racial sanction is invoked when violations of racial boundaries of the kind considered a failure to "know one's place" has occurred in the realm of race relations. Racial sanction occurs when whites punish other whites for trespassing into nonwhite geographic spaces or, conversely, for escorting nonwhites into white space.[43] Blacks are similarly punished for geographic trespass. The Jim Crow era in the United States and the apartheid era of the Republic of South Africa offer clear historical examples of formally legislated racial sanction. Both regimes designated punishments for interracial liaisons, and whites felt free to punish blacks who were found wherever or with whom they were not "supposed to be." Extralegal examples of racial sanction abound, most grisly and recently in the deaths of Willie Turks (a New York City transit worker beaten to death in 1982 by white youths because on the way home from work he stopped to buy a bagel); Michael Griffith in New York City (in 1986 Griffith and friends drove to pick up Griffith's paycheck when their car broke down in Howard Beach and he was chased onto the Belt Parkway by whites wielding bats, tree branches, and tire irons, shouting, "Get out of our neighborhood!"); Yusuf Hawkins (beaten by a mob and then shot in 1989 for traveling to Bensonhurst, a white Brooklyn neighborhood, to purchase a used car); Stephen Lawrence in London (while waiting for a bus in 1993, he was attacked and beaten to death by a group of white teenagers); James Byrd Jr. in Jasper, Texas (in 1998 beaten then chained to the back of the truck of twenty-four-year-old white supremacist Lawrence Russell Brewer, then dragged "whip-like" down a bumpy road until his head, neck, and right arm were severed); the eleven immigrants (and others) killed by members of Germany's National Socialist Underground in their twenty-first-century rampage; and Everett Gant in Florida (in 2011 shot between the eyes when approaching Walton Henry Butler to discuss the racial epithets Butler spewed at Gant's family; Butler allegedly closed the door on Gant's bleeding body, finished dinner, and after the police had arrived questioned why he was subject to the inconvenience of an arrest since he had "only shot a nigger").[44]

Of course, one does not have to die to be the victim of racial sanction. Take, for example, the beating of Vishal Wadhwa, an American of Indian national descent beaten in 2007 when enjoying a Lake Tahoe, California, beach with his fiancée. There are countless other beatings, slights, and shames that persons of color have had to endure and still live with.[45] Perhaps the first instance of racial sanction occurred when laws were put in place in the time of England's attempt to take over Ireland to punish (or racially sanction) any English person who adapted to Irish culture and was daring enough to practice parts of it.

These sanctions ranged from styling one's hair like the Irish do to intermarriage. When family elders issue warnings about the love lives of young ones with comments like, "Don't you ever bring any [fill in the racial blank] into this house, you hear?" they threaten racial sanction. But perhaps this last might also be characterized as emerging from racial commonsense.

Racial commonsense consists of the rules that help everyone to "know their place" and keep race relations going with diminished conflict. Other parts of the racial commonsense might explain why racial attitudes prevail ("blacks are more athletic/lazy"); why particular groups stay on top and others seem always to remain on the bottom ("Asians are good at math"); and the creation of racial universes in which orbits of identity mark areas of inclusion and exclusion ("black" music, "mainstream" media, etc.). Racial commonsense also varies across paradigms. The rules defining who is who, who is allowed to socially mix with whom, and who is discouraged from mixing at all are all different in Brazil than in the United States. These differences are often attributed to a historical moment centuries ago, when the Spanish and Portuguese chose to follow a racial politiculture that did not force separation of inflexibly distinct racial groups; indeed, they even allowed and expressed a desire for race mixing that was explained away as an ideal means to achieve population "whitening."[46]

Charles Mills's (1999) book *The Racial Contract* explains that racial commonsense is made by whites for other whites to know how to treat one another and nonwhites.[47] He argues that whites agree to a social contract that creates whiteness as the basis of a group that dominates over others and covers the social mores that make the racial machinery run. Nonwhites may be fully aware of but need not agree to the politics and culture of white supremacy since they are racial subordinates and not party to the contract. (Perhaps France Winddance Twine's [1997] *Racism in a Racial Democracy*, which uses ethnography to describe how Afro-Brazilians go out of their way to avoid labeling their interpersonal relations as racist or race-related, is a case in point.[48]) The intriguing part is that the racial contract is one that whites agree never to acknowledge. Barbara Flagg said it eloquently and succinctly: "The most striking characteristic of whites' consciousness of whiteness is that most of the time we don't have any."[49]

To say, as someone recently told me, that one might really enjoy "antebellum architecture" without having to acknowledge or even understand the racial overtones in the construction of these buildings is another such commonsense.

It's not that these properties and buildings are not beautiful. But there's a reason we say "antebellum" and not "nineteenth-century Southern U.S." architecture. The "antebellum architecture" phrase is meant to signal that we're to visit lands run by slaveowners on slave labor (and on these plantations, the slave quarters are normally torn down; it is only the slaveowners' homes that are restored). It is also commonsense to expect these gems to be beautiful sites that are perfect backdrops to weddings, as they're "antebellum" and not really graveyards for the lives of women, men, and children forced to serve their masters' foibles. (Do Spaniards similarly wed on Inquisition torture chambers? Or do people picnic on German lands where mass graves of Jews now are covered with wildflowers and lawns?) The idea that we should have so easily forgotten the multicentury horrors that helped create these places, which now serve as eye-candy for tourists' happy nostalgia—that makes racial commonsense.

Then where does racism fit into all this? If the reader comes to this book with some knowledge of the sociology of race, you already know that racism exists—and some would even say it is "alive and well." But race is one of the perpetual falsehoods still promulgated by those who many might call charlatans of science. Many people write, then, that race is not "real" (in the sense that it has no proven basis in biology or genetics) but that racism is "real." Some go so far as to say that race does not exist but racism does. Indeed, race is a socioeconomic system that goes beyond individual beliefs, as this chapter has explained. Racism, instead, is the belief system acted upon by institutions and individuals who enforce, reify, or struggle against the racial structures described here.

Race and racism may have a relationship, but one does not necessarily have a direct link to the other. One need not have agreed with Adolf Hitler's "Final Solution" program or even be a virulent anti-Semite to have supported his government. All one had to do was vote for the Nazi Party, or do nothing as Nazis began to tear down government and abuse and destroy innocent human lives. We are mistaken to continually link concerns for individual preferences with their expression and support, however benign or behind the scenes, for a system that allows one set of humans to oppress another while a third set looks on. Thus, one may support racism without stating obviously racist beliefs; in the appositive, one may be a racialist (a believer in racial difference) without behaving in racist ways toward others. Indeed, Michael Omi and Howard Winant track racial thinking in politics and culture through the idea of the racial project, defined as racial agendas promulgated by identifiable groups vying for increased political power—these groups need not be racist to use race as a political tool.[50] On the other hand, it is surely the case that race and racism coexist more often than not, for racism came into being when races were created and their hierarchical nature established.

HOW DOES THE CONCEPT OF ETHNICITY ENGAGE RACIAL THINKING?

Ethnicity is commonly thought to be an identity category, a self-knowledge process that results in self-naming that joins an individual to a group and that is the answer to such questions as "What are you?" or "Who are your people?" It provides a shorthand reference to one's people, culture, heritage, history, and homeland. Race is ascribed more than chosen; it links one's "blood" and phenotype to personal characteristics that reference such things as the propensity to succeed or fail in facing common challenges or opportunities. Pundits of racialized thinking now believe these characteristics are rooted in cultural strengths or failings and presume they are as much a part of our makeup as our DNA.

Race and ethnicity, as concepts used for categorizing human beings, actually developed together. Africans and Indians—these are groups wholly fabricated by amalgamating disparate nations that predated European conquest. Race and ethnicity are sibling mechanisms of human oppression in the sense that they developed together in the Imperialist West (the lands of Europe and North America in the time of European conquest and domination), when wealthy men of European descent worked to gain wealth and power through military might and retain it through political control.

While race and ethnicity are separate systems of classification, they do interact with one another in very important ways. Race is assigned or ascribed—it's a way of defining others. Ethnic group members, on the other hand, assert ethnic identifiers for themselves. The way these concepts interact can be illustrated with the example of my own life. When someone looks at me, they cannot see those ethnic categories I might use to identify myself: Unionite, since my people are from Union Island; Vincentian, since Union Island is one of the islands comprising Saint Vincent and the Grenadines; American, since I was born in the United States; or even New Yorker, since I was actually born and raised in New York.[51] Most Americans looking at me would say they see a "black" woman, and it does not matter to them much whether or not I ever want to call myself "black" or consider myself to be wholly different from what people might think the mass of black people to be.[52]

Race is a power relation, based on a hierarchy, whereas ethnicity is not necessarily so. The reason race exists is because it creates a hierarchy designed to justify the unequal distribution of resources (material goods, power, well-being). Race classifies "whites" on top, and "blacks" on bottom (or "reds," if we were in a different era); if other races exist, they are ranked somewhere in between. Ethnicities (at least in twenty-first-century American thought) are presumed to be more linear—we wouldn't consciously rank Hopi over Navajo or Nimipuu, or say that the Cherokee is superior to the Chinese who is superior to the Chilean; peoples simply are who they are as far as their ethnic classification is concerned.

In a way, ethnicity has always existed. For as long as people have been on the planet, they have had culture and ancestry and named themselves. Yet, race is "new," having emerged as conquering European travelers deemed it necessary to make classifying distinctions between themselves and others. Then again, as I explained in the first section of this chapter, the word "ethnicity" did not appear in the *Merriam-Webster Dictionary* until the 1950s. Come again? Surely it cannot be the case that only in the 1950s did English-speaking Westerners decide that it was time to give some recognition to the names and culture a people might have for themselves.

Newcomer ethnicities become salient when a significant number of "outsiders" (persons who don't fit well into the racial frame operative at the time) join their geographic communities. It is as the "stranger" that they are first identified as equivalent to the "bottom of the barrel," racially speaking. How is it that some ethnic groups rise to the top and become white? Which groups have managed that, and which have not, and why? Physical difference/similarity alone cannot be the answer, because many now-white (or nearly white) groups were once hardly thought of as "white." How a group attempts the racial uplift that could whiten them is the tale of the ethnic project.

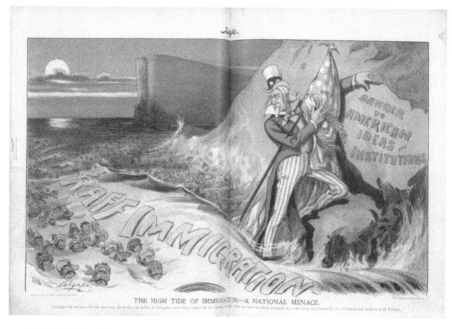

THE HIGH TIDE OF IMMIGRATION—A NATIONAL MENACE.

The High Tide of Immigration—A National Menace, cartoon by Louis Dalrymple, published in *Judge* magazine (1903). Caption: "Immigration statistics for the past year show that the influx of foreigners was the greatest in our history, and also that the hardworking peasants are now being supplanted by the criminals and outlaws of all Europe." Source: Art Resource, NY.

CHAPTER 3

ETHNIC WINNERS AND LOSERS

This is race talk, the explicit insertion into everyday life of racial signs and symbols that have no meaning other than pressing African Americans to the lowest level of the racial hierarchy. . . . Only when the lesson of racial estrangement is learned is assimilation complete. . . . Although U.S. history is awash in labor battles, political fights and property wars among all religious and ethnic groups, their struggles are persistently framed as struggles between recent arrivals and blacks. In race talk the move into mainstream America always means buying into the notion of American blacks as the real aliens. Whatever the ethnicity or nationality of the immigrant, his nemesis is understood to be African American. . . . There is virtually no movement up—for blacks or whites, established classes or arrivistes—that is not accompanied by race talk. Refusing, negotiating, or fulfilling this demand is the real stuff, the organizing principle of becoming an American. Star spangled. Race strangled.

Toni Morrison, "On the Backs of Blacks"

I wish that white people had never come into my country.

Flint Knife, Blackfoot, "A Wish"

The history of ethnic inequality in the United States is unique, but not solely because of America's fabled history of immigration.[1] In the United States people think differently about ethnicities than they do elsewhere, and perhaps they do not even comprehend fully their importance. Amy Chua, in her book *World on Fire,* writes, "Perhaps because of beliefs in the 'melting pot' and the United States' own relatively successful—though halting and incomplete—history of ethnic assimilation, Americans don't always understand the significance of ethnicity, both in the United States and especially in other countries."[2] Stephen Steinberg, in *The Ethnic Myth,* offers a somewhat different position, arguing instead that North Americans take great pains to perpetuate myths about ethnic heroes (who are socioeconomic successes and class achievers) and ethnic villains (whose presumably deficient cultures are blamed for keeping them at the lower end of the class structure). This mythology obscures the socioeconomic structures that create and perpetuate inequalities among groups, allowing Americans to persist in their belief that cultural difference (rather than inequality) drives ethnic conflict.

How are ethnic groups racialized in the United States? When newcomers enter the United States, their group is labeled in ways that help natives to "read" the members of the group rather quickly. A racialized fiction about the newcomers' origins, prospects, culture, and physical appearance indicates their status position. They are ascribed a race that becomes identified with the ethnonational label they are either forced to adopt or self-identify with once they are on American soil. That ethnonational label may seem somewhat "objective" (e.g., the labels "Italian," "Polish," "Jewish," "Chinese," and "Indian") and probably doesn't readily evoke racialized emotion. But soon after their first experiences in the new country, these ethnic groups find themselves placed at the bottom of the racial hierarchy (where group valuations apply). In due time, their ethnic label becomes nearly synonymous with their place at the bottom of the racial hierarchy. A recounting of a group's history of racial inclusion is nearly a chronologically organized list of that group's social, political, and economic outcomes realized after initial incorporation.

Indeed, the inequality experienced by ethnic groups in the United States persists because of the way the United States structures its racial hierarchy. This is not because ethnicity and race are identical, synonymous, or interchangeable concepts, but because ethnicity in the United States takes the place held (perhaps only temporarily) by racial categories that comprise the racial hierarchy of the United States. A hierarchy requires top and bottom positions to anchor the rankings of more and less privilege; at minimum, then, two racial categories are required for a racial hierarchy to exist. The simplest racial hierarchies, then, are binary—for example, where the categories of significance are white and nonwhite. Many scholars argue that although one may name many races that are operative in the United States, the U.S. racial paradigm is basically binary.[3]

As explained in the preceding chapter, race is best understood as a racial paradigm—a system with two components. First, there must be racial categories organized in a *racial hierarchy*; then there must also be rules under which the system operates. I propose the term *racial politiculture* for this system, which encompasses the list of privileges reserved for the top category and denied to those in the bottom; the means of keeping the categories and privileges separate; and a way to distribute the rules so everyone in the system knows what they are. All that is required for a paradigm to be operative, then, is whiteness (the superior or normative condition), its opposite (the inferior condition, to be nonwhite or "of color"), and a working politiculture (involving a means of categorizing individuals into one racial box or another).

Race is based on a system of institutional practices that denigrate "racial" groups in order to privilege one particular group above others. Racism, then, is the fuel that keeps the system or race operative and contemporary. As racism changes, so does the racial system, and vice versa. Racial systems rank groups into racial categories, forcing them to vie for unequal positions of power in a zero-sum game of racial hierarchy. These systems also produce and justify racial inequalities via mechanisms in the racial politiculture. This chapter explains how this struggle for racial power happens in the United States and how ethnic competition fuels the U.S. racial system.

THE FIRST U.S. RACIAL PARADIGM

The story of the first U.S. racial paradigm begins with the English—before they ever arrived.

The Europeans that colonized North America were Northern Europeans who lacked sophistication in understanding other humans with whom they shared the planet. (By contrast, Southern Europeans had encountered and intermingled with diverse populations and were therefore more sophisticated about the range of human variety in the Old World.) When Northern Europeans began to encounter human physical and cultural differences, they were wholly unprepared.[4]

Even as they began to come up against human differentiation, Northern European societies were themselves transforming. These shifts occurred in England well before the rest of Western Europe. The feudal organization of social and economic life waned, wage labor gained prevalence, and money began to dominate exchange. Opportunities for acquiring wealth through merchant capitalism increased, and a philosophy of possessive individualism and a market mentality gained prominence.[5] These socioeconomic changes displaced people from the land and created a class of jobless poor who degenerated to begging in the streets, thus becoming a class that was punished for their poverty and forced to work in systems of indentured servitude.[6] Conversely, property ownership eventually became so valued as to be equated with the fundamentals of religious Protestantism. These ideas about poverty, property, and servitude helped to formulate Northern Europeans' racial thinking and the forms of oppression they imposed on those they (later) decided were racially beneath them.[7]

The English's first attempts at colonization began in Ireland. They first invaded Ireland in 1169, and by 1200 they controlled the country (except for a few scattered clans who could not be conquered). The Irish were despised because of their nomadic and pastoral culture, which relied upon animal herds and collective land use. By contrast, the English had long depended on acknowledged land boundaries and farming with very ordered social relations that had become increasingly hierarchical in class terms—the propertied lorded over the propertyless.

The English were Catholics just as the Irish were until 1534 when the Church of England broke away after Henry VIII failed to receive annulment of his marriage. Not long afterward the English justified their oppression of the Irish by the denigration of the religion to which they used to belong. That the Irish enjoyed Catholic forms of Christianity and organized themselves in communal economic relations came as a shock to the English, who professed a Protestantism that sanctioned the divine right to individual wealth and equated poverty with devilishness and damnation.

From the standpoint of English cultural values, Irish utilization of the land was a monstrous waste. The rich soil that their animals trampled could be put to better use cultivating grains, vegetables, and other goods to market abroad in expanding urban centers. Moreover, the younger sons of English gentlemen who had no hopes of inheriting paternal lands could earn their fortunes from great estates established in Ireland with the aid of Irish labor. Yet all attempts to force Irishmen to settle on the land were rebuffed. When the English met their intransigence by confiscating and destroying their cattle, the Irish fled into the forests and let it be known that they preferred starvation to life as forced laborers on English farms.[8]

Of course, not all the English agreed with this plan; social relations are always contested. Since Irish conquest was achieved by settlement, repatriated Englishmen and -women encountered new ways of living, and many found these ways attractive. Some chose to assimilate to Irish culture; these cultural converts were considered degenerates on the wrong side of laws against such mixing. The 1367 Statutes of Kilkenny made it punishable for English persons to trade with the Irish, intermarry with them, wear Irish dress or hairstyles, or speak the Irish language. They even "outlawed Irish games, poetry, and music, apparently under the assumption that these cultural features were too seductive for young Englishmen to resist. These prohibitions and others stayed in effect until the seventeenth century."[9]

The English experience with Irish persons on Irish lands was a precursor to the atrocities they inflicted on those who lived and loved in North America, Africa, the Caribbean, and the South Asian peninsula (the other English colonial projects). But from the perspective of the times, the Irish experiment was all new. Attempts by the English to force the Irish to change their lifestyles, and to submit to enslavement on plantations in agricultural operations that were more capitalist than communal, resulted in failure. The English responded to Irish resistance with a campaign of murder and propaganda about

the unsuitability of the Irish for civilization. . . . They cited Spanish practices of exterminating Indians not only as a justification for policies of killing Irish men, women and children but also as an appropriate solution for dealing with those who refused to be enslaved. In the English collective consciousness, "the savage" was thus a kind of composite of these streams of negative ideas and images that flourished during a period of great social disorder, change, and unrest. The savage came to embody all of those repulsive characteristics that were contrary to English beliefs, habits, laws, and values. The imagery induced hatred for all things Irish, which persists among many English people right up to the present.[10]

The English planned a plantation system to be run with permanently forced labor from their supposedly savage inferiors, the Irish. They believed the Irish to be "heathen" despite their being Christians. According to the English, the Irish communal and pastoral lifestyle was proof enough that Catholics were insufficiently pious to be anything but heathens, and worse, they were sure "that the only way to bring them under some form of civilized control was to enslave them. Indeed, Irish people formed the bulk of the servile peoples who were eventually transferred to the New World English plantations during the seventeenth century."[11] In Ireland, as Edward Burke wrote in 1792, "Roman Catholics were obliged to submit to [Protestant] plebeians like themselves, and many of them tradesmen, servants, and otherwise inferior to some of them . . . exercising upon them, daily and hourly, an insulting and vexatious 'superiority.'"[12] To the ire of the English, their project for Irish enslavement, a plantation system, and colonization failed. But their attempts to subjugate others for profit, and their belief that they had a God-given right to do so—even if that included the murder of men, women, and children—would carry on.

When the English migrated to North America in their second colonization project, they brought with them their contemptible views of the Irish. They imposed on the local "Indian" populations a similar system of hierarchical thinking, along with a new merchant capitalism, fueled by attempts at enslavement, and the replacement of communal customs of survival with plantation production. Only the paradigm's categories had changed, adding the label "Indian" to the "ethnic" or "minority" groups that made up the nascent nation.

Initial contacts were not full of racial prejudices, however. Englishmen and cousins John Hawkins and Francis Drake, although involved in plunder and kidnapping in African villages and trade in African and Native American slaves, showed no obvious racial prejudice in these dealings with native populations. Other English explorers (such as Walter Raleigh, ca. 1552–1618) plundered from Indians, Africans, and Spanish alike—that is, they did not single out Native peoples for especially heinous treatment. At the time the English made no reference to race when justifying their equal opportunity pillaging, nor did they consider any of these ethnicities to be racially charged in the extreme.

Early contacts with the Native Americans were marked by altruism. The Europeans were welcomed, fed each day, and generally aided by the Natives, and settlers were taught survival skills and encouraged to trade. It was only later, "when some of the English colonists began to help themselves to food in the fields and in storage areas, to cross into Indian lands that were not open to them, and to generally ignore Indian rights and customs, [that] the latter began to withdraw support. Many even decided to flee from the strange ingrates who made such arrogant demands of them."[13] The European settlers' gratitude devolved into wariness, for they distrusted the motivations of those who helped them survive. It is then that racialized thinking became applied to Native groups. When Europeans were newcomers in need of Indian services, Indians were seen as ignorant and primitive; but when their land and goods were desired in a context of conquest, the Indian became the "savage" of the New World for whom no defense from aggression, subjugation, and enslavement should be allowed. The Natives' communal behavior was condemned in ways similar to that of the Irish before them, but even those Indians who assimilated and converted to Protestant ways of life were not spared.

Here again, as happened in Ireland, some Europeans joined communities of colonized peoples. It is even suspected that some of the early European settlements in North America that seemed to disappear with no trace actually may have been absorbed by Indian societies. What is clear is that many English who were captured by Indians preferred the lifestyle of their new culture.[14] But the English in power would not attempt to understand or remain indifferent to these cultural converts. Their explanation for whites' attraction to Indian life was that they all cavorted with Satan. Nothing, it seemed, would show the English that the Indian could be worthy of rights to land and freedom or to use that land according to their own choice of lifestyle. The English remained intractable in spite of the evidence of Indian assistance to the English settlements, Indian conversion to English lifestyles, and the repeated protests of captured whites who refused to stay with the English once offered "rescue." Indeed, Indian communal regimes, the diversity of Indian nations, predilections to nudity and polygamy, and a general refusal to convert to Protestantism and "civilized" ways were all considered proof that the Indians were savage—as savage as the "wild Irish."

The English subjugation of Africans in North America is the third iteration in the creation of the U.S. racial paradigm. Here, I focus only on the incorporation of African bodies into that paradigm. (Other colonial enterprises over African and Indian-subcontinent peoples happened in other lands, but my purpose here is to derive the origins and trace the development of the U.S.

racial paradigm.) Africans slowly, over time and in contested ways, descended into slavery and were designated to be "black." The "African" as a concept is invented, for the masses of people shipped as chattel from the West Coast of the continent did not think themselves united in any particular ways—except in the ways of subjugation.[15] They were not united by race as yet, for race as we know it did not exist. In fact, Africans' physical differences were not the basis of their descent into lifelong enslavement. The reasons for judgments of African inferiority were the same as for the "Indians" and the Irish: savagery and non-Puritanism. By this time, "many colonists of the seventeenth century believe, or vindicated their actions with the belief, that enslavement was a major step toward saving the souls of the Africans."[16]

In 1640, the first Virginia law demarking difference between black and white rights prohibited blacks from bearing arms. Soon thereafter, lifetime enslavement became the fate of the black man, woman, and child. Discriminatory treatment was allotted to those men and women whose love caused them to cross the color line into sexual affairs. A 1691 law in Virginia ordered a fine (and five years' bondage if it remained unpaid) for a white woman who bore a biracial child, and interracial marriage was prohibited altogether. Alternatively, punishments were nonsensical for white men who sexually violated black women; neither the women nor the black men to whom they may have been attached had a right of self-defense. Blacks who had been able to resist slavery because they adopted Christianity, or because they could claim free white paternity, over time lost their rights to freedom. "Lawmakers [and readers of the law] were beginning to see blacks as a people apart."[17] Africans were not enslaved because they were black; they were made black because they were made slaves.

In the evolving racial hierarchy, the Irish was deemed a savage, a beast with a wild animal nature (hence the term "wild Irish"), whose nation need not be recognized. The evolution continued, and the Irish made way for the "Indians" (a name bequeathed by a geographically disoriented Columbus), with natural but not civil rights that any white man need recognize. The Indian was deemed a heathen, the unenlightened person of an unrecognized religion who lacked morals and principles. The next heathens became the "Negroes," and Negroes deserved no rights at all. They were deemed inhuman, with no country of origin, invoking all that was dark, black, and unfathomable. This racial hierarchy evolved along with the new nation.

Max Weber, theorist and father of sociology, wrote that Protestantism was the key to the success of the English enterprise in North America and central to the way they viewed the world. To him, the marrying of modern capitalism ("the rational organization of formally free labour") and Protestantism (the idea that one might be driven to accumulate wealth, but at the same time have little interest in the "worldly pleasures it can purchase") brought about a great self-discipline among the colonizers.[18] Anthropologist Audrey Smedley thinks little of this idea, and instead argues that the New World invaders actually *chose* capitalism *over* religiosity and piousness. English Protestant religiosity became a source of protection and comfort when used to identify friends (Protestants) and foes (others—including other Christians) in Europe but was hardly a driving force of their action. When Protestantism was evoked in intergroup relations it was used mainly to make excuses for the brutalizing of others.[19] In fact, the racial thinking of the day took Protestant religiosity (and the delineation between the heathen and the saved) and added to it the Spanish belief in the heritability of social status.[20] (Recall from chapter 2 that the term "ethnicity" is in its origins synonymous with "heathen.") Together, religion and blood created a heritable racial character, and the lore about the tainted races was plastered on any enemy in order to downgrade them from fully valued human status.

Continually contested at the national and local levels, the bottom category changes and is reshaped. Here the racial pariah involves those who are "red," those who are "black," and so on.[21] In 1908 the Louisiana Supreme Court first declared that, "there are no negroes who are not persons of color; but there are persons of color who are not negroes."[22] But then in 1910, the court changed its ruling to nearly equate the terms (persons of color and Negroes) in order to fully ban the intermixing of blood (through miscegenation[23]), one of many steps made to solidify the racial binary in the United States between whites and others. This act not only had great historical significance but also indicates the permanence of the dominance of racial thinking in American life. After all,

people of non-Caucasian, non-Negro ancestry had been labeled *persons of color* throughout the nineteenth century. But to continue to call them persons of color in the twentieth century would mean that [all such persons, former non-Negroes included] would assume all legal disabilities intended only for those with African ancestry. The relabeling of Indians and Filipinos was part of the movement to clarify the intentions of anti-miscegenation statutes.[24]

Other laws follow, whereby white men are unable to allow their mixed-race progeny to inherit. Thus, the net was cast wide to include all such "darker races" as inferior to whites. By the time they were done, they had perfected race well enough that it was systematically imposed to denigrate all such "persons of color."

This sounds very much like the ethnic project that I defined in chapter 1. These are the campaigns that groups of people, variously identified as "ethnic groups," created in order to fight for rights and privileges in the competition for racial status. Difference is not immediately seen as hierarchical, so racialized thinking is required to make a hierarchy of difference. This history suggests a template for what could be the very first ethnic project operative in the very first racial paradigm. In three different historical settings (Ireland, North American encounters with Native persons, and Africans captured and used as goods for trade), English colonizers chose for themselves markers that identified them as culturally different in order to place themselves in the superior position of the very first racial paradigm. They succeeded in uplifting themselves socioeconomically and defining as inferior their opponents in colonial and enslavement enterprises. Race was an English social experiment in domination that was tried in several settings but was not perfected until English race-makers reached North American shores and had (what they in the end named "black") African bodies upon which to experiment. By the late mid-1700s they had managed to create a system of racial categories, which included "white," "Negro," and "Indian" but sometimes were interchangeable with the colors white, black, and red; a hierarchy that was based on the premise of systematic white male supremacy, which was now divorced from property ownership but did not require redistribution of property to those made newly white; and a racial politiculture that designated systems for distributing knowledge about the new racial rules and a means for punishing those persons who refused to live by the rules of racial delineation (including the imposition of antimiscegenation rules that somehow allowed for nonconsensual sexual relations with women "of color" and punishments for consensual relations with "white" women who dared to cross the newly drawn color lines). When "white" is fully formed as the category at the hierarchy's topmost position, race is systematic, paradigmatic, and unmistakably North American.

HOW WHITE AND BLACK CAME TO BE

The term "white" as a social status doesn't actually appear in the historical record until a Virginia rule became law in 1691. Thus, Theodore Allen is justified in writing that "when the first Africans arrived in Virginia in 1619, there were no white people there."[25] Propertied classes argued that the colonies would be under threat should alliances form among persons native to North America, European indentured servants, and unfree Africans.[26] Indeed, in the mid-seventeenth century, bondsmen conspired to flee their bonded condition. Today we would say they were of different races (white, black, and perhaps also mulatto), but there was no such thought then. Allen argues that race was formed to create a buffer class between those who would rule society and those who would be ruled. To discourage unions among those of different classes and stations of bondedness (e.g., slaves with indentured servants), whiteness was created and rewarded. The people later to be known as "white" had suffered enslavement themselves but ideologically joined with those white planters and government officials who created race. The elites deepened their ability to extract lifelong labor in the most extreme of ways and excluded nonelite whites from the life sentence.[27] In 1660 for the first time the terms of servitude for citizens of Christian nations were limited to five years—by which time persons in Ireland qualified, having established the Anglican Church there. In 1640 a group of runaways were sentenced: African American John Punch was sentenced to lifetime servitude (wherein the court cited his condition as "Negro"), while his European American runaway counterparts were not similarly punished. Punch's fate is the first recorded instance of unequal treatment for bondsmen of different races. Inequalities began to be applied to African Americans with increasing regularity. Repeated resistance to sentences of lifetime servitude by way of flight, uprisings, court petitions, and adopting the Christian faith had little effect on the increasing racial inequality. Race in the United States was created by the application of systematic inequality to groups into which one was deemed a member by birth and for life (a side effect of which was that persons of European origin and descent began referring to themselves as "white" and others as "Negro").

Humans have hardly been on the planet long enough to have bred out the biological similarities we inherited from our common ancestors, and therefore certainly nowhere near long enough to have created separate races from a single human genus. Europeans had been "known by vague tribal names: Scythians and Celts, then Gauls and Germani," but they became the "white race" only recently.[28] It was only in the 1780s that for the first time "American" and "European descendant in the Americas" became synonymous. This connection was reified racially in the writings of Thomas Jefferson (1743–1826) and Samuel Stanhope Smith, (1751–1819) who both argued (albeit quite differently) that Saxon ancestry made Americans of European descent deserving of freedom and independence.[29] The superior beauty of "whiteness" was given additional credence from the writings of scientists and skull observers Charles White (1728–1813) and Johann Blumenbach (1752–1840), and these authors of race infused Northern Europhile literature: Anne Louise Germaine Necker de Staël (1766–1817), Charles François Dominique de Villers (1765–1815), and Ralph Waldo Emerson (1803–1882).[30]

Before whiteness existed, humans were known by nationally rooted, ancestry-based cultural markers with which they identified. Once whiteness was created, there was an idea that this new brand of human being was different from humans that once were or could ever be. Whiteness is a club you cannot marry into or join through naturalization; whiteness can only be bestowed. In the racialized United States of America, whiteness is the only attribute that really counts. White ethnics have been accepted into the melting pot of American-ness, but perpetually thought of as "other" are those who descend from Thai, Nigerian, Pakistani, Jamaican, Peruvian, or some other ancestry understood as nonwhite in its roots.

Whiteness was a fiction created by elites who wished to protect their own class position of extreme wealth.[31] The English developed slave codes and applied them to an invented black race in an attempt "to squeeze out class similarities between blacks and whites by bringing racial distinctions to bear against the former."[32] Elites purposefully created whiteness to suppress disquiet and pacify poor Europeans and their Euro-descendants by racially raising the status of the poor without having to share any of the wealth. The elites used their power to create laws that established rights and privileges for propertyless bond laborers and other "whites." This included "the presumption of liberty, the right to get married, the right to carry a gun, the right to read and write, the right to testify in legal proceedings, the right of self-directed physical mobility, and the enjoyment of male prerogatives over women."[33] Indeed, racial chaos ensued when the once-held right of self-defense was taken away from these humans "of color." This legal move led directly to the ability for men deemed racially white to forcibly extract sexual acts from women of color with impunity—acts that neither they nor men of color could prevent, inhibit, or cause to cease. White women and men who saw this depravity and wished to protest against it did not get very far, and most did not even attempt to do so.

As Africans descended into racial debasement, European bond labor was deemed unnecessary.

The [indentured] servant trade began to dry up during the 1660s, when the material conditions of servants made Virginia unattractive to the English poor. Former servants complained of poor diet and long hours in the field. They also objected to laboring and suffering alongside blacks, an indictment against how degraded their life had become. . . . By the end of the 1660s, white laborers began showing their discontent by running away.[34]

This caused planters to revisit the idea of the slave trade, with the purposeful and conscious goal of forcing captured Africans to living as chattel. Says Allen, "The choice of slavery was deliberate, odious, and foul. Census takers had already marked off blacks as different twenty years before the courts in the 1640s recognized them as enslaved . . . [and] slaveholders had already consolidated a slave code twenty years before they began masking slavery behind ideology and religion in the 1720s and 1730s."[35] Allen is saying that blackness was deliberately and knowingly created in order to get away with as much abuse as was necessary to extract labor cheaply enough to enrich themselves; and whiteness was deliberately and knowingly created in order to make the majority of the poor say nothing about it, even as their own livelihoods disappeared and their poverty was made semipermanent.

To accomplish this, they began making racial distinctions in the censuses, creating slave codes, and then advertising the differences between the newly created blacks and whites. Bonded Africans could be used and abused, bequeathed, sold, or rented, but (by 1691 statute) they could not be set free.[36] Christians (read "Europeans") could not be whipped and could raise their own cattle; African bondpersons had their cattle confiscated. By 1723 no non-European could own a baptized Christian (again, read "European"). Negroes lost the right to testify in cases against whites and then also lost the right to defend themselves, a ruling that simultaneously enabled white male sexual assault of Negro women an oxymoronic phrase in legal terms.

Importantly, European bondsmen generally failed to protest their loss of work and means of survival. They also generally failed to protest the conditions their fellow humans from the African continent endured, even as these conditions put them out of work. They did not rise up against the abusive conditions that made brutal lifetime enslavement of these newly minted "blacks" cheaper for the planters and slaveowners. What they did instead is agree that they too would benefit from being able to join in the abuse of other humans, though they paid a price for this with the loss of their own food and shelter. Europeans of means ensured that all poorer Europeans in North America knew of this new state of inequality, for they advertised well the poorer Europeans' roles in the new racial structure.

Exclusive measures were put in place to guarantee that the people were systematically propagandized in the moral and legal ethos of white supremacy. . . . To prevent any "pretense of ignorance," the laws mandated that parish clerks or churchwardens, once each Spring and Fall at the close of Sunday service read ("publish") these laws in full to the congregants. Sheriffs were ordered to have the same done at the courthouse door at the June or July term of court. If we presume, in the absence of any contrary record, that this mandate was followed, the general public was regularly and systematically subjected to official white supremacist agitation.[37]

The important achievement was to align the interests of European or Euro-descended labor (both bonded *and* chattel) to those of the landholding and wealthy Europeans or Euro-descended gentry, to the exclusion of blacks who soon became the sole human chattel. The eureka moment for elites came with the creation and legitimization of whiteness, which allowed them to accomplish this feat of interest alignment without having to give up any of their riches!

At the time of these proclamations there was no answer (yet) to the question of how to determine who would be considered sufficiently European. After all, humans from all parts of the world intermixed, intermarried, and bore children, as humans had always done and will always do.

Although lawmakers tried, they could not reconcile slavery as consistent with the conditions of religious conversion or of mixed-race ancestry. As they grappled with Christianity and interracial sexual relations, they began making distinctions between whites and nonwhites with dogged determination. Indeed, in promoting a society based on race, the great planters had recognized the need to diminish distinctions made among Europeans, English-born or not. The authorities, attempting to create solidarity among poor whites and the great planters through racial consciousness, prohibited blacks from owning or supervising whites regardless of their status. White and black slaves and indentured servants were once not only equal, regardless of skin color, but friendly! Then, race was hardly a mature concept. But at this point race matures: it means more than skin color; it means denigration of blacks below the status of anyone white, no matter the occupational station of either. Thus the wedge between the newly formed races was driven deeper.[38]

Just as whites were created in the United States, so were blacks. The rule of hypodescent developed first in Virginia; then in Maryland, Pennsylvania, and New Hampshire; and only much later was it accepted in South Carolina and Louisiana after much resistance.[39] However, hypodescent is now so accepted that to this day we see that people who look like Vanessa Williams and Mariah Carey can claim blackness, despite how "whitelike" they may appear physically, because they have that "one drop" of black blood (i.e., red blood from a black ancestor) that qualifies one for blackness in the United States. Thomas Jefferson, that stalwart of human dignity and freedom, was never quite sure about the inferiority of the so-called black race. He asked scientists to provide proof one way or another—and scientists are still looking for the answers.[40] Audrey Smedley aptly described all this racial business as the transformation of racial "folk wisdom" into a racial "worldview."[41]

What came afterward was the maturation of a divide-and-conquer racial politiculture that solidified the North American view of racial difference. Rules about the appropriate categories to use, who fit in which ones, and the pseudoscience that made it all look legitimate—these matters took quite some time to disseminate and even longer to come into wide use as if agreed upon by everyone. Johann Blumenbach, the antiracist scholar, created out of whole cloth a race of Caucasians in his dissertation, using mumbo jumbo for his theory that the color of skins must somehow match the color of skeletons. Perhaps he would not be so horrified to see what use we have made of the term "Caucasian," which he made up to get his degree. Although he thought differently when he coined it, Blumenbach surely defended the way the term was used later in his life.[42]

RACE AS PURPOSEFUL FICTION

Racial categories in the United States are always in dispute and undergo continual change. If we look to the U.S. government's listing of possible answers to the census race question, over the years the unique categories among which census takers could choose are between 2 and 17 in number (not to mention that now a respondent can choose any combination of these categories they embrace, or elect "other" and write in a term of their own choosing). David Hollinger is credited with coining the term "ethno-racial pentagon" to describe the five-category standard to which the U.S. government would adhere on racial matters.[43] Karen Brodkin uses "ethnoracial" as a descriptor for U.S. categories of persons in the United States; her suggestion is that we began with a color-based system of black and white, moved to a system that included black and white and red, and finally arrived at what we have now, which includes many more "colors" of persons.[44] Perhaps this incorporation of all colors into North America is what William H. Walker meant to convey in 1907 when he drew the cartoon *The Father of Our Country as Seen by His Children* for *Life* magazine.[45] (Or perhaps he had in mind something more cynical, for he shows in the last frame Theodore Roosevelt as the colonial father of the Philippines.)

Just as racial categories are a fiction, so must be the rules for determining who fits which categories. Most people in the United States may think the average person's race is "obvious." But if someone sat down and attempted to delineate the rules about who is in which race, then it becomes quite clear that it's not so obvious after all to decide who is in which group. Even worse, a group's race can change over time—for example, the Irish were once considered "black" in the United States but now are "white"; conversely, when the 1848 Treaty of Guadalupe Hidalgo was signed, Mexicans were made "white" by legal decree (ostensibly because only for whites could property rights be enforced, as such rights were promised by the treaty). But few in the United States would now agree that all Mexicans are white and all Irish are black. Similarly, a single individual can change races, so to speak, by simply moving to a new location where racial categories are differently organized than they were at the place of origin (e.g., a light brown person moves from the United States to Brazil or Europe, and "whitens"). Follow any of these lines of thinking for a long enough time and you will question whether anything about race holds true. If race is so nonsensical, but persists so strongly and is believed so deeply, it is because there is systematic societal support for the structure (or paradigm) of racial/racist thought.

Certainly, there's a great deal of convincing research that supports the idea that none of the so-called science supporting the existence of true racial differences is to be believed. Collectively, the scholarship on the idea that a social group (i.e., "whites") constructed race in their own interests is compelling. It is far more valid according to the rules of the scientific method than any of the work that suggests that racial categories exist, that we can decisively declare a person to be in a single race, that we know that one race is better than another in certain things, and that we should all support various social policies that reward or punish behaviors that are presumably native to one race or another. Yes, the preponderance of evidence says that this whole system is a trick played on all of us, to ensure that we agree to use and abuse people and support racial policies that actually go against our interests.

Theodore Allen's body of work explains that what we really all ought to be questioning is the idea of whiteness—for that is the basic building block for the whole racial system. It is because privileges must be reserved for the few (whites with wealth and property) that the category is created. Allen argues that the creation of race was absolutely necessary for elites to continue to rule as they did precisely because there were too many poor whites in the incipient nation to allow a stable level of inequality among whites of different classes. Race was the poor whites' reward for accepting the new unequal status quo and joining elites in struggle against Native Americans or American (but enslaved) blacks. Allen argues, then, that the creation of race was purposeful—it was meant to conjoin ethnic European interests with those of the landed and wealthy gentry without the latter having to give up any of their land, wealth, or gentrified status nor to forfeit any of their own privileges to the lower classes. Indeed, the lower classes become the enforcers of the racial status quo because they agreed to make "race, and not class, the distinction in social life."[46]

Allen suggests that the demographic composition had much to do with this choice—in other words, there were too many poor whites in North America for elites to ignore. He notes that the rules for the British colonies Virginia and Jamaica were very different. Jamaica's Assembly in 1721 offered twenty acres to any laborer who would participate in the colonial project and move there, plus five acres more for each slave the laborer brought with him to settle there—and "every free mulatto, Indian, or negro" who liked could participate in the offer. By the early 1830s, "free blacks and coloreds" owned 70,000 of the nearly 310,000 bond-laborers in Jamaica.[47] Jamaica also required the militia service of black freedmen, as the British army in the colonies was too small to offer adequate defense. Soon enough, however, they created a buffer mulatto class—not surprisingly because there were too few Europeans of laboring class to make up a buffer.[48] By contrast, colonial Virginia Governor Sir William Gooch sought "fixing a perpetual brand" on African Americans. There were too many Europeans without property, too many who labored in competition with members of the bonded class, who could never be contracted for labor. The ruling elites feared the possibilities that poor European laborers, whether free or bonded, would join together with poor non-Europeans to contest their rule. Further, the ruling elites used the promise of race to manipulate their compliance. They seemed to say, "You might be poor, but because we're white we're better; hang on, and soon enough you can be rich just like me!"

In earlier times, and even today, poor whites tend to side with wealthy ones, although siding with racial nonwhites who share their social position would benefit them far more. Today, whites vote for lower taxes for the wealthy—for they believe that they will each at some point become wealthy themselves—they may not be rich, but they are certainly "pre-rich." "Americans read magazines for people more affluent than they are (*W*, *Cigar Aficionado*, *The New Yorker*, *Robb Report*, *Town and Country*) because they think that someday they could be that guy with the tastefully appointed horse farm. Politicians proposing to take from the rich are just bashing the dreams of our imminent selves."[49] Perhaps Americans believe these ideas because rather than critically examining the system that helps a small elite to their own detriment, it is easier to buy a story (with racist overtones) that falsely says wealth for whites is just around the corner and poverty and governmental assistance is what is in store for undeserving nonwhites.[50] The majority of persons on welfare are white, but both whites and blacks in the United States falsely believe that the majority on welfare are black and that blacks make up the majority of poor people.[51] More ironically, a very large portion of people receiving social security, unemployment, or Medicare benefits report never having received any government assistance! Perhaps this is because they fail to comprehend their own relationship to the government or believe the racial hype they have been told about government supporting slouchers and moochers who cannot in their minds be white.[52] Indeed, the U.S. system of social welfare was first created to protect *white women*, but it has for the most part been dismantled because the U.S. racial politiculture construed the welfare system as a set of programs designed to protect lazy women of color.[53]

In the United States we are revisiting (again and again) the choices that nonelite whites made in the 1700s that hurt them while helping the wealthy and propertied. Solidarity across (fictionalized) racial boundaries seems to me to be a far better choice than eroding one's own socioeconomic stability, but it seems not to have been the popular choice throughout American history. Nor has much changed up to today, for there is much evidence (presented in the subsequent chapters) that nonwhite nonblacks (those neither white nor black, e.g., Mexicans, Chinese, and Native Americans) have learned to follow—for they too seem to be eschewing cross-race solidarity.

No one is born with a knowledge of race. It is growing up and living in the Americas as a racial being that teaches one how to give up the innocence and un-Americanness of the raceless life. For some, the way to white racefulness is through great shame—the shame of learning who not to befriend, love, or care for, at pain of losing the love of those who gave birth to and raised you, or who befriend you as peers. Those who claim the label "white" are not always proud of that stance. Indeed, the pain for those who embrace the label has been documented.[54] This pain is not accepted lightly, and with most who end up accepting whiteness, some form of indoctrination must take place repeatedly and continually. Punishment for crossing color lines may come from persons on either side of those lines, but the racial lessons one learns first are likely taught by one's own racial compatriots. Shame for complying is internalized by those who silently accept their superior racial station, and shame is inflicted upon those who would openly question the illogic in racial hierarchy.[55]

John Hartigan Jr. discusses the exception that proves the rule in his cultural study of the status extremes "white" and "white trash." He writes, "Whiteness is not simply a racial identity and that race is not an absolute social condition. No single cultural figure makes this clearer than 'white trash.' Understanding how whiteness works requires grasping how the visage, speech, and actions of certain whites can so disturb notions of belonging and difference that they are simultaneously marked as white yet expelled from the privileged social domain of whiteness."[56] The experience of white immigrants like the Italians and the more modern "white trash," that is, demeaned whites, problematize the homogeneity that is assumed in many of the writings on whiteness and immigrant assimilation.

The term "white trash" (synonymous with "mean whites" or "poor whites") was first used in the mid-nineteenth century in Southern states to distinguish white others from the planter and wealthy classes that made up only one-quarter of the white population. The enslavement of and trade in Africans created the terms "white," "black," and "white trash" as markers of racial conditions, and it was in the slave states of the United States that the term "white trash" was born and most widely used. Evoking both sympathy and scorn before the Civil War, in subsequent years those seen as "white trash" were universally derided. Suddenly they were found in the Midwest and soon thereafter nationwide. White trash sightings seemed to coincide with the increasing volume of eugenicists' concerns about the impure element in the white race and the pseudoscience that backed those ideas. Knowing the history of the fears whites had of other whites can help in making sense of the thinking behind the 1790 naturalization law that restricted post-birth acquired citizenship to "free whites" of "good character." This thinking soon evolved to the idea of "race suicide," which became a "central trope in the eugenical discourses."[57] Hartigan's point is that race is not always about "othering" but is also about naturalizing "anxieties" about white "self-constitution."[58]

Remember, however, that the U.S. race game is not only a game for whites to play. With ethnic projects, it seems that everyone in the United States is stuck playing a version of the quest for increased status, as seen in the case studies that show how history has repeated itself. It is in the interests of those at the top of the racial hierarchy to maintain their position—and these same interests are served if those of us who struggle to survive with far less material wealth, political clout, and socioeconomic resources (factors not unrelated to one another) continue to busy ourselves with ethnic infighting for only slightly improved social (read racial) status.

RACIAL PARADIGMS AND ETHNIC AGENTS

Racial ideas (like the fact that races exist, and that no one is without a race) are perpetuated because we continue to live racial lives and subscribe to our local racial systems. Racial systems are perpetuated under a system of racial hegemony (where discriminatory practices are not forced upon us all) because not enough people stand up and say "no more" when they are not the victims being targeted at the moment. To say that all participants in the paradigm have a stake in having that system perpetuate or change is to say we all have what sociologists call "agency." As Evelyn Hammonds explains, "We made it [race], and we can unmake it," and by "we" this black female professor did not mean just white folks.[59] While race may have been invented by Europeans—who themselves did not have a unified understanding of what it was but developed it in hot contests over a very long period of time—race does not perpetuate itself. We all have agency, and use it racially, whether or not we actively or consciously intend to support or contest the paradigm in which we live.

People from the United States—especially "whites"—tend to think that racism has to do (mainly or only) with individual prejudices and individual decisions to discriminate.[60] But sociologically speaking, racism is much more than that. Herbert Blumer argues that we might grasp "a more realistic and penetrating understanding of race prejudice" if we see that race prejudice occurs between *groups who vie for position*, and not simply between individuals who dislike or discriminate against one another for a presumed racial membership.[61] Blumer proceeds, then, to explain how this group competition works. First, he says, in order to have racial prejudices at all, we have to have racial groupings. That is, each person has to see him- or herself as a member of a racial group and to see others that way also. Second, he or she must believe that each of these groups stand in relation to another. Blumer explains that people learn about racial positioning through experience and through the media (whose representatives are spokesmen for accepted racialized understandings). He further explains that people hold four basic types of feelings, which transcend individual feelings about the racial enterprise. These are: superiority, a sense of difference from the subordinate race(s), a deserving of their privilege, and fear that the subordinate race threatens the dominant group's position. Thus, group position is a "historical product."[62]

Other scholars have followed in Blumer's mindset. Eduardo Bonilla-Silva notes that Lawrence Bobo, James Kluegel, Jim Sidanius, and Mary Jackman have all put forth similar arguments.[63] However, these scholars focus on the actions of whites and, in particular, white prejudice and white dominance. What I argue here is that nonwhites also play the dominance game, but because they do not all have access to "whiteness," per se, they use a myriad of strategies to strengthen or increase the value of their racial position.

Ethnic groups take a gamble, and in this they have little choice. When they begin the process of being "incorporated, "assimilated," or "acculturated" they generally are treated exceptionally poorly. They are labeled with ethnic slurs, and popular discourse suggests that keeping them in the society would bring down the quality of life of the entire society. Attempts at repatriation or wide-scale segregation result. Any given ethnic group in the process of "assimilation" becomes associated with the worst of what humans have to offer. The loss in status is not lost on the members of the ethnic group, even if they don't care to become a permanent fixture in the United States, and even if they fully intend to return to their homelands. So, they take a gamble and embrace the ethnic identity being imposed upon them, and they use their agency to make assertions for themselves about what that ethnicity truly means.

But organizing group efforts to employ group agency toward racial uplift in a singular way is no straightforward task. One reason is that it's not always clear how a racial system behaves, for the ways that racial systems operate are deliberately masked. For instance, we learn to use ethnic identifiers to reference positions in the racial system (e.g., "Irish" means "white"), but these things change. We learn the contradictory lesson that racial and ethnic identifiers are not synonymous, but at the same time, are mutually referential. For example, when you say "black" you know what that (presumably) looks like, and similarly, when you say "Irish" we know what that (presumably) looks like, but we're not (or no longer) taught to think that there are persons who fit into both categories. Even more confusing, we learn that the Irish were once considered racially "black" and used violence, and political and workplace organizing, to change their racial category to "white."

In making efforts toward racial uplift, the Irish were certainly not alone. Other ethnic groups relied on different manipulations of the racial system to increase their racial status. The historical chapters that comprise most of the book will make very clear that manipulations of these kinds have happened repeatedly as the United States of America has moved forward in history. To understand how these projects succeed or fail, however, one must first understand the workings of the racial system and see the possibilities of our agency within it. Examples from American cultural and political history will show how ethnicity works and why it is the perfect tool to raise or lower a group's racial value.

The Ignorant Vote—Honors are Easy, cartoon by Thomas Nast, published in *Harper's Weekly* (1876). Paul Hester, Houston, TX/Menil Foundation, Houston, TX. Reprinted with permission of the W. E. B. Du Bois Institute for African and African American Research, Harvard University.

THE IRISH, CHINESE, ITALIANS, AND JEWS

Successful Ethnic Projects

Alex Haley [the collaborator on Malcolm X's *Autobiography*] describes being in a U.S. airport with Malcolm and admiring an arriving family of European immigrants. They are, Malcolm predicts, about to learn their first word of English: nigger. The weight of U.S. racial division must be learned. The drama and tragedy arise from the knowledge that American realities were such brutal and effective teachers of [U.S. racial] division and that immigrants were such apt and ready learners of a word which, as Ralph Ellison wrote, "made them feel instantly American."

> David Roediger, "The First Word in Whiteness"

At one time, the Irish and the blacks were equal on the scales that weighed their value in the United States.[1] Today, however, one group is white, and the other is—still—black. The Irish were certainly not alone in raising their racial value relative to African Americans; other similar groups achieved whiteness in full, along with a degree of ethnic erasure. Scholars mark assimilation by the extent to which an *ethnic* process (i.e., erasure or weakening of ethnic difference) has occurred, as measured by markers of spatial dispersion, socioeconomic status, language attainment, and intermarriage.[2] But the case studies in this chapter lend an interpretation of assimilation that reads differently: a group becomes more "American" and less "foreign" by *whitening*, a racial process that has a side effect of making ethnicity less salient and allowing for these measured characteristics of "assimilation" to change. Measures for the whitening metaprocess include: a marked differentiation of gender roles, with masculine men and feminine women (whereas nonwhites have emasculated men and masculine women); segregated labor, for whites do not work alongside blacks; intermarriage with those who are deemed white, not with blacks; and sanction for those who cross newly constructed racial boundaries.

The story of whiteness-attainment in the United States goes back to the formation of the nation. There were thirteen original colonies, each with its own peoples and style of government, conjoined in a federation of sorts.[3] New York City and most of what we now call the "Mid-Atlantic" states were predominately Dutch; Pennsylvania was largely German and Scotch-Irish; the Delaware River Valley was Finnish and Swedish; Rhode Island, North and South Carolina, and Virginia were settled by the English; and so on. Each colony had a seemingly homogeneous population—"seemingly" because a singular origin could only be lore given the acknowledged presence of many persons of different origins and ancestries in the colonies. The English eventually dominated the new nation and were responsible for shaping the nascent nation's racial paradigm, but they certainly did not view the coming together of groups as a laudable kind of pluralism. Stephen Steinberg explains, "Non-English colonials were typically regarded as aliens who were obliged to adapt to English rule in terms of both politics and culture. . . . Though the English tolerated non-English in their midst, there was no question as to their exclusive claim on the state. Determined to avoid the cleavages that engendered wars in Europe, the founding fathers placed high value on the homogenous origins of the American people."[4] So when the English propertyholders created whiteness, they did so with homogeneity determinedly in mind.

Because the North American colonial enterprise required both an invasion of settlers and the labor to make profits accrue, the English colonizing operation required a reluctant tolerance of people the English would long consider "outsiders." Each of the European colonizing operations had difficulties furnishing labor for their projects in the "New World." Colonists had little intention of doing all the dirty work themselves for the projects they had planned in the Americas. To enrich themselves, colonials from Spain, Portugal, France, and Holland used (and abused to the point of genocide) the labor of the natives they encountered; later, they moved on to exploiting African labor.

The English were the only colonists to also use European labor to fuel their American exploits. Desperate Europeans were in abundance, their numbers increased by the ruination of the English cloth-making industry and by land displacement when agricultural production was destroyed in order to make way for sheep production. British rulers used two methods for relocating European undesirables to North America: expelling "the Protestant masses of Europe and Ireland" through indentured servitude, and expelling "paupers, vagrants, and convicts."[5] These conditions made for a surplus of unemployed English ready for export. Social control of these "housed beggars"—as statesman philosopher Francis Bacon (1561–1626) called them—was ensured by making them into a middle class of "yeoman constables, church wardens, Overseers of the Poor, jailers, directors of houses of correction, etc." in North America.[6] The nonworking remainder was at risk of being declared vagabonds and vagrants. For a brief time in the sixteenth century this group was punished by temporary enslavement, and attempts to escape were further punished with a lifelong chattel status. Making slaves of Englishpersons was temporary and widely looked down upon, but it opened the English mind to thinking that enslavement might work in the long term under the right circumstances.

In comparison, the style of enslavement in the United States accomplished a very important thing in the development of the racial hierarchy and politiculture. Making enslavement a venture in which to involve whole swaths of society solved the problem of labor extraction. Theodore Allen invites us to imagine the problem of a slaveowner wishing to extract forced labor from another man. Who could go out each day to torture and berate a single individual face-to-face until they do as you say? Perhaps a few might be able to do it, but a system run on this method might not succeed. Instead, an entire class of people could be employed in the abuse sector. They would be paid to torture. It would become their job, from which they could gain a distance from the horror. They would abuse and torture a person, then "clock out"—with no need to see that person again for they would not be required to cook your dinner "after work." In fact, the person who eats the dinner that the tortured worker must cook is not the direct perpetrator of the violence. This arrangement eliminates the problem of forcing labor out of individual humans on a daily basis as a means of production and survival, and keeps the production of black enslavement running smoothly.

It also solves the problem of what to do with the white labor that is displaced. Suddenly there is employment for whole swaths of workers who became un-employed once black slave systems were put in place. If one hires one-half of the population to make the other half work unremunerated under torturous conditions, and convinces the former half that they "deserve" that work because of their superiority to the latter, then the labor and cooperation of the former is more readily ensured. Lower-economic-class Europeans became a racial middle-class of jailers, wardens, and overseers. This half of the population had jobs that ensured the other (black) half toiled as slaves. To keep things running smoothly, the state intervened to enforce labor control, both lowering slaveowners' costs and giving state support to the value of whiteness.

This style of enslavement in the United States also achieved a more com-plete racial denigration than perhaps anywhere else such a denigration-enslave-ment linkage had been tried. This American labor system directly coded racial categorization into one's work (and still does!). As Karen Brodkin explains, we justify our ideas about who deserves their low station in the inequality realm with a tautology: one is tainted and besmirched by demeaning work, but doing demeaning work means one is deserving of inferior status.[7] Said another way, Africans were not enslaved because they were black; they were assigned the denigrated category "black" because they were enslaved. Their status as humans was lowered by the demeaning manner in which they were forced to perform work in order to survive. The case is not much different, Brodkin argues, for any group that does demeaning work—European immi-grants included, whether they come as convicts via labor contracts made in the eighteenth century or by immigrant networks that led them to Ellis Island in the nineteenth and twentieth centuries. Whether voluntarily arriving and laboring or not, degrading work degraded the worker and racialized him/her.

Captured Africans arrived in great number in the Southern part of North America, and the racial paradigm evolved to the point of creating the catego-ries "white" and "black." Whites debated their own origins, creating myths of Anglo-Saxonism, for example, to preserve even greater privilege for the fewest. The non-English, non–Anglo-Saxons were grist for the growing economy's mills, so to speak, and those who dominated reserved the top slot for them-selves, defining their position as opposite the bottom (African). This was one great race-making enslavement machine.

At first the English's supposed superiority deemed them the only "ethnicity" deserving of whiteness, but as other groups began arriving in greater and greater numbers, the racial paradigm required adjustment. Dominant "whites" began distinguishing among, on the one hand, Protestant newcomers from nations in Europe's North and West and, on the other hand, the mainly Catholic and Jewish immigrants from the South and East, separating them into "Euroraces."[8] It took the arrival of the Southern and Eastern Europeans in great numbers before the idea of the "more familiar" Northern and Western European culture became idealized, and this process did not develop until the 1880s.[9] Beginning with the Great Compromise of 1877, and continuing with the system of Black Codes and Jim Crow laws, Northern and Southern politicians agreed to tie African blacks to agriculture in the South and exclude them from Northern factories; industrialists had to seek labor from external sources. Southern and Eastern European immigration reached such great numbers in the early twentieth century precisely due to the purposeful racial segregation of the nation's labor, which was meant to keep in near-enslavement the newly freed descendants of African slaves. It took the negotiated incorporation of many immigrant groups, a quite long process, to set up the racial system we know today. Let's look at the histories of racial incorporation of four groups to see how it worked.

THE IRISH

The story of the Irish in the United States begins with the story of the English in Ireland. The Anglo-Norman English occupied Ireland from the early thirteenth century until 1315 and imposed English law. The Irish were no party to the law, and Irish tribes sought equal treatment by inviting the Scots to invade. Their petition charged the English with Irish genocide and decried English actions: the murder of Irishpersons with impunity, the disallowing of Irish testimony against the English, the denial of inheritance to the Irish widows of Englishmen, and the ban on the rights of Irishmen to bequeath property. Theodore Allen explains that the Irish experience with the English in the thirteenth century parallels the African experience with the English in North America. The Latin term for Irishman was *hibernicus*, and it was also the legal term for "unfree"; in like fashion "Negro" was the near synonym of slave (unless modified by the word "free" before it).[10] In courts, Anglo-Normans were found not guilty of rape or murder when the victims were Irish, just as (in later times) whites would not be convicted of similar crimes against Africans. "Anglo-Norman priests granted absolution on the grounds that it was 'no more sin to kill an Irishman than a dog or any other brute.' . . . [In] Anglo-Norman Ireland, [the] native Irish of the free classes were deprived of legal defense against English abuse because they were not 'admitted to English law,' and hence had no rights which an Englishman was bound to respect."[11]

At the time that Columbus was exploring the New World, the English under Henry VII in 1494 began a new policy designed to settle the Irish problem once and for all through forced colonization. . . . [There was a widespread belief] that the Irish were better off becoming slaves of the English rather than retaining the brutish customs of their traditional culture. . . . The significance of this brutal treatment, and the transport of large numbers of captive peoples of both sexes to the sugar plantations in the West Indies, rested upon the growing image of the Irish as something less than human, as a people whose capacity for civilization was stunted. This view took form slowly but was perhaps common among the English elite by the early seventeenth century. Unremitting disdain for the customs and habits of the "wild Irish" is found throughout the literature of the sixteenth and seventeenth centuries.[12]

For four centuries of colonial project (i.e., until 1613), "the Irish were regarded by English law as foreigners in their own land."[13] The Irish had been so dominated by the British that they subsisted only on potatoes. During the famines of the 1830s and 1840s the crop was blighted to the degree that more than a million starved, and two million left their homeland and emigrated to the United States.[14] In 1830 the number of Irish Catholics in the United States surpassed the number of Irish Protestants, and the North American British colonies responded by administering anti-Catholic legislation.[15]

The Irish certainly began their time in North America near the bottom of the racial hierarchy. As Celts, the Irish were considered a race apart from and inferior to Anglo-Saxons, and some writers speculated that the Irish were of African descent.[16] The Irish and African Americans were both lynch victims and targets of race riots (like that in Boston in 1829, which targeted both groups simultaneously), and the two groups toiled together in degrading work in domestic service and transportation. They lived as neighbors in U.S. urban slums in the 1830s, danced together in times of leisure, and were lovers. The evidence suggests that sexual liaisons and love relationships between African Americans and the Irish (especially African American men coupled with Irish women) were hardly rare. Noel Ignatiev's rough calculation suggests that in Pennsylvania at the time of the 1850 Census, about 1 person in 30 in the Irish district of the state was the mulatto offspring of an encounter between an African American and an Irish; nor were "'mixed' matings" uncommon in either New York or New Orleans.[17] Both groups were living under mind-numbingly heinous circumstances far from their homelands; return was nearly impossible.

By the 1850s, more Irish than any other European ethnic group did service work or unskilled manual labor, especially in U.S. cities. The Irish did exactly the kind of denigrating work described above. Irish gangs were used as substitutes for slave labor in Southern states, and Irish youths served under indentured contracts.

They took the opportunity they saw to vie for whiteness in the United States and made use of the chance to register themselves superior to the blacks to which they were once compared. By 1843 it was clear that the poorest class of Irish in the United States had become proslavery and aligned themselves with politicos in the Democratic Party who took the same position. Even émigrés who may have left Ireland with antiracist ideas after the famine were silent on the issue once stateside. The Irish didn't mind referring to the British enslavement of Ireland, but they would not tolerate being considered slavelike in the Americas too. They sought to get rid of black workers by their side in order to rid themselves of the accusation that the Irish did "nigger work" and to free themselves from references to their being "smoked Irish" and "niggers turned inside out."[18] The Irish in the United States began to participate in antiblack race riots and lynch mobs, despite (or perhaps because of) their history of being at the victims' end of these kinds of attacks. They came to use "blackface" minstrelsy to demonstrate differences between themselves and the African Americans and to publicly show derision for the "blackness" they were once accused of embodying.[19]

Irish gangs in New York and Philadelphia used violence to intimidate the black workers with whom they once worked alongside. But this was not violence stemming from job competition—although many scholars have read it that way. Noel Ignatiev cautions against this erroneous reading of history. He says that indeed the Irish were simply willing to work for less than blacks were paid in order to undercut black wages. Ignatiev agrees that Irish immigrants replaced blacks and came to monopolize New York's unskilled labor market and domestic service jobs.[20] But "now it was the black workers who were hungry and desperate, willing to work for the lowest wage. Why then, were they not hired to undercut the wages of the Irish, as sound business principles would dictate?" Ignatiev's answer: the Irish formed trade unions and purposely excluded black labor, shouting, "White men will not work with him!"[21]

The Democratic Party—at that time both proslavery and white supremacist—took to Irish declarations of whiteness, unifying the immigrant and the American Northerner in a bloc of white voters. This political move also consolidated Democratic power among slaveholders in the South and whites in the North. "Conflict with Mexico, and to some extent the rise of Chinese immigration, made it possible in the 1840s and 1850s for leading Democrats to develop racial schemes unequivocally gathering all European settlers together as whites against the "colored" races just when belief in polygenesis was on the rise.[22] The Catholic Church was amenable to white supremacy as well. The Church supported the call for the Irish to be recognized as whites in the United States, as when official papers of the Church noted that Negroes were what the Creator made them (i.e., not Caucasian).[23] Thus, support from large political and religious institutions gave standing to Irish claims to whiteness.

By 1863, the Irish not only participated in but led mobs targeting African Americans. The Draft Riot in New York City was infamous. The Irish lynched free African Americans, mutilated their bodies, and then prevented the authorities from retrieving the corpses. The Irish mobbed places and times where freed blackpersons led temperance parades. And where the Irish and black danced and played and made love together, they had "a monomaniacal focus on race, and particularly on race mixing."[24] In 1872 Daniel O'Connell, an abolitionist activist in Ireland, circulated an antislavery and antiracist petition signed by 70,000 persons there; he cautioned the Irish in America to "side with the abolitionists" and "treat the colored people as your equals."[25] O'Connell warned, "Dare countenance . . . and we will recognize you as Irishmen no more," but America's Irish chose to ignore O'Connell and other Irish antislavery leaders in Ireland, in print denouncing abolition and calling it "niggerology."[26]

Upon arrival, gender differences among the Irish were said to follow one set of racialized stereotypes before they became white, and another afterward.

Irish women arriving in New York after the famine helped to strongly define domestic service as women's work. They comprised 74 percent of New York City's servants, although they were only a quarter of the city's population; by contrast Germans were 15 percent of the population and 15 percent of the domestics; Jewish and Italian working women were domestics in proportions of 14 percent and 9 percent, respectively.[27] Those women who were born in the United States thought this work degrading, and perhaps it was so, for Irish girls and women fought over wages and working conditions with the bourgeois "ladies" who employed them. Antebellum Irish domestic servants worked long hours at hard labor, and were at the constant scrutiny of women in the Victorian era who burdened them further with rules about their manner of work and dress and use of what little leisure time they had, for they were perceived as constantly trespassing outside of the confines of proper womanhood. Still, they suffered it all, using their savings to help support families back home and even send for others to join them in America. Many interpreted Irish women's domestic work as a cultural feature—that the Irish were tolerant of it if not willing to do it. The real appeal was more structurally based: since many immigrants from Ireland were unmarried women, live-in situations were practical, although the work meant living in isolated, near-feudal conditions.[28]

With some notable exceptional individuals, most Irish in the late 1800s were working poor, a rise from the destitution they'd suffered in the early part of the seventeenth century back in Ireland. Still, anti-Irish sentiment persisted: the American Protective Association "pledged not to employ, work with, or vote for Irish Catholics."[29] When Irishmen won elective offices in Jersey City's state legislature, the offices were abolished; and when an Irishman won the seat as Boston's mayor, the Boston police force was removed from the city's control.

But by 1900, 65 percent of employed Irish men were blue-collar workers.[30] Irish men and women were to some degree ambivalent about their social integration and rise to the upper classes, ruing the cultural transformations brought by increased wealth and property ownership (i.e., overvaluing money and becoming slumlords). Postfamine émigrés' letters back home spoke poorly about life in the United States, cautioning potential followers that in the United States one must "do a lot of things against his will in trying to make a livelihood" for people must become "hard hearted and selfish" to survive.[31]

By the 1930s, the Irish were dispersing and Irish neighborhoods began to disappear. Segregated housing, "traditional" work, Irish/African American sexual union and intermarriage, and racial tolerance—these were no longer part of their lifestyle. They had created and lauded ethnic differences between themselves and the persons at the bottom of the racial hierarchy, whom they publicly denigrated. The Irish segregated themselves from their former neighbors and coworkers, with the justification that the Irish were the racial betters of African Americans and should no longer be associated with people at the racial bottom. As their racial status increased they transformed the gendered differences between males and females in the ethnic group. And finally, the Irish expected group members to show loyalty to the racial uplift program and they sanctioned ethnoracial trespassers who (for example) refused to self-segregate. As is normal for ethnic projects, the Irish ethnic project did not threaten the U.S. racial paradigm as a whole. Indeed, the Irish ethnic project actually reinforced the racial system by simultaneously denigrating African Americans while petitioning for a new Irish status within. In all this, they prevailed. The Irish had achieved whiteness.

THE CHINESE

John Sutter and James Marshall were partners in Sutter's Mill in Sacramento County, California, when in January 1848 Marshall discovered gold flakes, which the two men vainly tried to keep secret. Thus began the California Gold Rush. One month later Mexico signed the Treaty of Guadalupe Hidalgo, ceding California to the United States. In that same year, three Chinese persons entered the United States through California.[32]

The Gold Rush caused the number of Chinese in the West to skyrocket. White racists provoked anti-Chinese riots, which replaced the welcome that the Chinese enjoyed when they were few in number. By 1852, the number of Chinese in California reached 25,000; many of them had come to evade the aftermath of the Taiping Rebellion (1850–1854) and try their luck finding gold.

Chinese immigrants were poor and were "accused of 'accepting' a lower standard of living" that in turn lowered white miners' wages. But the migrants' poverty looked like relative wealth when compared to the standard of living in Chinese villages from whence the immigrants had come. Still, most did intend to return. The Chinese were entangled in a "coolie" (indentured) labor system that was first used to undercut wages of former slaves in former Spanish and British colonies, but white racists used abolitionist rhetoric to argue that Chinese immigrants were "half-civilized beings" in "a more abominable slave traffic than that of the African slave trade in its most odious features."[33] The "six companies"—the term for labor contractors who paid passage for and served as middlemen employers for the indentured Chinese migrants—did enforce debt repayments and labor contracts. Laborers were organized into gangs that depended upon gang bosses to distribute wages (who did so in an often exploitative fashion). "Slave" workers were also said to be unfair competition to those (whites) who would otherwise be employed in the apprenticeship system that dominated artisan craftwork at the time.

In the nineteenth-century United States, there were two kinds of sentiments about the Chinese. While there was respect for their ancient culture, there was also a disdain for the Chinese people, who were seen as a "stagnating, perverse, semi-civilized breeding ground for swarming inhuman hoardes."[34] A Senate investigating committee was formed in 1877 to determine the nation's opinion on the migration. The general sentiment was clear: the Chinese had an inferior style of life that harmed whites who lived and worked near them; the Chinese encroached upon whites' jobs; and the Chinese threatened the entire social order. The committee's report said, "an indigestible mass in the community, distinct in language, pagan in religion, inferior in mental and moral qualities, and all peculiarities, is an undesirable element in a republic . . . [and worse yet,] there is not sufficient brain capacity in the Chinese race to furnish motive power for self-government. . . . [They are] a menace to republican institutions upon the Pacific, and the existence there of Christian civilization."[35] Former California Governor Frederick F. Low (who had also been a minister to China) as well as Henry George (a state inspector of gas meters) testified before the committee, both noting that the Chinese were much like the Negro biologically, although Low noted that the Chinese could keep himself from falling into servitude. Attorney James P. Dameron testified that the Chinese and Negro had similar brain capacity (far inferior to that of the "Indo-Germanic" race), and that Chinese civilization had "thousands of years ago [risen] to the highest attainment of their brain capacity" and would progress no further.[36] George also argued that because "the number of negroes in the country is fixed, while the number of Chinese may be increased indefinitely," the nation was at great threat.[37]

When the California legislature in 1850 made it illegal for blacks to testify against whites in court, this decree banned Chinese testimony as well. The Chinese were also denied the ability to naturalize and become citizens.

In 1852 the State of California issued a tax against foreign miners (but not white citizens). By the time this tax was declared unconstitutional, the sources of individual mining were exhausted. Lode mining was developed soon afterward, run by companies that required the use of explosives, drilling, and tunneling. Chinese who formerly worked as individual miners became wage workers hired by the companies at unequal wages. Chinese wages were between one-half and one-third those of white miners. Still, whites protested the Chinese in mining. Whites more readily accepted Chinese labor in what was considered women's work, such as cooking, housekeeping, laundry, and domestic service. On the West Coast, the dividing line that normally was drawn between women's work and men's was transformed into a division between white and nonwhite workers.[38]

Railroads began recruiting the Chinese, first as strikebreakers but later on for any blue-collar job. By the time the Central Pacific Railroad was complete about 90 percent of their workers were Chinese.[39] These newly unemployed Chinese workers again competed for mine wages. And once again, the Chinese were forced into manufacturing jobs that on the East Coast were filled by women and children.[40] "In 1869, leaders of the agricultural and railroad industries from throughout the South attended the Chinese Immigration Convention in Memphis, Tennessee, forming companies and hiring agents to contract Chinese workers from California, Cuba, and China and transport them to Southern locales."[41]

Ronald Takaki summarizes the racial position of the Chinese in this way: "Racial qualities that had been assigned to blacks became Chinese characteristics. . . . Heathen, morally inferior, savage, and childlike, the Chinese were also viewed as lustful and sensual. Chinese women were condemned as 'a depraved class,' and their depravity was associated with their almost African-like physical appearance[: they were] 'fair [of complexion] but [physically] a slight removal from the African race.'"[42] Occasionally, the Chinese, Native Americans, and Africans were all racially lumped together; indeed, white workers referred to the Chinese as "nagurs."[43] Legal scholar Ian F. Haney López explains it this way:

Unsurprisingly, this early social treatment of the Chinese as akin to Blacks also found legal expression. For example, in the 1854 case *People v. Hall* the California Supreme Court heard the appeal of a White defendant challenging his conviction for murder. He appealed on the grounds that he was convicted only through the testimony of a Chinese witness, and that this testimony should have been excluded under an 1850 statute providing that "no Black, or Mulatto person, or Indian shall be allowed to give evidence in favor of, or against a White man." The court agreed with the defendant that the Chinese witness was barred from testifying by the 1850 statute, reasoning that Indians originally migrated from Asia, and so all Asians were conversely also Indian, and that, at any rate, "Black" was a generic term encompassing all non-Whites, and thus included Chinese persons. This legal equation of Chinese and Black status was not temporally or geographically unique. Three-quarters of a century later and across the country, Mississippi's Supreme Court reached a similar decision, holding in 1925 that school segregation laws targeting the "colored race" barred children of Chinese descent from attending schools for white children.[44]

Starting in 1870, discriminatory state and municipal ordinances legislated minimum lodging spaces; placed bans or taxes for using poles to carry laundry or vegetables and on wearing braids; and prohibited the Chinese from owning land or laboring in municipal works. These actions culminated in the Anti-Chinese Alliance of 1876–1882, which reintroduced racially discriminatory legislation that had already been declared unconstitutional. By 1877 the percentage of Chinese in California well exceeded the national average.[45] In 1882 Chinese immigration of unskilled labor was banned altogether when Congress suspended immigration from China in response to racially motivated backlashes against the Chinese. The ban was set to be revisited every ten years to ensure the ability to increase Chinese immigration should Europeans fail to arrive in sufficient number. But this suspension was continually renewed until 1924 when, in an effort to cease Chinese immigration altogether, the National Quota Immigration Act was installed—with no quota for China.

Once again, rather than choose to join with laborers facing racialization and discrimination, white low-wage workers made racial alliances with white capitalists in the hopes of ensuring their own socioeconomic position. Interestingly, some whites petitioned for the Chinese to gain equal pay, but scholars have argued that this was only a ruse, carried out in the hope that employers' racist sentiment would win out and the Chinese would never actually reap those earnings.[46] Instead, employers offered to hire white workers' children, with the idea that both the children and their parents would earn low wages. Indeed, creating a ban against Chinese immigration was also a move to stem unionization—campaigning for exclusion of the Chinese was one of the unions' strongest organizational tools. Eventually, declining employment and active recruitment induced the Chinese to move from California into other states; anti-Chinese sentiment followed the Chinese internal migration and dispersal.[47]

Some Chinese were recruited to work on plantations in the Mississippi Delta after manumission of enslaved Africans and their descendants left farm labor in an unsettled state. Most of the migrants in the Delta region originated in the Sze Yap district of southern China.[48] Many of these Chinese transplants were men who married black women (who were overwhelmingly if not exclusively from the upper classes of black communities) and bore children with them. But while they found love and family there, the Chinese migrants soon enough realized the predicament that sharecropping brought to them. Clearly, they were to replace the Africans whose enslavement had been a casualty of the Civil War, and the goal was to exploit the Chinese even further by a combination of labor control and racial subordination. The editor of the *Vicksburg Times* explained the prevailing sentiment: "Emancipation has spoiled the negro, and carried him away from our fields of agriculture. Our prosperity depends entirely upon the recovery of lost ground, and we therefore say let the Coolies come, and we will take the chance of Christianizing them."[49] Southern planters were at times even clearer in their answer to Reconstruction's promise, for another journalist at the time explained that with Chinese recruitment "the tune . . . will not be 'forty acres and a mule,' but . . . 'work nigger or starve.'"[50] The Chinese resisted this oppression with protests, risking injury or death from planters armed with guns. In one instance "the labor gang was so enraged by the false promises that had been given them that when the Chinese agent who had initiated the transaction visited the plantation, they attempted to lynch him."[51]

At the time of Chinese incorporation into the Delta, the local racial paradigm was bifurcated. The Delta community was aware only of the racial categories white and black, and upon entry the Chinese in the Delta were equated in status with blacks. Interchange between whites and blacks was restricted by racial segregation and racial etiquette, and whites who became "too familiar" with blacks were chastised and castigated. Whites didn't care if the two low-status groups "fornicated" with one another—indeed, they nearly saw them as one, at least in the early period. Because of severely restricted Chinese immigration there were nearly no available Chinese women. As one Chinese respondent interracially married in the 1930s said, "If a Chinese man *did* have a woman, it *had* to be a Negro."[52] In fact, the Mississippi Chinese intermarried at a rate of 20 to 30 percent before 1940, far less than their Chinese counterparts around the world.[53] The Chinese in Java, Britain, Jamaica, and Trinidad all intermarried to far greater degrees. Even more strange, then, is the low Delta intermarriage rate, because in these other regions the Chinese were not put exclusively into the bottom of the racial hierarchy. In the Delta, Chinese-black sexual liaisons were all that the Chinese migrants had available to them.[54]

The extreme racialization drove numerous Chinese to leave sharecropping. Many became "middlemen minorities" by opening shops in black neighborhoods, with black clientele; whites also patronized these stores. Even after entering the grocery occupations Chinese racial status did not change much, perhaps because the groceries were the only sites of integration at the time (sometimes black women were hired to work in these stores), and strict racial etiquette frowned upon integration. The Delta Chinese were also expected to go to segregated schools. Negro schools were always inferior (and even when on an equal financial footing with white schools, they were not accredited). Hires were not often made among graduates of private black Tougaloo College, for (as the white county school superintendent said) blacks schooled there "have too many *ideas*—they give people *ideas*."[55] Chinese children could go to Negro schools, or cross into Arkansas to board with the few families that had succeeded in sending their children to white schools despite the laws against it.

By the 1920s the Delta Chinese had begun seeking alternative schooling for their children. They began by working with the few white schools that had admitted one or two Chinese children, boarding their children with families of admitted children. When the school system pushed back, the Chinese appealed to the courts but lost: in an important 1927 test case that went to the

U.S. Supreme Court, Chinese grocer Gong Lum sued to force the Rosedale school system to admit his daughters but the final ruling agreed with the Mississippi Supreme Court's decision to bar them. The schools won with the argument that white schools were for white children, which Chinese children were not, thus they should go to the colored public schools. The real concern, some say, was that the Chinese had mixed with the African American population, and allowing Chinese in the schools would allow mixed-race Chinese, which would in effect desegregate the schools. Indeed Lum's failed petition assured that his daughters were not mixed.[56] In the end, Lum moved his family to Arkansas. In 1936 a Chinese Baptist Mission School was built with funds collected from local merchants and other Chinese communities around the country. With some notable exceptions (one where five "pure" Chinese students were allowed to attend a white school on a test case basis), Chinese were segregated in schooling until the 1940s.

Occupationally, the Chinese grocers did well.[57] They treated black patrons better than white grocers did, and blacks did not have to travel to frequent these stores. The Chinese also extended credit to blacks whereas whites did not, and patrons and sellers addressed each other with status titles such as "Mr.," "Mrs.," and "Miss." But those Delta Chinese who had reached adulthood by the 1950s (most of whom had inherited their occupations and wealth) ostracized the families who had intermarried with blacks. They would not condone marriages between their children and blacks (and would only reluctantly abide intermarriage with whites). The men of this generation now "see themselves at work as a group of successful proprietors in a triethnic community."[58] Between these generations, in the 1940s, the Mississippi Chinese crossed over the color line to the white side of the racial paradigm, literally leaving behind those who (legally or in common law) intermarried with blacks and refused to abandon the Chinese-Negro families they helped to create. The community ostracized Chinese-Negro families, and allowed only severely limited contact with any Chinese man who had a black family. "The pure Chinese found it in their interest to exclude them; indeed, such a policy was in some instances explicitly required of them by the white establishment."[59] By contrast, when Chinese intermarried with whites, it was almost always a male shop owner marrying a white woman of the lower classes. Still, and especially after World War II, the Chinese community accepted these Chinese-white unions and not the Chinese-Negro families (even when formed with a Negress of a higher class). The newer generations didn't understand that the Chinese-black liaisons in earlier times didn't jeopardize social standing, and in fact were considered "good for business." It was only "when entrance into white society came to be viewed as the overriding concern was there any 'threat,' and that only then was the action morally condemned."[60]

How did the Chinese orientation to the racial system change? What changed the position of the Chinese on Chinese-black liaisons? It is clear that the Chinese had long appealed their black or near-black treatment in the workspaces in which they were allowed—they rebelled against sharecropping because, as *sojourners*, the goal was to earn money to send back to family in China. (Perhaps those who married black women may not have been sexually faithful to their wives back home, but this was not a problem as long as they were still financially faithful.[61]) It may be that they considered themselves outsiders here to survive and make a buck, intending to return home again, and therefore they lacked a dog in the fight to build the U.S. politiculture. But when the Chinese settled, stopped looking homeward, and became *immigrants* instead, they seemed to reach the limit of their willingness to live inside the confines of blackness. Embracing life in North America meant buying into the racial paradigm, and the position of blackness was untenable. After all, race is a social construction, so one may not be able to construct a whole new system, but it is possible to construct a new place for oneself. Like the Irish before them, the Chinese community as a whole refrained from making attempts to overturn the racial hierarchy or substantially change its politiculture, only to fit within it in a better place. Becoming shop-owning entrepreneurs in black communities posed no threat to the racial status quo, even as it allowed them to leave behind "black" occupations. The Chinese and Irish histories have another quality in common: the Chinese community sought to increase its racial status by leaving behind those men who had intermarried or formed common law bonds with black women. Affinities with those compatriots and companions in the black community were not forbidden, but certainly they were disallowed. One businessman said of such couples who stayed together: "We didn't have anything to do with them, that's all. We didn't try to break up their marriages."[62] As for whites, they merely had interests in maintaining their own superior position and not in keeping the Chinese black. So, while they did not allow the Chinese to integrate white schools, they did allow the Chinese to create their own schools. The Delta Chinese quest for increased status did not threaten white superiority, and this was key.

Today, Delta Chinese young people say they prefer white lifestyles and seek acceptance in white society, whether or not they qualify for middle-class status (for most do not live in white middle-class neighborhoods).[63] Real estate discrimination is not as rampant as it once was, but the practice of lying about one's true address in order to get one's child into a white school has become ineffective. Chinese professionals say they have little contact with blacks—men report that the current state of race relations is fine, while women report a desire to be more white-affiliated.[64] Today, among the Mississippi Chinese, intermarriage means a Chinese female married to a white male. The Chinese have experienced an upward trajectory that is marked by application of the term "model minority," often used to describe groups who have achieved enough to be a "model" (and without resorting to political agitation or reliance on government programs) but failed to achieve enough to erase the group's "minority" status.[65]

The racialization of the Chinese continues, and the Chinese (sociologically speaking) continue to respond. Across the U.S. mainland, today it is neither uncommon nor impolite to refer to the Chinese as "Asians" (despite the fact that the term "Asian" lumps together the Chinese with persons from many different nations on the southern and eastern end of Eurasia) or even "Asian-Americans" (despite the fact that "Asian-American" still indicates "otherness" for North Americans by birth who have Chinese ancestry). This categorizing as a single group persons with differing cultures, heritages, ethnoracial alliances, and conditions of birth is a new twist on a very old style of racialization. Wesley Yang wrote passionately about it in the *New York Times*:

Sometimes I'll glimpse my reflection in a window and feel astonished by what I see. Jet-black hair. Slanted eyes. A pancake-flat surface of yellow-and-green-toned skin. . . . It's my face. I can't disclaim it. But what does it have to do with me? . . . I, for instance, am the child of Korean immigrants, but I do not speak my parents' native tongue. . . . I have never dated a Korean woman. I don't have a Korean friend. . . . And although I am in most respects devoid of Asian characteristics, I do have an Asian face. . . . Here is what I suspect my face signifies to other Americans: an invisible person, barely distinguishable from a mass of faces that resemble it. A conspicuous person standing apart from the crowd and yet devoid of any individuality. An icon of so much that the culture pretends to honor but that it in fact patronizes and exploits. Not just people who are "good at math" and play the violin, but a mass of stifled, repressed, abused, conformist quasi-robots who simply do not matter, socially or culturally.[66]

Yang's statement is most certainly a statement of racialization, not so different from that W. E. B. Du Bois describes in his classic book *The Souls of Black Folk*, as he explains what it is like to learn that one is on the wrong side of the veil of race that hangs between blacks and others. Yang's commentary is different from Du Bois's because Yang's racialization presumes him to be superior in intellectual ability, but simultaneously not to matter. Yang hints that perhaps the "traditionally Asian upbringing is the problem" that is stopping Asians from reaping the ripe fruits that would come with full incorporation, that is, hitting the "Bamboo Ceiling." This is how he explains the rise of programs like LEAP—Leadership Education for Asian Pacifics—that offer courses and workshops to teach Asians and Pacific Islanders networking, self-promotion, and assertiveness to succeed in the capitalist workplace. One lawyer participating in the program explained:

White people have this instinct that is really important: to give off the impression that they're only going to do the really important work. You're a quarterback. It's a kind of arrogance that Asians are trained not to have. . . . Someone told me after I moved to New York that in order to succeed, you have to understand which rules you're supposed to break. If you break the wrong rules, you're finished. And so the easiest thing to do is follow all the rules. But then you consign yourself to a lower status. The real trick is understanding what rules are not meant for you.[67]

In his *New York Times* article Wesley Yang also discusses the ABCs of Attraction, a group focused on success in the U.S. dating market. They teach Asian males how to model (white-style?) charisma via the "alpha male" stance (shoulders back, legs apart slightly wider than shoulder-width), use of the "kino escalation" ("you must touch her"), and use of "the intonation exercise" (where students repeat the phrase "I do what I want" in a variety of moods).[68] Cosmetic surgery is also an option. Asians are just over 3 percent of the U.S. population, but they garner 6 percent of cosmetic surgery procedures in the United States (and this figure does not count those who get procedures done in Asia). More Asian Americans choose cosmetic surgery than any other ethnoracial group, including American whites.[69] Most often, they choose implants to make their noses more prominent, or double-eyelid surgery to create folds above the eye. In fact, scholar Eugenia Kaw notes that "for many . . . the surgeries are a calculated means for socioeconomic success [and] most [of my respondents] described the surgery as something to 'get out of the way' [at an age younger than 18] before carrying on with the rest of their lives"; moreover they said that they were empowered, not oppressed, in making choices about how they use technology to change their look.[70] Although many who opt for such changes refuse to characterize their surgical choice as a response to racialization, Kaw sensitively doubts their rationalizations, for in a climate where beauty is singularly "Caucasian," so to speak, how can paying to change one's appearance—not to be youthful, but to round "slanty" eyes that are said to make one look to be "sleepy" or of less "wit"—be seen as based on something other than race?[71]

Thus does this ethnic project march forward into the twenty-first century. Wesley Yang ends his article by laying out his own path: "I see the appeal of getting with the program. But this is not my choice. Striving to meet others' expectations may be a necessary cost of assimilation, but I am not going to do it."[72]

THE ITALIANS

Four Italians—John Cabot, Amerigo Vespucci, Giovanni da Verrazzano, and Christopher Columbus—sailed to the Americas with the support of patrons from other states, for when these men traveled, Italy as we know it did not exist.[73] A fragmented Italy was declared unified in 1861, but the unification process was not completed until ten years later. An estimated four million Italians emigrated between 1890 and 1920, most leaving from Southern Italy because of their disappointment that Italian unification left unfulfilled the promise of a liberal Italian state.[74] Southern Italians were racialized as nonwhite during the premigration period, when anthropologists in the late nineteenth century produced racial "proof" that the Southern Italian was racially inferior to the Northern.[75]

The 4,600,000 Italian migrants who moved to the United States between 1820 and 1930 constitute the second-largest group of European immigrants in that period (while the 5,900,000 German immigrants were the largest); and between 1880 and 1920, Italians made up the largest group of European immigrants to the United States. Eighty percent of these were Southern Italians.[76]

The Italian government considered laws to restrict emigration, and opponents to the exodus worked to frighten prospective immigrants with tales of

American horrors. At the beginning of the migration flow these immigrants were tolerated, but as the nineteenth century came to an end and Italian immigrants outnumbered other nationalities, "open hostility became more pervasive than tolerance."[77] Educated Americans knew about and admired Italian culture (at least its contributions to arts and architecture) even before there was an Italian nation, but that did not preclude the formation of anti–Italian immigrant sentiment in the collective American vision.

Most Italian émigrés came to the United States, and most of these entered through Ellis Island, where as many as five thousand were processed through immigration in a single day. Only about a quarter of those who landed moved away from the industrialized Northeast.[78] By 1900 Italians comprised the largest group of foreign-born Philadelphians, but groups were much smaller in Baltimore or Boston where they lived packed into tenements. Southern Italians dominated Chicago's Italian immigrant pool after 1880, and by 1919 made up 75 percent of Chicago's Italians.[79]

Italians who migrated to the United States in the earliest part of the twentieth century were not always permanent migrants, for this period was marked by Italian migrants moving to the United States to work and send back money, then return to Italy; up to half of all these travelers to the United States returned.[80] Perhaps this circular migration could be partially to blame, but soon enough there was hysteria in the United States about the hordes of Italian newcomers. Once again, the immigration story followed a predictable pattern, as the Italian migrants were believed to be racially inferior carriers of African blood, prone to violence, and from societies morally and socially "reminiscent of primitive and even quasi-barbarian times."[81] Italian immigrants rarely spoke their own national language but instead used regional dialects. They were not a homogenous group. But Johann Blumenbach, the inventor of the term "Caucasian," determined at the time of its definition that Italians belonged in the Caucasian group—and however undesirable they may have been, they were considered to be and remained white.[82]

Recruiters (who were often fellow Italians) offered desired but less than appealing labor contracts, but migrants' exit from Italy was also aided by hunger, drought, and a severely depressed Southern Italian economy.[83] The Italian transplants were generally peasants who strongly supported union movements and affiliated themselves (when they did make political affiliations) with socialist or anarchist groups.[84] They worked the lowest-paying jobs, doing menial work—but they did not occupy society's lowest rungs.[85]

Up until 1910 Sicilians were recruited to rural Louisiana (some from other parts of the United States, some direct from Italy) to cut cane, pick strawberries, or toil at cutting lumber up.[86] Some of these migrants did wage labor, and others sharecropped as growers sought to replace African American workers they believed to be less dependable and productive. At first, African Americans and Sicilians in Louisiana lived together and worked peaceably alongside one another for the same pay, and the Italians suffered violence and terror (including lynching) from Southern whites. Sicilians adapted to the United States' style of racism, but those Sicilians "who worked or mingled with blacks [were seen] as inferior and suspect."[87] Jim Crow and the Black Codes kept African Americans tied to the land in ways Italians were not, so Sicilians left or protested when faced with very poor working and living conditions.

After 1900 they moved into entrepreneurship, getting a leg up from planters who created a tenant system (similar to sharecropping, but allowing farmers to keep half the harvest) intended to stabilize the labor force, and this system even encouraged some Sicilians to become landowners. "[By] 1902, sugar planters complained that it was difficult to keep Italians in the cane fields for more than two seasons, for 'by that time they have laid by a little money and are ready to start a fruit shop or a grocery store at some cross-roads town.'"[88] They also ran saloons or became peddlers to African American clientele.

Sicilians were also recruited to Bryan, Texas. Entrepreneurial migrants purchased land and had access to even more land in exchange for clearing the land of lumber for the state government. They offered one another mutual aid in times of crises (as in 1899 and 1900 when the Brazos River flood devastated the group), but intermarriage between Sicilians and non-Sicilians was rare. By 1905 these migrants comprised three-fifths of the town's population. Independence, Louisiana and Bryan, Texas were model towns for the Italian immigrant experience, but deception, devastation, and destitution faced those who left the Northeast and went to those towns and elsewhere in the South. Italians who went West fared better mainly because "the population [there] consisted largely of newcomers who tended to be more accepting of foreigners."[89]

Some scholars argue that Italians' racial status was complex, not straightforward. Though declared white, in some ways they were treated as black.[90]

Italians' denigration and degradation made them "nonvisibly black."[91] They, like African Americans, were subject to lower wages and suffered lynching and segregation. But they were never barred from naturalization (which, starting in 1790 and up until 1952, was available only to whites), nor later from the benefits gained through the New Deal.

"Is an Italian a white man?" a journalist asked a West Coast construction boss in the 1890s. "No sir," he answered, "an Italian is a Dago." Similarly, a *Harpers' Magazine* piece offered a guided tour of "Italian Life in New York," exoticizing Italians and comparing them to Africans: "It is no uncommon thing to see at noon some swarthy Italian . . . resting and dining from his tin kettle, while his brown-skinned wife is by his side."[92]

Whites mobbed against Italians in New York in 1862 and New Orleans in 1891. Italians had an uneasy dance with whiteness—and some go so far as to say they were slow to embrace it, at least until World War II when 4,000 Italians were arrested and interred as the United States declared war on Italy.[93]

Italians, although labeled "white," simply did not "*act*" white."[94] They accepted their racialized post–Civil War economic niches in degrading farm labor and tenancy farming, and they lived and worked among blacks with ease. There is some evidence that they intermarried with African Americans, but on this point, Italian scholars don't seem to be consistent. Still, intermarriage and sexual liaisons between Italians and African Americans in Chicago were frequent enough that they were quite casually announced in the ethnic paper *L'Italia,* which also reported on black lynchings.[95] Italians were victims of lynching in Louisiana, Mississippi, and West Virginia. More famously, mob violence (justified in the national press) killed eleven Italian immigrant prisoners in retaliation for the murder of the New Orleans police chief. As a group they were marked by the epithet *dago.* James Barrett and David Roediger cite a 1906 Italian government report finding that "a majority of plantation owners cannot comprehend that Italians are white," particularly when they and blacks were doing the same agricultural or manual labor.[96] Italians were "white enough for naturalization and the ballot," but Southerners saw Italian immigrants as similar to African Americans though occupying perhaps a racial middle ground.[97]

Being white by law (e.g., being given rights to naturalization, voting, homeownership, and New Deal benefits all denied to African Americans) may be what counts in the Italian case. But these "white on arrival" Italians saw the need to position themselves against African Americans.[98] Vincenza Scarpaci argues that writers have made much of the Italians' involvement in Louisiana's history of protecting the (white) immigrant vote and disenfranchising African Americans, but he counters that history is complex—in some cases the Sicilians supported black disenfranchisement, and in others they were against it.[99] Further, "In Louisiana, while Italians did move along the trajectory from 'inbetweenness' toward social acceptance by shedding some of their outwardly different cultural practices, their conformance to the dominant system was one of compliance of the outward forms, and not necessarily the full weight of racism."[100] David Roediger notes that Italian nationals certainly had experienced exchanges with and explorations in Africa, participated in the slave trade, and worshipped black Madonnas.[101] Roediger explains that when W. E. B. Du Bois analyzed and assessed the Italian Americans' path to whiteness in an article published in *Foreign Affairs*, Du Bois read Italy's October 1935 invasion of Ethiopia this way: "Economic exploitation based on the excuse of race prejudice is the program of the white world. Italy states it openly and plainly."[102] Du Bois argued that Italians sought whiteness because it is a power relation that has global effects, and those African Americans who rioted in 1930s Philadelphia against Italians in America who supported Italy's invasion of Ethiopia perhaps supported Du Bois's view.[103] By contrast, in Chicago in 1936, according to an article in the *New York Times*, "'4000 daughters of Italy married their husbands anew . . . in celebration of their homeland's conquest of Ethiopia . . . donning "iron of empire" rings' Mussolini provided in exchange for their gold wedding bands, which they sent to the fascist state."[104] Roediger continues, "The justification for Italian empire led some Italian American editorialists to dismiss African American grievances in the United States and to imagine that both Italian and U.S. ventures in white supremacy brought blacks into the 'school of progress.'"[105] For them, surely, racial whiteness always made the difference; it is of little consequence that Italians as an ethnic group were looked down upon by other whites in the room. Said another way, race always trumps ethnicity in the global domination game. But legal whiteness was apparently not enough, for Italians were not so assuredly white that there was no need for an ethnic project of their own.

Where Italians struggled against the racial hierarchy and its racist status quo—for example, Italian anarchists' antiracist writings and campaigns in New Jersey—they were "attacked, murdered, and silenced."[106] While racialized as the lowest of whites, Italians learned to accept American racism and support it and, further, to silence those members who professed antiracist stances.[107] Italian migrants were arriving in large numbers during the post–Civil War Reconstruction era, and the "constitutional evil" of racism was revived in legislation.[108] Italians participated in their own U.S. racialization, albeit in complex ways, by constructing "their own sense of place in the racial hierarchy to the extent they could."[109]

Scholars like Richard Alba declare that Italian upward mobility (through occupational mobility and increased suburban residence) signals a waning of ethnicity across the broader Italian population,[110] but I suggest too that waning ethnicity is a signal of *racial* incorporation. Most scholars who write on Italians focus on Italians as an ethnic group among other ethnic groups, or Italians as whites among other whites, but tend not to understand Italians as white ethnics in a racial hierarchy with other whites of varying ethnicity, and also with blacks who are basically denied ethnicity altogether.[111] There is a common error of failing to see that groups and individuals hold both racial and ethnic positions at the same time.[112]

There was one period in which whiteness didn't matter as much as Italian birth. This period began November 9, 1939, when FBI director J. Edgar Hoover ordered "the compilation of a Custodial Detention List of persons of Italian, German, and Japanese ancestry to be rounded up and imprisoned in concentration camps in the event of a national emergency."[113] The list was activated in December 1941 in response to the attack at Pearl Harbor. From then on, being a hyphenated American without citizenship who was on this list meant internment—even for someone living a long, recognizably American life but without documentation. Even some Italian naturalized citizens were interred. "Italian Americans had to prove their loyalty. The way to do that was to *forget*—forget what they knew, forget who they were. To become American, that is, to be trusted as loyal Americans in the crisis at hand, a kind of cultural amnesia was required."[114] In one fell swoop, 600,000 Italians without citizenship became suspect. They all were required to carry identity cards, and thousands were arrested and tested to determine the extent of their loyalty and the danger they posed. (By contrast neither citizenship nor birth on American soil protected Japanese and Japanese Americans from internment.)

Why would a group designated as white from the start ever need to have an ethnic project for racial uplift? In what ways may Italians be said to have had an ethnic project at all? Perhaps Italians mark the embryonic stage of ethnic projects in the United States. They were white, but segregated from other whites by the persistence of the denigrated ethnic lore that was regularly if not consistently applied to their group. They may not have needed a full campaign for whiteness, but they certainly took on the task of stepping on those below them in the racial hierarchy to indicate their elevated status, thus not only accepting the racial system but also validating and cementing it. On the whole, they favorably compared themselves to African Americans and other groups of color while noting their similar mythological ability to succeed without assistance of any kind.[115]

It is quite possible that Italians in the United States are sociologically analogous to the Irish in Britain who, Mary J. Hickman argues, suffered from their "forced inclusion" within a "myth or homogeneity." That is, the ethnic group's image shifted over the years, but they still did not earn equality among those in the superior category.[116] Jennifer Guglielmo and Salvatore Salerno named their edited volume *Are Italians White?* to challenge the idea that whiteness for Italians is a "done deal," and also as a query as to whether Italians in the United States are willing to continue to carry the burden of whiteness.

Italians' designation as "white" was meaningful in that it ensured their position in the topmost drawer of the U.S. racial hierarchy, yet the denigration to which Italians were subjected put them at the bottom of that drawer. It is only in this sense that Italians can be imagined as occupying some sort of "middle" place, if the middle can include people at the top of the heap (as the "middle class" in the United States appears to be).[117] Aiding this middle-race feeling may have been Italians' class history. They remained working class longer than most European immigrant groups, and this image helped Italians in the United States to "stand in for the very image of white ethnic working-class right-wing conservativism."[118] A rhetoric of self-righteousness about their own struggles and of blaming African Americans for society's ills of poverty and crime helped elevate Italians racially, but (as with other American ethnic groups) this same rhetoric caused them to fail to make alliances with groups who might have otherwise helped them fight the racism and oppression to which they had also been subjected.[119] Standing in the early twenty-first century and looking back on the vista of the Italian American experience, I see what looks like an ethnic project, one that is well on its way to success.

THE JEWS

In 1880 Jews were one-half of one percent of the U.S. population and concentrated in South Carolina. By 1920 they comprised more than 3 percent of the U.S. population and were concentrated in the New York City area. Between 1881 and 1924, 2.5 million Jews from Eastern Europe entered the United States.[120] That Eastern European Jews were coming in large numbers worried the wealthy Protestant pundits of the day, who mixed anti-immigrant and anti–working class sentiment in their public speech. President Woodrow Wilson feared revolution because of their presence, Senator Henry Cabot Lodge sought the cutoff of immigration altogether, and Theodore Roosevelt warned of "race suicide." Madison Grant published *The Passing of the Great Race* in 1916, which rooted the lower races of Europe in the lower classes. Grant joined with eugenicist Charles Davenport to form the Galton Society in 1918 to promote eugenics and restrict immigration. Lewis Terman, Henry Goddard, and Robert Yerkes developed the "intelligence test," which coincidentally proved their belief in the "feebleminded" nature of Southeastern European immigrants, African Americans, American Indians, and Mexicans. These men were hardly in the radical fringe—they carried the mainstream views of the time.[121]

In sum, when Jews first arrived in large numbers from Europe, they were unwelcome. One hallmark of their status was the lynching of Leo Frank and the racial aftermath that absorbed the nation. In 1913, fourteen-year-old Mary Phagan's body was found in a factory basement in Georgia, and Jews clearly fell on the wrong side of Georgia's "white over black bifurcation."[122] Evidence pointed to the (black) night watchman as the evildoer, but Frank was tried and convicted instead; a white mob hanged him in 1915 when the sitting governor Nathaniel Harris commuted his sentence. Harris, noting a new rise in anti-Semitism in Georgia, conceded "that Jews had 'banded together as a race or a religion to save a criminal,' and had thus 'ranged themselves in opposition to men of other races and religions'"—for Governor Harris, these defensive actions clearly showed Jews to be nonwhite, for whites need not engage in such behaviors.[123] Although others at the time commenting on the case argued that Jews were white, Jeffrey Melnick (the foremost scholarly expert on the case according to scholar Matthew Frye Jacobson) argues that Frank was clearly nonwhite once charged with such a crime, for his Jewish religion, Jewish "look," and perversion were argued by many to be conjoined.[124]

Karen Brodkin traces the Jewish transformation from "not-quite-white" to whiteness in her partly autographical book *How the Jews Became White and What That Says about Race in America*. She explains that her family has to "learn the ways of whiteness," since their normal behavior did not qualify them.[125] The transformation to whiteness—not just for Brodkin's family but for all Jews in the United States—required changes in the ways the sexes related inside and out of the Jewish household (requiring an embrace of white womanhood that meant the removal of power from the strong ethnic Jewess) and where they lived (suburbanization was required whether or not desired), among other things. In the history that Brodkin presents, she acknowledges Jewish ethnic pride, stick-to-itiveness, and "bootstrap" mentality, but acknowledges that these are not sufficient to enable Jewish success. Jews and others of the darker "Euro-races" faced barriers to their success, and each group had to be whitened before those barriers would fall.

One marker of Jewish nonwhite racialization was their level of segregation in the labor force. Where immigrant and white workers were jointly employed, they were still segregated, both in their occupations and in company housing. That Southern and Eastern European men did degraded forms of work (that no white man would do) only helped prove the inferiority of the worker; and the women did factory and domestic work (that no white woman would do). Jews were largely skilled premigration but were frozen out of the occupations for which they had skills, and they merely moved to the jobs they were able to do: as tailors, furriers, hat makers, bakers, carpenters, bookbinders, and build-ers. Jews were also excluded from professions in corporate management. Their labor-market exclusions caused them to enter entrepreneurial occupational niches, setting up small shops as doctors, pharmacists, and other independent businesses that did not then have the cachet that they do today. They did work that was considered degrading for it was menial. The work was undifferentiated by gender, with women and men working alongside one another, and thought of as requiring no skill. It has been already noted that doing degrading work is an important marker of racialization. Those that had jobs in the garment indus-try saw their jobs deskilled and thereby degraded even more. In response, Jews unionized, forming the International Ladies Garment Workers Union (ILGWU) and the Amalgamated Clothing Workers Union (ACWU), and they unionized other trades as well (e.g., the Typographical Union and the Jewish Butchers

Union). (Jewish women comprised the majority of garment workers when the infamous Triangle Shirtwaist Factory fire in 1911 took 146 lives; the doors were locked to keep the young female workers in and the union organizers out.[126]) Jewish workers' organizations created a heavily socialist political culture that—along with Jewish builders—resulted in residential cooperative apartments and housing projects and a respect for working-class culture and lifestyles. The 1919 Red Scare was another marker indicating the degree of unwelcome facing the Jews and their organizing behavior. That Jews were working class, willing to organize in unions and community organization, and willing to strike—coupled with the Russian Revolution, a series of labor strikes, and more post–World War I immigration—fueled fears of communism in the United States.

Brodkin maintains that gender relations are also important contributors to racial status. When Jews in the United States were still nonwhite, working-class Jewish women who were young and single contributed to family wages, as did their single brothers and fathers. "Single Jewish women were not seen as sexual beings in need of social and/or ritual regulation"—it was the "sexually wise" married women who were the "potential seducers."[127] Married women needed to be monitored and regulated, and they performed home-based work to earn income. Racialized women are strong. Anti-Semitic stereotypes emphasized racialized gender differentiations, labeling Jewish women as coarse and aggressive and Jewish men as effeminate and lecherous.[128] Prewhite Jewish women organized strikes, food riots, rent boycotts, and other protests. Giving new meaning to the phrase "upsetting the apple cart," a Jewish woman overturned a peddler's cart of vegetables when he asked his wife to beat a female customer arguing over the price of onions, then overturned other carts and pelted with produce the police officers who came on the scene.[129] (Jewish men were also involved in political parties, unions, and other community-centered organizations.)

Between 1885 and 1913 social science scholarship debated the question of whether Jews were a race or another type of social group, but they certainly leaned toward "race" as the answer. Nineteenth-century notions of race, immigration, and peoples were invested in Lamarckian science that promoted beliefs in the heritability of acquired traits. Race, culture, and nation were all conflated, reflected in the physical, and heritable. Thus, debates of the time questioned from where Jews got such things as their long-headedness (was it through heavy use of the brain?), "Jewish nostrility," and "the Jew's eye."[130]

Creating and promoting the idea of ethnicity was in large part a self-serving exercise. Jews were an immigrant group with no nation to put on the left side of the hyphen, and fears of anti-Semitism made them reluctant to embrace the term "Jewish-Americans." Jews started "to construct a new discourse of ethnic difference in which they eschewed the twin pulls of assimilation and cultural separatism," but the idea really took root in the public discourse only in the 1940s and 50s.[131] These are the years Irving Berlin (b. 1888 in Russia; moved with his family to the United States in 1893; d. 1989) wrote some of his most famous tunes, such as "God Bless America" (written after World War I but first publicly performed in 1938), "Easter Parade" (published 1933, sung by Bing Crosby in the 1942 film *Holiday Inn*), "There's No Business Like Show Business" (published 1942, performed by Ethel Merman in the 1954 musical of the same name), and "White Christmas" (written in 1942 and reperformed in the 1954 film of the same name).[132]

Jewish thinkers contributed the idea of "ethnicity" to this debate—a contribution that could only happen when race was separable from culture and nation. That could only happen with the twentieth-century demise of Lamarck's ideas. Key figures in this creation were Louis Brandeis (1856–1941) the anti-assimilationist, pluralist, and Zionist Supreme Court Justice; Horace Kallen (1882–1974), the professor who advocated for political and economic assimilation with maintenance of distinctive culture; and many famous others involved in the Intercollegiate Menorah Association (established 1913) and its official publication, the *Menorah Journal*.[133] They used these forums to debate the meaning of being a Jew and an American and to further secure the idea that race (fixed, heritable, and different) was distinct from ethnicity (based on nation and reinforced through cultural institutions and practice). "It was an amazing forum in which issues of subnational identification and politics were debated at the highest levels. It was here that reference to ethnic groups and loyalties first appeared. Interestingly, the *Menorah Journal* became the site of a high-powered intellectual exchange precisely at the moment when American universities and magazines were closing their doors to Jews."[134] Jewish access to higher education was severely restricted, and in some cases, discrimination against Jewish applicants was flagrant. College in the early-twentieth-century United States "was not about academic pursuits. It was about social connection through its clubs, sports, and other activities, as well as in the friendships one was expected to forge with other children of elites and these were reserved for white Protestants."[135] Columbia University, Harvard, and the Seven Sister schools all excluded Jews—and other institutions emulated Columbia's model of Jewish exclusion. (Those Jews finally admitted after World War II were the children of Jewish elites.) Thus many Jewish scholars petitioning for Jewish ethnicity were at the same time also declaring the group's racial whiteness; some (like Brandeis and Maurice Fishberg [1872–1934]) argued that assimilation into whiteness was ethnic suicide so that great care must be taken to hold onto ethnicity, but that Jews were white all the same.

Perhaps the publicity campaign from these and other Jewish intellectuals worked, or maybe guilt from having barred for so long Jewish refugees fleeing Nazi oppression had an influence. Whites acquiesced to Jewish efforts at mobility and even became philo-Semitic.[136] In the 1940s, Jews like Milton Berle, Sid Caesar, Sam Levinson, and Jack Benny were widely visible because they were in the arts and the new medium of television.[137] In the 1950s we saw the rise of New York's Jewish intellectuals, "interpreters of white America" of the times: Lionel Trilling, Irving Howe, Philip Rahv, Norman Podhoretz, Daniel Bell, Irving Kristol, Norman Mailer, Sidney Hook, Nathan Glazer, and Martin Peretz. Almost all came from working-class families, almost all were educated at City College or Columbia University, and almost all of the white-interpreters were male.[138]

The 1950s conversation took a new bent when it directed an antiblack discourse. In the public arena of "high culture and public policy, . . . [they] invented their own Jewish form of whiteness by reinventing blackness as monstrous and proclaiming their distance from it: I'm good, you're bad; I'm white, you're black."[139] Put another way, "postwar intellectuals . . . knew that they were not to the manor born and needed to create a place for themselves there."[140] Jews created the idea of ethnic pluralism and constructed Jewish whiteness by propping up Jews as a model minority and contrasting themselves against blacks who they deemed culturally deficient. This was the time when Nathan Glazer (not Daniel Patrick Moynihan, as is widely believed) created the myth of the black matriarch—the woman who destroys the black family and ruins the black child by her domineering attitude and demeanor and whose single-mother household is contrasted with a strong two-parent Jewish family.[141] Daniel Bell and Irving Kristol argue that the black middle class does little to aid in solving "Negro social problems."[142] Norman Podhoretz projects his fear of the black male into a discourse on masculinity.[143] Even Jewish participation in the civil rights movement has been interpreted as "part of their effort to present Jews as more American than were native-born whites, precisely because Jewish concerns with social justice heightened their dedication to American ideals of social justice and democracy."[144] Assimilationist impulses made it easier to support the civil rights movement rather than openly and publicly fighting growing anti-Semitism.

Postwhite Jewry looks significantly different from its prewhite image. Jews took prewar themes in Jewish culture and gave them new postwar assimilationist spins to claim Americanness. Self-made Jewish moguls project Hollywood versions of Jews as virtuous, hardworking self-sacrificers.[145] There was a sharp decline in Jewish small business ownership, and a corresponding increase in professional occupations held by Jews; many became doctors and college professors. Jewish whitening required the creation of a parallel Jewish bourgeois universe. Expectations of bourgeois white women differed significantly from the prewhite era. When whiteness has been achieved, male occupations are considered skilled and exclude women. In the heyday of radio, Jews lived in the ghetto, but on TV Jews live in the suburbs. Jewish girls no longer work for wages but now become Jewish American Princesses. Jewish mothers do not organize, protest, or riot but instead coddle and overprotect from inside the home. New Jews don't loudly protest anti-Semitism for fear of entrenching images of difference. Even Jewish socialists sought to eliminate the Yiddish-speaking branches of the Socialist Party. Wholly new Jewish icons can be found in Calvin Klein and Ralph Lauren, Norman Podhoretz and Nathan Glazer, Philip Roth and Barbie and Ken. In this 1950s–1970s transition, Jewish whiteness became American whiteness.[146]

The postwar period also brought to returning war veterans economic opportunities that wholly changed the racial and economic structure of the United States, and the outlook for Jews changed as well.[147] The G.I. Bill of Rights (i.e., the 1944 Servicemen's Readjustment Act) gave eight million returning soldiers benefits to higher education (but also lowered the value of said education, which before the war was a mark of upper-class status). Similarly, the Federal Housing Authority (FHA) opened the doors of suburban home ownership to soldiers returning from the war. (Prior to that time, homes were bought with cash. The FHA introduced the 20-percent-down option with which we are all now familiar.) Many scholars nicknamed these programs "white affirmative action" for the impact they had on elevating new whites like the Jews to much higher socioeconomic status. This nickname may also be apt because access to these programs was consistently denied to nonwhites. The opportunities offered to whites to purchase homes in new and affordable ways (e.g., paying in installments on a thirty-year mortgage), and denied to blacks, increased racial segregation in housing and labor markets and also in investments to already segregated education and housing.

Jews sought an ethnic identification that could comfortably rest between full assimilation and separatism without upsetting the prevailing racial hierarchy. Victoria Hattam suggests Jews created and popularized the term "ethnicity" as a useful way of writing about their in-group loyalties without emphasizing their religious differences or framing their efforts as staunchly opposed to anti-Semitism. Karen Brodkin argues that Jews took to this new status with some ambivalence and uneasiness with capitalist-infused affluence, and an edging away from a full embrace of American-style whiteness, rooted in the memory of the Jewish Holocaust and a companion allegiance to Israel. Jewish writers on ethnicity took pains to make crucial distinctions between ethnicity and race, and to make Jews explicitly ethnic, "because [in their thinking,] if one is raced, one is not an ethnic."[148] They used the formation of a strong ethnicity to get away from race; in their thinking, deracing is also whitening.

THE SUCCESSFUL ETHNIC PROJECT

I have presented four ethnic histories that show evidence of ethnic projects—concerted efforts by an ethnic group to increase their racial status. These projects merit the label "successful" because of the trajectory of the group history: each group ended in a higher status place in the racial hierarchy than where they began. The groups vary on so many important levels, but they each waged successful ethnic projects under wildly varying circumstances. Each group entered different regions of the United States and came at different time periods. Some went West, some East, some North, some South. Some entered at the nation's inception, some came in great numbers only fifty years ago. And all these ethnic histories are tales of contestation—for there was neither a straightforward nor a singular way to use group agency to respond to racialization. Still, we may mark these histories as having many similarities.

The histories are similar in that these ethnics used migration in their quest for a better life; no matter that they entered the United States under quite different circumstances. They variously came as indentured servants, as free labor, or as refuge-seekers. While migrants are always somewhat better off than those they leave behind, these groups all entered the United States under dire circumstances and sought to improve their lot in life.

The histories show that each group entered the United States with very different senses of their own ethnic identity, but each created a unified ethnic identity with the aid of their ethnic project. Many came from places that were only forming nations; some only saw their nation formed after World War II. Some were grouped together ethnically despite speaking different dialects and languages. Italians certainly did not all speak the same language. Neither did Jews. One should note that Ireland became part of the United Kingdom in 1801, the modern Greek state was born in 1830, Italy didn't become a unified nation until 1861, Romanian independence was not achieved until 1877, and Poland became an independent state in 1918. Each group entered with different senses of ethnic identity, and all these Europeans moved from places that *were becoming places* at the same time they were becoming immigrants in the United States. Similarly, sojourners, like the Chinese, began with an orientation that looked outward and changed their perspective on race when they began to call the United States home and embarked on their ethnic project.

Each group faced negative racialization on arrival, but managed to raise their racial status. These ethnicities were created in a new nation obsessed with race, and they could not be born without a racial taint. Victoria Hattam puts it this way: "New immigrants underwent racial categorizing at the same time they developed new identities, and the two sides cannot be understood apart from one another."[149]

Italians were always white, but perhaps full status attainment was elusive. The Irish, by contrast, were understood to be savages at first, but crossed over into whiteness. The Jews were notoriously racialized by Germans in the Nazi Party and their sympathizers—partly as a direct result of U.S. pseudoscience "proving" the racial superiority of whites—but ultimately waged so successful an ethnic project in the United States that they achieved whiteness. The Chinese in Mississippi were originally racialized as black, but succeeded in raising their status by seeking inclusion not as fully white, but only as nonblacks.

Part of that racialization perversely included a denigration of the contributions of the community's women, who were seen as strong—in a bad way, as if they were out of control. Whitening meant relegating the women to a place behind men, where they were more cloistered and their contributions were less-valued and sometimes the target of ridicule.

Each group had formed close relationships to African Americans upon arrival in the United States at the time they formed their ethnic identity; yet each group changed their orientation to African Americans. Initially, most groups intermarried and worked side-by-side with African Americans. Some even joined the movement petitioning for civil rights for all. The members of each group have carried out plans to create a far more distant relationship to African Americans than the one they had at the time of their entry to the nation and succeeded. And (perhaps because of that very success) each group now has reached a higher racial station than where they began. Each one, we may say, had very successful ethnic projects.

It is hard to imagine an immigrant group who before arrival had clear understandings of the U.S. racial paradigm. No matter, for they learned, and even after facing persecution and denigration themselves, "still got caught up in this racial thing."[150] When they caught onto the ways the U.S. racial paradigm worked, and how they might benefit, many European and Asian nationals and their descendants contorted their own ethnicities in order to improve or preserve stations higher-ranked than African Americans. The newly ethnicized made determined decisions to make those changes happen, and continue to act as if they are status seeking, despite feeling great ambivalence toward their newly attained higher statuses. David Richards sums it up well when he writes, "American racism could not have had the durability of the political power it has had, either in the popular understanding of American culture or in the corruption of constitutional ideals of universal human rights, unless new immigrants, themselves often regarded as racially inferior, had not been drawn into accepting and supporting many of the terms of American racism. We cannot begin to understand or protest the unjust terms of American racism unless all Americans, whatever their ethnicity, have some sense of how their multicultural identity has been importantly deformed or even suppressed in service of this injustice."[151]

The Proposed Immigration Dumping Site, cartoon by Frederick V. Gillam, published in *Judge* magazine (1890). Caption: "Statue of Liberty: 'Mr. Wisdom, if you are going to make this island a garbage heap, I am going back to France!'" Source: Art Resource, NY.

CHAPTER 5

THE NATIVE AMERICANS, MEXICANS, AND AFRO-CARIBBEANS
Struggling Ethnic Projects

Not once have the Civilized been able to honor, recognize, or
describe the Savage. He is, practically speaking, the source of their
wealth, his continued subjugation the key to their power and glory.

James Baldwin, *Notes of a Native Son*

The ethnic projects of the groups discussed in this chapter are marked by two
features: the groups' struggles for racial uplift; and an inability to successfully
and permanently raise their status above the color line that divides whites
from nonwhites in the racial hierarchy. To understand these struggles, think
of a trend line that summarizes statistical data. Where the trend is positive,
that is a successful ethnic project, moving upward toward higher racial status.
Struggling ethnic projects have trend lines that are neither clearly positive nor
clearly negative in the algebraic sense. Said another way, for such groups, the
trajectories measuring racial status are not uniformly positive over time. These
ethnic groups begin their racialization at a low point in the racial hierarchy and
have seen both upward and downward movements in racial status over time.
In those periods where increments in higher racial status attain, the upward
trend does not persist long enough for me to name them as wholly successful.

I discuss here the histories of Mexicans and Afro-Caribbeans in the United
States, along with those of several Native American nations, including the

Choctaw, the Cherokee, the Creeks, and the Nez Percé. These groups have a long history of racial incorporation in the United States, although this incorporation has never reached the point of embrace. Sometimes the extreme violence that characterizes their experience looks less like "incorporation" and is more reminiscent of genocide.

But first, I must provide a word of caution. In some ways, it is quite odd to speak of Mexicans, Native Americans, and African Americans as distinct ethnic groups. Of course, my argument in this book is that we create ethnicities in much the same way as we create races (omitting, perhaps, the pseudoscience that would be included in the recipe for race). We add a mix of ancestry, heritage or tradition, mythology, and folklore but also ignore a great deal of admixture. In this case, the admixture ignored is significant. It goes without saying that the Native American groups discussed here were nations on the land now called the "United States of America" and that their nationhood predated European conquest. Since the Europeans arrived, there have been many types of "miscegenation" that have resulted in admixtures of Native peoples, Europeans, and Africans.

Jack Forbes has written extensively about the fallaciousness of believing African Americans and Native Americans to be distinct peoples. They are quite conjoined in their history and in their progeny, and therefore even to think of them as distinct groups is to think erroneously. Forbes writes:

By the nineteenth century it is quite certain that Afro-Americans (in the broadest sense, whether living in Latin America, the Caribbean or in North America) had absorbed considerable amounts of Native American ancestry. Similarly, many North American and circum-Caribbean native groups had absorbed varying amounts of African ancestry, from New England to the entire rim of Central and South America. But in many cases we are dealing with 300 to 400 years (twenty generations) of intermixture of a very complex sort. Very seldom would we be looking at, for example, a half-[Native]American, half-African person in the later nineteenth century, but rather at a person both of whose parents might have varying amounts of African and American ancestry derived at different intervals and from extremely diverse sources—as from American nations as different as the Narragansett or Pequot and the Carib or Arawak, or from African nations as diverse as the Mandinka, Yoruba, and Malagasy.

The ancestry of modern-day Americans, whether of "black" or "Indian" appearance, is often (or usually) quite complex indeed. It is sad that many such persons have been forced by racism into arbitrary categories which tend to render their ethnic heritage simple rather than complex. It is now one of the principal tasks of scholarship to replace shallow one-dimensional images of non-whites with more accurate multidimensional portraits.[1]

If the progeny of Africans and Indians permeate the North and Central American world, then Mexicans and Afro-Caribbeans must also be considered hybrid groups, well beyond the meager evidence of intermarriage and admixture I present below. Many Mexicans—admixtures themselves—can hardly be called "immigrants" to the United States for they instantaneously joined the U.S. polity when states were formed on the lands on which they lived. Thus it is inaccurate and perhaps even deceptive to treat these groups as distinct from one another, and this is crucial to keep in mind as one reads these ethnic histories. The fact that their ethnicities are understood to be distinct might be taken as clear evidence that these ethnicities, too, are social constructions. They have less to do with who the group members are and with whom they procreate than with how outsiders have constructed them and how they have constructed themselves. In this book I am wholly unequipped to untangle the "true" ethnic origins of the groups discussed here. I am not a historian, anthropologist, or archeologist, so I must review published literature to explain these ethnic histories. In some ways, then, I am bound by the same constructionist paradigm that created the ethnic group, even as I search for evidence of the ethnic projects that mark the quest for greater racial status. Still, it is particularly sad to note—especially in light of this history of Native-black admixtures—that these peoples who are far from "pure" chose to deny ties to African Americans or acknowledge their brethren and sistren who share African American blood. Many Native American groups have extirpated ties to African Americans who were once tribal members. Similarly, Mexicans have denied ties to blacks and emphasized ties to Europeans, while simultaneously deemphasizing their own *mestizaje*, or cultural and biological hybridity.[2]

NATIVE AMERICANS

A miscalculating Christopher Columbus, while looking for "the Indies" so he could grab its gold and spices, veered off course and landed in the Americas in 1492. In the United States, children are taught that Columbus "discovered"

America that year, but there were people on these lands who had discovered them way before he did. His first visit landed him in Haiti, where he was greeted by Arawaks bringing food, water, and gifts. Some were wearing gold flecks they had found. Columbus and his crew captured these people to force them to reveal where the imagined stores of gold were hidden. A tax of sorts was instituted: Indians who failed to bring their quota of gold had their hands severed and bled to death. In 1495, having returned to Europe and back on his next expedition, Columbus rounded up and enslaved 1,500 Arawaks, taking the best 500 back to Spain. Only 300 arrived naked and alive; they were sold at auction. In two years, half of the 250,000 Arawaks on Haiti were dead.

The colonial project that had begun with Columbus continued. "What Columbus did to the Arawaks of the Bahamas, Cortés did to the Aztecs of Mexico, Pizarro to the Incas of Peru, and the English settlers of Virginia and Massachusetts to the Powhatans and the Pequots."[3] In U.S. public schools children are also taught about Tisquantum (a.k.a. Squanto), the Patuxet Indian, enslaved in England and thus English-speaking, who taught the Pilgrims to catch eels and grow squash and survive their first winter. These events are commemorated in the United States with the annual November Thanksgiving turkey feast and the pardoning of one live turkey by the sitting president of the United States. Children are normally taught neither about the European treatment of these "First Nations" (as Canadians call them) nor the causes of population decline that in no time brought the Natives' numbers down to one-tenth their size.[4] From the perspective of the Native population, colonization did not change with U.S. independence in 1776; 69 percent of the signers of the Declaration of Independence had held colonial office under England's rule.[5]

Although genocide was the ultimate result of the meeting of Indians and Europeans, the populations native to the Americas had varying lifestyles and radically different orientations toward white America. Some nations, known as the "Five Civilized Tribes"—comprising the Cherokee, Choctaw, Creek, Chickasaw, and Seminole tribes—accepted cultural assimilation, owned slaves (albeit under reportedly different conditions from white American slaveowners), and even fought for the Confederate Army. A few, like the Nez Percé, are known for having refused to assimilate. (There are also a few Seminoles who held out; their descendants are still trying to live a Native lifestyle in the Everglades today.) Whether these tribes were agricultural and sedentary, or dedicated to keeping Native ways, religions, and nomadic movement that followed seasons and migrating herds, Indians were racialized and criticized as "savage."

Whether sedentary or roaming, Native Americans were equally denigrated and damningly racialized. A strong test of the ethnic project hypothesis would be to search for evidence of ethnic projects among these diverse types of Native populations. For the studies in this section, I selected Native nations from across the spectrum of these varied lifestyles, and I found evidence (however fragmented) of ethnic projects among them.

THE FIVE CIVILIZED TRIBES

Two themes mark the parts of the history of Native American groups that I highlight here and consider as elements of their ethnic projects. Each of these groups fought hard for recognition from the U.S. federal government and also for their rights to property and liberty. They had relations with African Americans—not always as a separate ethnic group, but as members of these same tribes. These groups' ethnic projects, then, confirm the denigration they suffered during "incorporation," underscore their acceptance of "white" ways, and show their subsequent willingness to purge themselves of the African American element within their nations.

In 1540 the Choctaw in Mississippi encountered Hernando de Soto's company and their knives, and many thousands died as a result. After these first meetings, however, several whites intermarried with the Choctaw, and these unions created children that rose to tribal leadership in subsequent generations. One such leader was Chief Moshulatubbee, who himself was believed to have both Indian and white wives. Whites desired Choctaw land, but the Choctaws were agricultural—they were sedentary homebuilders and farmsteaders, as were the Cherokees, Choctaws, Creeks, and Chickasaws.

The War of 1812 was fought between the United States and Britain, and at its end many Americans likened it to a second war of independence. At this time most of the Cherokees, Choctaws, Creeks, and Chickasaws were still on their homelands and intended to stay, but obstacles to winning that fight were great. None of these nations posed a serious military threat to the expanding United States, and each nation was divided in that a minority wished to maintain traditions while an increasing majority embraced white material culture.[6]

It could be argued that the Cherokees became the most acculturated to white ways. They had accepted Moravian missionaries in 1801, and in 1817 they accepted others from the American Board of Commissioners for Foreign Missions.[7] Sequoyah, also known as George Gist or Guess, invented the Cherokee alphabet in 1828, and the Cherokees rapidly became literate. They appeared to live very much like whites did in their own settlements. Both Cherokees and whites had farms, plantations, and slaves; some Cherokees were Christians who read a translated New Testament and followed the Sabbath; and the Cherokees also had a written language, a constitution, their own newspapers, and tax-supported schools.[8] Also, in 1828, the Cherokees adopted a political system modeled on the United States, with three government branches; a court system; and an elected chief, mixed-blood John Ross. Ross was educated by missionaries and preferred to dress like a white planter, but he was committed to his people and could argue against the whites' laws.[9]

The Creeks were named thus by whites because they were subtribes of a nation of people in Georgia and Alabama who lived along rivers and streams. Although they watched in horror as white men killed animals for fun, they readily traded with whites (to the point of dependency upon that trade) and intermarried with them. Gloria Jahoda explains, "The Creeks had appropriated white customs that suited them—cloth dress, hunting weapons and ammunition, the keeping of peach orchards and livestock," but also "they took to the white man's ways so readily that they were considered a 'civilized tribe.'"[10]

Red Eagle, warrior leader of the Creeks nation, met personally with the partially paralyzed, war-wounded Andrew Jackson, Red Eagle's white counterpart, after the Creeks suffered multiple retaliations in return for an attack on Fort Mim in Alabama. They shook hands on an arrangement that would put the native peoples on (already occupied!) soil they did not know in the Great Plains. This set the stage for the Indian Removal Act, "a simple law: any Indian who remained on his ancestral lands affirming his Indian identity would be a criminal."[11] Although the Creeks, Choctaws and Chickasaws were all similarly acculturated to white lifestyles, it was the Creeks who were pressured to give up their land.

In varying degrees, the Choctaws, Chickasaws, and Creeks followed a similar road to acculturation, learning from missionaries, educating their young at schools, creating constitutional governments modeled after that of the United States, and developing stable agricultural economies. In each of the tribes, prosperous Indian elites emerged, wearing fashionable clothes, living in two-story plantation houses, owning slaves and handsome carriages, and rivaling the lifestyle of their most affluent white neighbors.[12]

But removal was imminent and a foregone conclusion:

The reasoning of the Long Knives [whites] was torturous. Indians only "infested" the land; they were hunters and did not farm it. (When one saw corn and cotton and squash and beans and peach trees and cattle in Indian towns, one turned the other way.) The hunters must be removed for go-getting farmers. On the other hand, the officially nonexistent Indians who were becoming go-getting farmers themselves were competing with white Americans. Therefore, they must be turned into hunters again, and hunters could not be civilized so they would have to go. The Indians were damned if they hunted and damned if they didn't. The more agricultural the tribes became, the more of an autonomous threat they were.[13]

Events in the life of Choctaw Chief Moshulatubbee are illustrative in explaining Choctaw attempts for recognition and incorporation as well as the rebuff these attempts garnered in return. In 1820 the Choctaw were already suffering displacement by encroaching "Long Knives" who had already settled on Choctaw land. Hopeful about the prospects for moving west, Moshulatubbee signed away the Choctaws' existing holdings for the promise of land in the Western United States. As a result the Choctaws suffered forced removal to the Western United States. Tribal leaders appealed to Washington, and the group was later granted citizenship at the cost of their own sovereignty. Believing the invitation to full citizenship to mean what it said, Chief Moshulatubbee ran for Congress, to the horror of white Mississippians—but he lost the election in any event. The Chief signed the agreement, and removal of the Choctaw from their land soon followed. This removal had the support, too, of white convert Greenwood LeFlore, who gave elegant speeches favoring removal even though he did not join them. LeFlore remained behind on an estate with his slaves and renounced his tribal membership.

Many groups suffered similar experiences with "removal," the euphemism that covered up the all-too-realistic violence and deception resulting in the murderous and forceful overtaking of a people's ancestral and historical homeland and destruction of their sustenance and livelihood. "The Potawatomis had called their journey the 'Trail of Death.' But the term used by southeastern tribes wrenched from farms and plantations became the general one. Because the Creeks and Cherokees and Choctaws had wept, the Cherokee called the forced removal 'The Trail Where They Cried,' from which the term 'Trail of Tears' is derived."[14] In 1832 the Choctaws of Mississippi were also on the move West, and many leaders had lost lands and other resources by signing treaties they could not read. Many died from exposure to winter cold and exhaustion and many others from cholera, but some did make it to a new settlement in Oklahoma.[15]

The Cherokees are also known for launching the most organized resistance to removal. It would not be possible to do justice to the story if I tried to detail the entire history of the Cherokee nation; so here I focus on their experience in Georgia. In 1817 several Cherokee leaders were bribed into signing a treaty that ceded a third of Cherokee lands in exchange for land in Arkansas territory; and in 1835 a fraudulent treaty agreeing to removal of half the tribe split the Cherokees and doomed those who remained, for it was enforced as if it bound the whole tribe.[16]

The Cherokees fought on both legal and moral grounds in an effort to retain their eastern homelands. They petitioned the Supreme Court of the United States, which in *Johnson v. M'Intosh* (1823) declared that Indians who owned land could do with it what they wished. This ruling came too late for those forced out onto the Trail of Tears where some 45 percent of the 22,000 removed lost their lives.[17] In response, Georgia passed its own laws foreshadowing Jim Crow: the Cherokees could neither pass any laws of their own, nor could the Cherokees or Creeks be considered valid witnesses against any white person. Moreover, Indians who discouraged Cherokees from leaving their land could be jailed.[18] In 1829 whites invaded remaining Cherokee lands in a rush for gold after it was found there, and Georgia's state government further made it illegal for Cherokees to mine gold or assemble for any purpose aside from ceding land.[19] In May 1830 Congress passed the Indian Removal Act and it was signed into law. In 1831 the Cherokee nation sued to show that the state of Georgia had no jurisdiction over their nation, but in *Cherokee Nation v. Georgia* the U.S. Supreme Court ruled that it had no jurisdiction in the matter. In 1832 they sued again, in *Worcester v. Georgia,* a ruling that fell on the side of the Indians, to which President Andrew Jackson responded, "[Supreme Court Justice] John Marshall has rendered his decision, now let him enforce it."[20] Prior to the Removal Act, approximately

8 percent of Cherokee households held black slaves.[21] These ethnic Africans walked the Trail of Tears with their Cherokee tribe.

By the early nineteenth century, white American public opinion had changed in many ways since the philosophically enlightened period of the writing of the Declaration of Independence and the founding of the Republic. Arrant nationalism and racism had struck deeply among the majority of white Americans, and the southern Indians would not find safety by modeling themselves and their republics on the idealism of the American revolutionists. Despite their successful efforts to become acculturated, they were still regarded as members of an inferior race, no longer feared but possessing what the whites wanted. Under the Jackson administration, they would fall victim to what in the late twentieth century would become known brutally, but candidly, as "ethnic cleansing."[22]

At the same time, the Cherokee had begun to create their own tripartite system of race, distinguishing between the blacks and whites with whom they had mixed. In 1855 the Cherokee passed a Marriage Law to govern intermarriages between Cherokees and whites—African Americans were not a party to this as they were excluded from citizenship until the Cherokee nation abolished slavery in 1862 (three years before the U.S. government). When black manumitted slaves were given Cherokee citizenship (without regard to blood quantum, or the degree of ancestry one can prove via bloodlines), they were named the "Freedmen." While Cherokee-black intermarriage occurred, blacks were not acknowledged as marriage partners and had a lower racial status.[23]

The relationship of the Creeks to blacks in North America was in many ways contradictory. Creeks held slaves who were used as interpreters in dealings with whites. "During colonial times and until the mid-nineteenth century, Creeks were efficient 'slave catchers' who sold black refugees to whites. By the beginning of the eighteenth century the Creeks were beginning to assimilate the white view of the black race. However, intermarriage (often called "miscegenation") was so frequent that numerous descriptive terms (*zambo, mustee,* black Indian, etc.) appeared in the sources."[24] Creeks and African Americans fought together in the Red Sticks War, and they also fled together to join the Florida Seminoles. In the 1820s the Creeks and the Cherokee both passed "slave codes" restricting the activities of blacks in their tribes, and in 1824 they forbade black-Indian progeny from inheriting.

Tribes describe their own mixed nature as something other than "black." The tendency for prerecognition mixing with blacks was seen as detrimental to the process of tribal federal recognition. Academics studying these communities tend to legitimate blackness and simultaneously erase indigeneity—it is easy to see that the degree of blackness, indigeneity, and mixing is difficult to determine.[25] Still,

> perceiving the potential effects of racialization with blacks under white supremacy, Indian people in the South have at times policed the boundaries between Indianness and blackness with equal vigor. . . . Each of the so-called Five Civilized Tribes of Oklahoma (Cherokee, Chickasaw, Choctaw, Creek, Seminole) has in varying degrees excluded people from tribal enrollment because of African ancestry, leading some of the remaining tribal members with African ancestry to hide their heritage behind particularly loud anti-black rhetoric."[26]

The Mississippi Choctaw historically "refused to associate with blacks" altogether. The Tunica-Biloxis (or Tunicas, a band of the Choctaw) with black ancestry were recognized by the federal government, but continued intermarriage caused that legitimacy to be revoked in the 1930s. The tribe itself was more accepting of mixing and believed that as a whole it dampened individual antiblack impulses. Still, overall, white-Indian intermarriage (never prohibited in Louisiana by antimiscegenation laws) is far more acceptable both to the U.S. government and to Indian tribes than is black-white intermarriage. Indeed, white-Indian intermarriage was promoted. The State of Virginia offered bounties to whites who would intermarry; and Georgia's Secretary of War William Harris Crawford recommended intermarriage for Indians who refused to relocate beyond the Mississippi.[27] Three states that had banned white-Indian intermarriage did so on the premise that those Indians had intermarried with blacks.[28] By contrast, the Mississippi government in 1865 outlawed intermarriage between whites and blacks and imposed a sentence of life imprisonment on those found guilty of the crime. Even in 2011 a poll showed that the majority of Mississippi Republicans still support antiblack, antimiscegenation legislation.[29]

Clifton-Choctaws, Jena Choctaws, Tunica-Biloxis, and Houmas Indians (all bands of Choctaws) refused to attend black schools when given the opportunity. "It was more important socially and economically to the Clifton-Choctaws to avoid being considered black than to receive a high school diploma, and avoiding racialization as blacks was vital to maintaining their identity as an indigenous group. . . . Though the Clifton-Choctaws had African ancestry, they maintained a strong social distinction between themselves and blacks, even if people outside their community inconsistently acknowledged the distinction."[30] The colonial encounter, continued white supremacy, and the power of the federal authority over Indian tribes still are influential factors. To assert Indianness, one has to not only deny African ancestry but also show aversion toward blacks more generally.

Federal recognition is one issue that causes denial of black members. For most of the twentieth century, Indian tribes had frantically sought members, for enrollments of substantial size were key in obtaining federal recognition. Tribes seeking federal recognition were aware that relationships with African-descendant members could affect the chance at recognition. Indian tribes without African ancestry were more likely to receive federal recognition than tribes who mixed with Africans; further, recognition has come more easily to tribes who denied black racial mixing.[31] First established in 1978, federal recognition allows for government-to-government interaction to which unrecognized tribes have no access, but it surely also acknowledges and validates the United States as a colonial authority over the Indian nation receiving said recognition. Moreover, recognition policy reflects the assimilationist pressures that tribes have faced, along with inconsistent application of requirements and a host of other problems.[32] The Cherokee was one of the few Native American groups that the U.S. government did not require to have federal recognition. This kind of acknowledgment only began for the Cherokee in the 1970s.[33] The last federal roll of the pureblood Cherokee was closed in 1906, and in 1990, the youngest Cherokee on that roll was more than eighty years old. Attorney Joel Thompson spoke on ending the practice of using race to determine whether or not someone is a member of the Cherokee nation, saying, "What other people in the world allow their ethnicity to be determined by blood quantum? As long as we allow the white man to determine who is an Indian, we are in trouble. Is being Indian a physical attribute or a state of mind? We must be allowed to define ourselves, to determine who we are."[34] The Cherokee may allow the federal government to determine who belongs, but they decided who does not. They struggled with the status of their Afro-descendant members for decades, but only recently eliminated entirely the Freedmen and African American admixtures from their tribe. "These are the descendants of black slaves owned by Cherokees, free blacks who were married to Cherokees and the children of mixed-race families known as black Cherokees, all of whom joined the Cherokee migration to Oklahoma in 1838."[35] They became full members of the Cherokee nation in 1866 as part of a treaty with the United States.[36]

When the 1887 Dawes Commission, charged with enforcing new rules of land displacement, created a census of Cherokee tribal members, they made lists of full members and Freedmen; but the commission abstained from counting at all any member who "looked" as if they were an African-descendant. "More than 75 percent of those enrolled in the Cherokee Nation have less than one-quarter Cherokee blood, the vast majority of them of European ancestry."[37]

A legal battle between the Freedmen and the Cherokee nation raged throughout the twentieth century and into to the twenty-first. In April 1906, the Indian Office of the Five Civilized Tribes voted to disallow any Freedmen from being transferred onto the Dawes Commission rolls listing "citizens by blood."[38] Then in 1986, the tribal council voted to remove the Freedmen's right to vote on the grounds that they were not "Cherokee by blood," but the Freedmen appealed this action and rewon their voting rights in December 2006. The council voted in March 2007 to expunge the Freedmen from the nation altogether, revoking the tribal membership of 2,800 descendants of the people the tribe once owned as slaves and eliminating about one percent of the membership of the tribe.[39] This vote was to exclude only the African American members, and no other tribal admixtures, and meant the denial of the Freedmen's access to tribal government funding (mainly housing and medical support) and sharing in tribal revenue. The council vote would allow membership for only those persons whose ancestors were listed among those on the Dawes rolls created 100 years earlier by the whites in government who decided Cherokee membership by bloodline. No white members, adoptees, or persons with white admixtures suffered similar revocation. The Freedmen filed a lawsuit in U.S. federal court in 2003 and also filed suit with the Cherokee Supreme Court. Marilyn Vann, lead plaintiff in the Freedmen's case against the Cherokee and a Freedmen member herself, says this struggle is about "racism and apartheid in the 21st century."[40]

At this stage two issues beyond federal recognition meant continued and increasing black exile. One is voting power. The blacks were ousted, as the nation was moving toward elections for a new chief. There was much legal movement around the time of the 2011 election. In January 2011 the Cherokee tribal court denied the ability to expel the Freedmen, but in August that same year the Cherokee Supreme Court ruled the opposite, upholding the tribal council's vote to expel. The U.S. Department of Housing and Urban Affairs followed through with some threats to withhold $33 million in funds if the preelection ousting were to continue. The Bureau of Indian Affairs threatened to ignore the results of the October 2011 election if the blacks' right to vote was not restored, so the parties seeking the ouster decided to back down.[41] The parties all came to a temporary agreement allowing the Freedmen to vote in the election but without resolving the membership issue. In that election the man who had held the chief's office for twelve years and led the move to oust the Freedmen lost his seat. The U.S. federal court dismissed the case of the Freedmen that same month, citing the sovereignty of the Cherokee nation; but the Cherokee nation had also filed suit against the Freedmen in federal court, effectively waiving their claim to sovereignty on this issue.[42] Thus, the legal battle continues.

A third issue surrounding black tribal expulsion is money. Note that the Cherokee are the second-largest Indian nation, annually generating $500 million in revenues and $100 million in profits in a billion-dollar gambling business.[43] For centuries, only very serious offenses merited expulsion, but eliminating members with black ancestry has now become something of a national trend, especially with regard to the question of distributing gaming revenue to tribal members.[44] The quest for federal recognition is an action that normally brings anti-Indian racism upon the group seeking gaming revenues, but the pursuit for tribal existence has become a referendum on gaming instead.

After gaming became a large-scale revenue source, recognized tribes reversed their enrollment-seeking behavior. American Indian enrollments in the 566 recognized tribes are actually on the decline overall because of these twenty-first-century disenrollments.[45] In 1967 the U.S. Supreme Court ruled in *Afroyim v. Rusk* that U.S. citizenship can only be given away, not taken away; but the Indian tribes can take it away, and apparently en masse.[46]

There is a clear recent history of Native American tribes eliminating African Americans from their midst, or showing prejudice against members with admixtures that show evidence of black ancestry. The Cherokee expulsion has been described. The Seminole won a legal battle in 2003 to remove their black members and as a result lost federal recognition of their sovereignty for the expulsion of black members nullified by their 1866 treaty. John Gomez Jr.

helped make Temecula, California's Pechanga megaresort, possible, working as a legal and cultural adviser, representative, and lobbyist for the tribe during the negotiations. The resort opened in 2002 and now brings in $1 billion per year. The Temecula/Pechanga Indians also "disenrolled" Gomez, 75 children, and 135 long-standing adult members who contributed to the tribe.[47] Tribe members had received $15,000 per month each in 2004 before the Gomez family was expelled; after the Gomez family was expunged, those payments rose to $40,000 for remaining tribal members by 2008. (The Gomez family represents 10 percent of the tribe. The extended family of Paulina Hunter, another 10 percent of the tribe, was disenrolled soon afterward.)[48] These expulsions also occurred right around the time of the election of leadership; eliminating 20 percent of the tribe also eliminated opposition to the consolidation of power in certain hands.[49] The Tigua disenrolled some of its members after 1996 when the tribe's wealth expanded when gaming revenues came in.[50] The Picayune Rancheria of the Chukchansi tribe also eliminated half of its members in the five years preceding 2012, and the Chukchansi disenrollments are not appealable.[51] The Oneida of New York, the Chippewa of Minnesota, the Sauk-Suiattle and Lummi of Washingon, the Sac and Fox of Iowa, the Paiutes of Nevada, and many others have seen increased disenrollments for reasons of blood quantum.[52] Thousands of Indians in California have been removed from the rolls, with that state's revenues from its more than 60 casinos nearing $7 billion in 2010.[53] John Gomez has since formed the American Indian Rights and Resources Organization and has become a leader for the disenrolled.

The Jena Choctaw (federally recognized in 1981) and the Clifton Choctaws (now petitioning for recognition) are now living in Central Louisiana. The Jena Band of Choctaw used antiblack racism to reinvent their identity in the twentieth-century South, and eventually they were integrated into white schools during World War II.[54] In the 1990s they sought federal acknowledgment in order to develop casino gambling. The Clifton-Choctaws (located nearby in Louisiana but southwest of the Jena) are unrecognized even after thirty years of organizing efforts. They were not allowed to attend white schools but refused to attend black schools, and the lack of education and economic prospects led to community disintegration in the 1960s as many found moving away was the best way to improve their lives. Indians in Louisiana were racialized as "colored" by Jim Crow–era whites who sought to erase or ignore tribal rights, and Indians employed antiblack racism to distinguish and distance themselves from blacks. (Significant portions of the Tunica-Biloxi and Clifton-Choctaw bands of the Choctaw tribe have African ancestry and, because of this, some outsiders consider them black, or "Redbone.")

Brian Klopotek explains that officials of the Bureau of Indian Affairs (BIA) claim blackness plays no role in the determination of federal recognition for tribal status, but tribes with black ancestry face greater obstacles to gaining federal recognition.[55] Today's federal Indian policy continues to encourage black-Indian distancing—even encouraging members who have no African ancestry to distance themselves from those who do—and in this way perpetuates the familiar distancing dance between blacks and Indians that has occurred between other ethnoracial groups.[56]

The peoples native to the Americas surely lost much in their North American encounters with Europeans. The Five Civilized Tribes did everything they could to preserve their way of life, if not all of their lands, against their resource- and land-hungry oppressors. These tribes even chose to adapt their lifestyle and culture, creating written traditions to match their oral ones, emulating the whites' governing structures, copying ways of dress and home construction, and even owning African slaves. Later, they chose to distance themselves from blacks to whom they assign a lower status than whites give the Indians. While there was a mixture of voluntary and forced inclusion of blacks among the Indians, the Indians of today understand very well the disadvantages of being associated with blacks.

THE NEZ PERCÉ

One group quite famous for its leadership in working to cooperate with whites so as to avoid deprivation and war is the Nimiipuu. In their language, this name means "the People"; but the French trappers who encountered them called them "Pierced Nose" or "Nez Percé," because when they saw some with shells in their noses they mistakenly believed them as a group to practice nose piercing. The Nimiipuu aided Lewis and Clark (who called them the "Chopunnish") in their expedition in late 1805. The Nez Percé's relationship with whites was so smooth that they boasted they had never killed a white man in seventy years. Numerous killings of Nez Percé by whites, however, are well documented, with no record of any punishment and few records of any trials.[57]

The Five Civilized Tribes' methods for dealing with whites might be called "the melting pot method," for they tried to assimilate into the style of life practiced by European-descended pioneers. By comparison, the Nimiipuu might be said to have tried the "ethnic pluralist method," which expected that people of different ethnicities could live side by side without having to give up their ways of life. This perhaps did not sit well with powerful whites in the mid-1800s, who strained white–Nez Percé relations with actions Francis Haines calls "compulsory civilization"; Jacqueline Fear-Segal called it "ethnocide."[58] Nez Percé children were taken away to boarding schools and learned to be subservient to whites. Parental visits and holidays were forbidden because they were thought to undo all that the schools were instilling in the children, who would otherwise resort to the Indian language and miss their ways of life. Men were expected to leave their ways to become Christians and pillars of the church. Whites infringed on their pasture lands, stole timber, burned fences, released cattle on Nez Percé's crops, and squatted with arms on Nez Percé lands when owners were away. For these trespasses, the Nez Percé won no justice in the courts. Although their treaties were ignored, it was a good thing that the Nez Percé had treaties with the whites, for those tribes with no treaties saw treatment far worse.

Most famous among the Nimiipuu are Chief Joseph the Elder (Tuekakas) and his son, Chief Joseph the Younger (Heinmot Tooyalaket).[59] In 1855 Governor Isaac Stevens told Old Joseph that the white men and Indian men should live separate, and for peace's sake, the Indians should stay in their own territory, to which Old Joseph replied that no man owned any part of the earth so no man could sell it. Many signed this offered treaty, but Chief Joseph instead took his band to Wallowa Valley—and they were again hounded for more land. Miners seeking gold in the rush overran the reservation, and during the 1860s miners are presumed to have stolen about $50 million in gold from the tribal lands. Even then, the Nez Percé avoided hostilities. A new treaty came in 1863, and some of the old signers who lived nowhere near signed again on the tribe's behalf. At his father's death in 1871, Young Joseph, now age thirty, stepped in to leadership, holding the same role and beliefs as Old Joseph but receiving more respect from whites and less from Indians who thought his father more impressive.[60] By 1877 these Nimiipuu were forced to move from Wallowa. Many battles and escapes followed. Those who did not flee across the Canadian border with the Sioux were captured under the pretense that soldiers would escort them to Lapwai; nearly a hundred died in Leavenworth, Kansas. Young Joseph was sent in 1885 to barren Indian Territory with the remaining 287 captives, many too young to remember or too old to rebuild; he died in 1904. Chief Joseph is remembered most for his speech of surrender, delivered before Congress, which many suggest is the most quoted of all Indian speeches. It is worth quoting at length.

The United States claimed that they had bought all the Nez Percé country outside of Lapwai Reservation, from Lawyer and other chiefs, but we continued to live on this land in peace until eight years ago, when white men began to come inside the bounds my father had set. We warned them against this great wrong, but they would not leave our land, and some bad blood was raised. The white men represented that we were going on the war-path. They reported many things that were false. . . .

For a short time we lived quietly. But this could not last. White men had found gold in the mountains around the land of winding water. They stole a great many horses from us, and we could not get them back because we were Indians. The white men told lies for each other. They drove off a great many of our cattle. Some white men branded our young cattle so they could claim them. We had no friend who would plead our cause before the law councils. It seemed to me that some of the white men in Wallowa were doing these things on purpose to get up a war. They knew that we were not strong enough to fight them. I labored hard to avoid trouble and bloodshed. We gave up some of our country to the white men, thinking that then we could have peace. We were mistaken. The white man would not let us alone. We could have avenged our wrongs many times, but we did not. Whenever the Government has asked us to help them against other Indians, we have never refused. When the white men were few and we were strong we could have killed them all off, but the Nez Percé wished to live at peace. . . .

We only ask an even chance to live as other men live. We ask to be recognized as men. We ask that the same law shall work alike on all men. If the Indian breaks the law, punish him by the law. If the white man breaks the law, punish him also.

Let me be a free man—free to travel, free to stop, free to work, free to trade where I choose, free to choose my own teachers, free to follow the religion of my fathers, free to think and talk and act for myself—and I will obey every law, or submit to the penalty.

Whenever the white man treats the Indian as they treat each other, then we will have no more wars. We shall all be alike—brothers of one father and one mother, with one sky above us and one country around us, and one government for all.[61]

Surely eloquent in language and moving in the extreme, this speech—and others famously published in the "noble savage" tradition—is largely fabricated, according to Thomas Guthrie's convincing analysis.[62] Noting that the Nez Percé made decisions (especially in war) by council, and Joseph was a horse trainer and tribal leader but no war chief, scholars Merrill Beal and Elliot West each echo the same sentiments.[63] Beal quotes adopted Yakahma Indian Lucullus Virgil McWhorter[64] as saying, "Why [Joseph] has received credit for engineering the great retreat is something of a mystery; symptomatic perhaps of the white man's great ignorance of his Indian adversaries."[65] In fact, most Indian speakers offered their speeches in a Native language that required translation, so Euro-Americans and not Indians wrote those words we like to quote. (In the case of Chief Joseph, very few were present to hear his actual speech—it was the English writings about that speech that were circulated and from which even I am quoting.) Actual speech is subordinated to written representations, and these texts further substitute for the Indians themselves. As Guthrie explains, "The appeal of wounded, bleeding Indian orators carried over into the production and collection of Indian texts. . . . If the words of past Indian orators live on in written records, their power depends on the ability of anthologizers to keep the dying, bleeding Indian in front of the reader, who then experiences the pathos of passing life . . . [it's] nothing more than a prolonged, textual death for whites to enjoy."[66] The production and interpretation of these fabricated speeches contribute to the subjugation of Native peoples because they were unable to defend their land claims *precisely because* speeches of this ilk were imbued with the aura of poetics, and not politics; speeches and treaty negotiations were for drama, not real dialogue. Whites could romanticize about the language of the dispossessed precisely because the dispossessed were (and are) subjugated. Said another way, there was "complicity between the Indian's rhetorical success and political failure."[67]

Although much has been written about the Nez Percé Indian tribe and their famous leader, the young Joseph, the flow of publications will and should continue. Joseph and his band remain an example and inspiration to those who today are seeking recognition as human beings, as worthy as any others on the planet, and therefore entitled to equal status among men. Those who recognize that such aspirations must not for long remain unfulfilled can derive from Nez Percé history examples of the consequence of policies conceived in ignorance and colored with disdain of the culture and way of life of minority peoples who are reluctant to renounce their heritage and values in order to become submerged in the society of the predominant majority.[68] As Chief Joseph is believed to have said in his speech to Congress:

I know that my race must change. We cannot hold our own with the white men as we are. We only ask an even chance to live as other men live. We ask to be recognized as men. We ask that the same law shall work alike on all men. If an Indian breaks the law, punish him by the law. If a white man breaks the law punish him also. . . . We shall all be alike—brothers of one father and mother, with one sky above us and one country around us and one government for all. Then the Great Spirit Chief who rules above will smile upon this land and send the rain to wash out the bloody spots made by brothers' hands upon the face of the earth. For this time the Indian race is waiting and praying. I hope no more groans of wounded men and women will ever go to the ear of the Great Spirit Chief above, and that all people may be one people.[69]

And herein lies the problem of defining ethnic projects among the first nations to inhabit North America. In some ways, their route to acceptance by "whites" was paved with self-denial. If physical annihilation were to be avoided, it would only be through spiritual and cultural annihilation. Thus, this first period of study of the ethnic project actually covers the efforts of so-called Indians to be accepted, that is, seen as honorary whites, rather than make an ethnicity of their own. History has taught us that this effort failed (despite cultural camouflaging as sedentary agriculturalists, and the aforementioned intermarriage). Feeble discussions and formal certificates foretold the creation of Indian states, but these, too, came to nothing.[70] In the second instance, the Nez Percé's pluralist model, however, an ethnocultural revival of sorts is obtained, but in a way bastardized; no longer as myriad peoples with unique and distinct identities, but a pan-"Indian" amalgam that is—purposely or not—more easily digestible by outsiders.

THE MEXICANS

Hernán Cortés set out from Cuba to explore the Mexican mainland, landing in February 1519 first on the island of Cozumel. Although two other Spanish explorers had been to eastern Mexico before him, many mark Cortés's arrival as the beginning of the Spanish colonial period. The Spanish called their colo-

nized land in the Americas "New Spain"; the name "Mexico" is derived from
the Aztecs, who called themselves *Mexica*.[71] Following Ian F. Haney López, I
use the term "Mexican" to mean Mexican migrants in the United States and
their descendants.[72]

As explained above, the Mexican incorporation story cannot be told without
repeated reference to admixture. Africans and their descendants were present in
Mexico from the time of Spanish colonization of the Native American people.
In Mexico City, it was a sign of great status for a Spaniard to have an African
valet, and many Africans intermarried with Indians although the Spaniards discouraged it, perhaps because under their rule the child of an enslaved man and
free woman would be free.[73] Spaniards found both black women and *mulatas*
attractive and at one point even preferred them to Indian women.[74] "It took
only one generation for *zambos*—people of mixed black-Indian ancestry—and
mulattoes—those of white-black mixture—to outnumber Africans in New
Spain. But by the 1570s, people of black ancestry still outnumbered mestizos
[admixtures of Spanish and Indian]. They made up the largest and most visible sector of *castas*, the generic term Spaniards used to refer to racially mixed
people."[75] Under conditions of this kind of mixing, an examination of ethnic
projects among Mexicans cannot ignore the absence of blackness. Observers
in the sixteenth century failed to record the presence of these admixtures in
colonial society. Because they did not fit into the existing racial order, and because they were in all social classes, Spaniards for the most part pretended that
castas did not exist except to note their perceived threat to societal stability.
The way racial admixtures were understood and self-presented varied: in rural
areas links to whiteness were emphasized; in the cities, they were associated
with blacks and thereby saw their reputations suffer.[76] Overall, Spanish colonial
society was two-tiered, with Indians in one tier, and in another the Spaniards
(along with mestizos born in wedlock or of aristocratic mothers or adopted
by fathers and therefore considered *criollos* [Spaniards born in the Americas]);
other *castas* and manumitted Africans had no place.[77]

Christian Spanish colonizers instituted a congregation policy forcing rural
Indians to relocate to villages segregated from Spaniards, mestizos, and blacks.[78]
The newly detribalized Indians were called *ladinos* and were culturally distinct
from rural Indians. The villages soon shrank due to decimation from illness and
the number of Indians who left to find work. A *sistema de castas* ranking groups

according to varying admixtures of Spanish, Indian, black, and *lipieza de sangre* (cleanliness of blood) was enforced by white elites trying to cling to superiority and power, but it was undermined by widespread miscegenation.[79] Colonizers began sending Indian Christians on a campaign northward to market the ways of the Christian Spanish, and newly acclimated Indians were made porters and guides and were transported to settlements even farther north. Admixtures followed, and some of these became the first Hispanic Texans.

Mexican independence came in 1821, along with a criollo nationalism born of Spanish descendants raised in the territory.[80] Texas and Arizona were Mexican states—and in Mexico, all races were declared equal under the law. Anglos entered the region and were ceded land, especially when they married Mexican women. Intermarriages were also common in New Mexico and California territories. While antislavery Mexico inhibited slaveholdings, it didn't prevent it entirely, and many Anglos brought their black slaves with them. Officials exempted Texas from the emancipation requirement, and Anglos got around what restrictions remained. Gerald Horne has written quite eloquently about African American participation in the Mexican Revolution and Mexico's popularity as a black refuge.[81] Runaway black slaves sought freedom in Mexico and runaways were often aided by Mexicans. ("There was no reason to *run* up north. All we had to do was to *walk* south, and we'd be free as soon as we crossed the Rio Grande."[82]) Despite U.S. requests for their extradition, escapes continued even after 1845 when Texas was under U.S. control.[83]

At the borderlands in the last years of the 1800s and early 1900s, blacks and Mexicans lived together and intermarried; but in some border towns, like Laredo and Tucson, blacks suffered as well as prospered. (Arizona didn't become a part of the United States until 1912.[84]) Negroes served as troopers to defend against Mexican military action along the border.

But the highly controversial Treaty of Guadalupe Hidalgo, which ended the Mexican-American War of 1846–1848, granted Mexicans in the United States equal civil rights and in return had the United States acquire territory up to the new border, the Rio Grande. These rights were not upheld, and each state had to decide the citizenship and racial status of Mexicans present. Only New Mexico followed the treaty, while California granted only white Mexicans the right to vote, and Texas granted citizenship to Mexicans who were nonblack and non-Indian. The first antimiscegenation laws in the Southwest appeared after the annexation, "[nullifying] Mexico's liberal racial laws and [reimposing] a hierarchical racial order more akin to that of colonial New Spain."[85] When Mexican territory was acquired by the United States, various ideas about what to do about the Negroes were considered—including Native-American-style displacement and genocide, military occupation, and "Saxonization"—but certainly not incorporation as equals.[86]

Citizenship was supposed to be the right afforded Mexicans who remained in the acquired territory, but it was not automatically given. Perhaps the origins of Mexican claims to whiteness might first be found in Mexican immigrants' petitions to be considered full citizens, against the U.S. government's insistence that citizenship through naturalization was reserved for whites only. Between 1878 and 1909, U.S. courts heard twelve cases questioning the limiting white racial designation required for application to naturalization, and it rejected eleven. The sole winner was Ricardo Rodríguez, who gained citizenship in 1897 by declaring himself as neither Indian nor Spanish but "pure-blooded Mexican."[87] The court ruled that "if the strict scientific classification of the anthropologist should be adopted, he would probably not be classed as white" (a necessary designation since only whites could be granted citizenship through naturalization), but it granted his citizenship on the basis of territorial cession resulting from the Treaty of Guadalupe Hidalgo.[88] The ruling meant that Rodríguez and other Mexicans should be treated as if they were white but never actually declared Mexicans to be so.[89]

Texas, the largest mainland state, was a slave state, and by 1890 also the largest cotton-producing state. Anglos were moving into Texas buying (and in many cases fraudulently stealing) land from *Tejanos*. Mexicans were immigrating as well, and newly arriving immigrants and Mexicans already in the United States were socially distant. Mexican immigrants mined and worked railroads, their employment aided by the closing of immigrant opportunities to the Chinese and Japanese. By 1910 two-thirds of Mexican migrants were arriving in Texas, mainly as farmworkers. Mexicans displaced both Anglos and blacks on cotton farms in central Texas at a time when beatings, lynchings, and other forms of violence terrorized blacks in Texas.[90] White Texans had a long history of invoking the color line in their social, economic, and political interactions with African Americans, but they had little experience in plantation society with what one contemporary sociologist called "partly colored races."[91] Relocated Southern whites new to the southwest, along with their descendants, fought hard to change the complex Mexican racial system into a binary one that respected "the color line" by instilling transplanted Jim Crow ideology and making Mexicans equivalent to blacks (despite the tendency for upper-class Mexican females to marry Anglos). Many Anglo Texans thus often wore two hats: the ten-gallon variety as well as the white hood of the "Invisible Empire."[92] Mexicans were marginalized "at varying rates of speed in different regions, depending largely on the size of the Anglo population and its ratio to that of Hispanics. In Texas, the process of subjugation had been completed by the beginning of the Mexican-American War."[93]

As former Mexican territories became absorbed into the U.S. racial paradigm, many blacks in the United States still believed Mexico to be a refuge from Jim Crow. Their beliefs were validated in 1919, when in June the Mexican minister of the interior, and in September the high-ranking Mexican official Juan Uribe, invited blacks to Mexico. This call was repeated in 1922 by Mexican President Álvaro Obregón who "cordially invited the Negroes [a delegation of leaders] to settle in his country." Many blacks in the United States had clearly concluded that life in Mexico could easily surpass life in the United States, but under pressure and fearing U.S. intervention, Mexico limited black entry.[94]

With the rise of U.S. racial science in the 1920s came a parallel increase in the belief in and use of standardized testing. Testing became a tool to help downgrade the racial characterization of Mexican Americans, solidifying their place as closer to "blacks," although class and skin color did mitigate the racial standing of Mexicans in Texas.

Mexican Americans were betwixt and between African Americans and white Americans in the supposed chain of racial being. They were in many instances accorded the Jim Crow style of apartheid reserved for African Americans throughout the American South, but treated as "white" when an urban, affluent, or middle-class background could be demonstrated. A lighter hue of skin pigmentation, however, was obviously important in this determination. In those instances it was concluded that testing performance and innate intelligence of those few Mexican Americans meeting the necessary class and skin color expectations were of an equal mental capability to white children.[95]

As with African Americans, standardized testing has both "opened doors for lower income and middle-class [minority] students in gaining admission into elite or exclusive institutions" but also solidified "the measurable underachieve-ment by minorities, particularly Mexican Americans and African Americans."[96] Carlos Blanton shows clearly how severely flawed even the most thoughtful and honest such research can be, concluding that "these IQ tests can not be sanitized by the notion that they were simply bad science that just happened to have had a peculiarly racist effect."[97]

From 1850 to 1920 Mexicans were classified as white; but whites recon-figured the racial paradigm by removing Mexicans from the white and right side of the color line and inserting them into a new and racially subordinated ethnic group. The racial incorporation of Mexicans in Austin, Texas, between 1910 and 1930 exemplifies the group's racialization experience in the nation as a whole.[98] In these years Mexicans had been moving into Texas sharecropping, first working alongside American blacks, and soon enough replacing them at even lower wages. Anglos believed that Mexicans were naturally well suited to cotton picking, and they were exploited more severely than blacks or Anglos in sharecropping.[99] Mexicans became subject to segregated public schooling when the first of these schools opened in 1916. In the late 1920s white nativists waged a successful campaign to reclassify Mexicans as officially nonwhite un-less definitely reported as white. But in the 1930s nativists were horrified to discover that they had successfully corked Southern and Eastern European im-migrants with the passage of the 1924 Immigration Act that instituted national quotas, but since Mexican migration was not considered significant at the time the 1924 Act never considered Mexican migration. So the quotas on other mi-grants had the effect of making Mexicans a far larger share of the newcomers to the United States. Policymakers viewed Mexicans as mixed-race half-breeds who regularly engaged in miscegenation and thus would "make the blood of all three races [black, white, and Mexican/Indian] flow back and forth between them in a distressing process of mongrelization."[100]

As a remedy, the California Joint Immigration Committee wanted to find a new test case that would reverse the precedent set by the 1897 *Rodríguez* case, and Timoteo Andrade's denied application for naturalization fit the bill. Andrade's 1935 case became an international incident. A very convoluted set of hearings ended with Andrade being classified as white and granted citizenship in 1936, but this did not settle the question for Mexicans as a group. Nativists fought to have the Census Bureau remove Mexicans from the list of white races on the

1930 Census questionnaire, and they won. Census enumerators in 1930 were told, "Practically all Mexican laborers are of a racial mixture difficult to classify, though usually well recognized in the localities where they are found. In order to obtain separate figures for this racial group, it has been decided that all persons born in Mexico, or having parents born in Mexico, who are not definitely white, Negro, Indian, Chinese, or Japanese, should be returned as Mexican ('Mex')."[101] Now, mixed-race Mexicans would be excluded from naturalization.

Mexicans responded to their racial categorization as black equivalents by further distancing themselves from blacks and asserting their whiteness. Mexicans "felt they had to distinguish themselves from blacks in order to safeguard the status and rights they had achieved."[102] They emphasized their European lineage, and in 1929 organized in groups like the League of United Latin American Citizens (LULAC) to fight the segregation of Mexicans as a nonwhite people. As Rodríguez explains, in this period Mexicans "were learning to negotiate the Anglo American racial hierarchy to their advantage" and, further, they "could be quite unsubtle and crass in their efforts to disassociate themselves from blacks," applying to blacks the racial attitudes they had adopted from local whites.[103] LULAC urged its members not to associate with Negroes, instructed them in the importance of maintaining the color line, and even expelled a member for having married a "Negress."

To complicate the matter of the racial categorization of Mexicans further, the U.S. racial politiculture changed in its relationship to Mexican immigration. In 1931 U.S. Labor Secretary William Doak launched a raid against illegal aliens in Los Angeles and other cities. While only 300 undocumented Mexicans were found (and only a very small portion deported), this move shaped the understanding of Mexicans as immigrants and launched the fear that they are migrants who can be presumed to take jobs away from "real Americans." Fearing reprisals, many more Mexicans left the United States in the 1930s than the raids ever targeted. The negative racialization of Mexicans had begun to take hold across the United States. In a reversal from ten years prior, 1940 census enumerators were instructed that "Mexicans are to be returned as *white*, unless definitely of Indian or other nonwhite race."[104] McDonald suggests that the state sought to recognize Mexicans as white at this juncture in order to divide them from African Americans in order to prevent their entering together movements to struggle against Jim Crow.[105]

In 1948 Mexicans established the G.I. Forum, which, along with the League of United Latin American Citizens, challenged in court anti-Mexican discrimination and school segregation. Even as their immigrant parents still called themselves *Mexicanos,* the U.S.-born children of Mexican immigrants fought for status as whites to rid themselves of the Jim Crow oppression of the times.[106]

Having failed to convince Anglos that the word "Mexican" denoted nationality rather than a separate race, LULAC members and other urban Mexican Americans constructed new identities as "Spanish American" or "Latin American" in order to arrogate to themselves the privileges of whiteness routinely denied to Mexicans, blacks, Chinese, and Indians. Becoming Spanish or Latin American also enabled Mexican Americans to distance themselves from recently arrived Mexican immigrants who were often illiterate, poor, non-English speaking, and dark-skinned. Mexican Americans thus began to object strenuously to being labeled as "colored" or forced to share facilities with black Americans. Increasingly, middle-class Mexican Americans during the thirties and forties began to call themselves "Spanish" and insist on their whiteness.[107]

In the decades leading up to 1968, overt anti-Mexican prejudice declined, but at the same time anti-Mexican discrimination persisted and helped to create a racial commonsense that darkened Mexicans in the average American's eyes. In these years (1930–1968) leaders in the Mexican community claimed to be white and promoted the term "Mexican American."[108] But 1968 brought about a sea change in their racial categorization of Mexicans, for starting with a 10,000-strong student protest against appalling conditions in East Los Angeles schools, Mexican insurgents shouting "Chicano Power!" claimed a Chicano identity. This development was path-breaking in ethnoracial terms because it was the first time Mexicans in the United States claimed to be brown. Legal scholar Ian F. Haney López studied the cases of the "East L.A. Thirteen" (accused of inciting the high-school students to protest) and the "Biltmore Six" (arrested six weeks after a fire broke out at a 1969 conference of the California Department of Education where then Governor Ronald Reagan was speaking; the group was accused of burglary, arson, and conspiracy).[109] At a conference organized in 1969 to protest these arrests, Chicanos constructed their own racial identity. Proclaiming it in the courts and having the cases and protests covered in activist newspapers, Chicanos propagated the idea for others to learn and understand it.[110] Those involved in the cases used evidence to show that Mexicans were inordinately excluded from serving on grand juries, and unduly victims of police brutality and bigotry, to prove that nonwhite status was the reality for Mexicans. "More than ever, we know ourselves by how the police and courts treat us. If we receive respect, courtesy, fair treatment, and due process, we are white; if we are harassed, beaten, arrested, or detained by executive fiat, we are black, brown, yellow, or red."[111] In this phase of their ethnic project, Mexicans went from Mexican Americans (i.e., "white persons with Spanish surnames") to Chicanos, brown militants rejecting *agringado* and *agabachado* (i.e., the Anglo and Mexican American varieties of whiteness).[112] In this case the embrace of brownness was not an embrace of a low status; indeed, Chicanos did not want to be likened to blacks. They instead were invoking primordial ties to the land and *Aztlán*, likening themselves to Native Americans more so than African Americans.

Mexicans and their descendants are currently 60 percent of Latinos, the largest and fastest-growing ethnic group in the country.[113] Their racial categorization has transformed over time, and different factions of the Mexican community have responded to these categorizations in different ways. The largest concentration of Mexicans is in California, but they are dispersed throughout the nation, and local responses to their categorization and assertions of their identity also vary. They have claimed whiteness, and brownness, but avoided claims of black ancestry. In this they are aided by others who seek to understand Mexicans as Hispanics or Latinos with no black ancestry. For example, while studying data from the 1980 Census, Frank Bean and Marta Tienda "corrected" the responses of Mexicans who answered the race question claiming blackness, justifying the change by noting that any Mexican who said they were black surely could not have understood the question.[114] Perhaps they in turn were aided in their perception by the new way the 1980 Census framed thinking about Hispanics—a new "ethnicity" question was developed for them to create a division among whites (e.g., "Hispanic" and "non-Hispanic"), and this frame is still commonly used among social scientists.[115]

Mexicans, as every people do, wished to create and enjoy their own identity, but racialization in the United States hindered the realization of that dream. To reach for a better station as white, Mexicans sought to have the state recognize them as white, and when the campaign to become white did not succeed, they sought to strengthen their position by identifying as brown—oppressed, but different from black. They too segregated themselves from black Americans, but that has not given them the success they sought. Still, their struggle is not over.

THE AFRO-CARIBBEANS

Black migrants from the Caribbean have been called "West Indians" for many years, despite the widespread awareness that Christopher Columbus was nowhere near the South Asian Indian peninsula when he landed in the Americas. The term has lumped together the Caribbean-born descendants of African and Native American freedmen and slaves, European colonizers and slave traders, Chinese and South Asian Indian contract laborers who populated the lands after Europeans decimated the native tribal nations of the Caribs, Arawaks, Tainos, and others. (Other groups native to the Americas, the Cherokee and Choctaw among them, have been recorded as captured and taken to the Caribbean from South Carolina, Florida, and Mississippi from 1670 onward.[116]) The term is used in the United States mainly to refer to immigrants from the Caribbean who are classified as black once they arrive on the U.S. mainland from a variety of island nations that are now independent from Dutch, French, Spanish, and English colonizers, as well as a sprinkling of U.S. territories and protectorates. While most persons from places that touch the Caribbean Sea but hold inhabitants who now speak Spanish are named according to the nation of geography—such as Dominican, Puerto Rican, or Cuban—persons from places as disparate as Jamaica (formerly British), Martinique (formerly French), Guyana (formerly Dutch, and geographically on the northern edge of the South American continent), and Saint Vincent (once held by each of these colonial masters) are all considered "West Indian."

Much is made in American sociology of West Indian immigrant ethnic "success." That is to say, scholars compare Caribbean-born immigrants to American-born African descendants mainly because they are presumed to share positions in the black race. For example, the politically conservative scholar Thomas Sowell gained fame in the 1970s by stating that West Indian success in occupational and educational attainment is proof that racial discrimination is inconsequential (if not nonexistent) in U.S. society.[117] The presumption of this positivist thinking is that in a comparison across the West Indian and African American ethnicities, race is "held constant" and everything else is allowed to vary. Therefore, what systematic group differences one sees would have to be something other than race. Apparently in such comparisons, the fact that one group is native-born and the other is immigrant is not considered to be crucial. Whatever differences in attainment appear in empirical data are usually attributed to differences in "culture," as if culture is as innate and heritable as race is fallaciously presumed to be.

West Indians, when compared to African Americans, do show differences in labor market outcomes, and they do achieve housing feats like integrating neighborhoods that are predominantly white, many of which attain from their status as *immigrants*.[118] Black West Indians form transnational social networks through which network members offer one another aid and resources that help them create occupational niches and proffer jobs to one another. Scholars interpret laboring in these niches as if they are based in a moral culture presumed to be superior to that of American blacks, even though obtaining the job took little effort on the part of the job seeker. Social pressure from the network requires good job performance—sometimes one's domicile and migration status are dependent upon the network, so losing one's good standing in the immigrant network can jeopardize one's shelter and migration status (and ability to stay in the United States), and put one at risk of being ostracized.[119]

The United States has no means by which money whitens, as it does in parts of Latin America where higher class standing earns a higher racial status than phenotype alone might otherwise confer. In a place and time where phenotype reigns (and it was not always so), West Indians would be wholly unsuccessful in petitioning for white status. But certainly, they too have been known for distancing themselves from African Americans.

Mary Waters studied New York City's West Indians and wrote about their distancing behaviors.[120] The West Indians she encountered claimed blackness (i.e., claimed to share a racial category with African Americans) but proffered differences between themselves and African Americans (such as claiming ethnic differences between the two groups), and they "wanted other people to know that they were not the same."[121]

They saw themselves as superior to black Americans, and they were disappointed and dismayed at the behaviors and characteristics they associated with black Americans.

Although some adopted the term "American" as part of their identity, referring to themselves as Jamaican American or West Indian American, they did not want to be seen as simply "black American" because for most of them assimilation to black America was downward mobility. . . . Both the middle-class and the working-class immigrants argued that West Indians were much harder-working than black Americans and that they were less likely than black Americans to engage in all kinds of wrongdoing, from being discourteous to using drugs and murdering people. The immigrants see many differences in the home life of black Americans and West Indians, arguing that West Indians have stronger, more intact, families and stricter upbringing of children. There was definitely a great deal of blame piled on black Americans for the negative circumstances they found themselves in and for their sense of entitlement.[122]

The immigrants defined criminal or nonworking West Indians to be exceptions to the rule, and black Americans with the same traits as flawed in character. Waters explained that the ideas that West Indians held about black Americans were drawn from a long-standing culture of racism, biased antiblack American media reports. Gross generalizations about black Americans were factually incorrect, but West Indian immigrants believed the differences to be real, even if they personally knew upstanding black Americans.[123]

Waters found class differences changed the sentiments immigrant black ethnics had about American blacks: middle-class West Indians were more likely to see black Americans as heterogeneous, and not as an undifferentiated whole, and some thought West Indians and black Americans to be the same. This makes sense in an ethnic project context. The black immigrants who feel most compelled to distance themselves are the ones who would benefit from employers, educators, landlords, real estate agents, and other socioeconomic gatekeepers' perceptions that they are undeserving of the racial denigration that goes with being "black"—the bottommost position in the racial hierarchy. If social distancing behavior earns only the next to last position—although far from the white side of the color line, not wholly black, not wholly racially contemptible—then perhaps more of society's rewards may accrue.

Perhaps, too, West Indian immigrants think that black Americans don't *want* to work because it was surely easy enough for the immigrants to get jobs if they had aid from a network. Many West Indians didn't have to look for work at all, since their friends and family could easily help them get jobs. (Surely these jobs were not the best U.S. society has to offer, but they were jobs nonetheless.) My own study of transnational networks had me interviewing black immigrants in the areas surrounding New York City and London. In both places, immigrants reported ease in finding jobs if the networks assisted them. In New York, an immigrant who was helped into the country and invited to live with her sponsoring hosts until she got on her feet, told me that she was told to "get dressed Monday" for she would then be brought to her sponsor's workplace and offered work on the sponsor's say-so.[124] On both sides of the Atlantic, immigrants also manipulated legal systems to get friends and relatives into the country and secure legal status or to stay and work illegally. Other ethnic groups have similar kinds of networks, and it is clear from immigrant studies that network systems help their own members succeed but fail to provide aid to outsiders.[125] Black Americans, when they do have connections to persons who can help them, find that those connections do not offer them aid.[126]

Caribbean immigrants to the United States hear the same stereotypes of African Americans that other ethnic groups have, and learn in a similar fashion to other ethnic groups how the U.S. racial system works. Black migrant groups may be presumed to phenotypically match other blacks in the United States, but as soon as they open their mouths and an accent comes out, they are able to show that they are "different" from the expectation. This difference—and the pressure networks give migrants to conform—makes for the ability to convince employers that the network's members are reliable enough that the employer should not bother to put out advertisements but should ask current employees if they know anyone to fill the slot. This kind of networking gets employers to think, "Wow, those [fill in the name of the ethnic group] are really great [fill in the name of the occupational niche]!" This kind of networking gets onlookers to say, "Wow, those ___ are hardworking!" for they are seen concentrating in jobs like nursing and construction. This only works for the group, however, in the immigrant generation, again because they are *immigrants*. Second-generation West Indians have no such accents to proffer when looking for work or housing. Their parents are West Indians, but to the average white American onlooker, the accent-less, network-less second generation is made up of just plain American blacks. Thus, their ethnic project may succeed for the first generation to arrive in the United States, but it is less effective in the second generation, and not visible at all in the third generation. As each successive generation is Americanized, each successive generation gets absorbed in blackness.

THE STRUGGLING ETHNIC PROJECT

Indians and Mexicans were the ethnic groups who most suffered from the geographic expansion required by the colonial project that built the United States of America. For Indian tribes, that expansion meant displacement, which was achieved through deception and violence that was oftentimes the equivalent of genocide. Mexicans too were duped of lands, particularly in the period when they were supposed to be protected in their land possessions under the Treaty of Hidalgo, when whites who cared to steal property from Mexicans did so with impunity. Within this history of geographic incorporation, there is also a racial one. Native Americans, Mexicans, and black Caribbeans—all admixtures of Africans, indigenous Americans, and Europeans—were incorporated as the United States was building its racial paradigm.

We can begin summarizing the ethnic projects in this chapter by noting that they are rather disparate in many ways. They involve different histories of racial incorporation. The groups discussed here are variously classified as red, brown, white, and black. Some are considered what the Canadians call "First Nations" with origins on North American lands that predate the arrival of European conquerors who faced elimination despite attempts at negotiation, battles on the legal front and on the war stage, and nearly complete acculturation. While Mexico was acknowledged as a nation with which the U.S. government needed to more straightforwardly negotiate with when acquiring territory, the people on those acquired lands were not as easily absorbed as was the land itself. They were transformed in the North American mind from a group with First Nation origins that mixed with Europeans and Africans to a group that is now synonymous with "immigrant." West Indians, too, are seen as immigrants, and though they too have mixed ethnoracial origins, they are today wholly understood to be black.

Several things unite these ethnic histories, however.

Each group segregates themselves from those at the racial bottom. In each case, African Americans were made unwelcome in the ethnic group itself—even when admixture was clearly a far from rare occurrence—and blacks were unwelcome as neighbors as well. Black expulsions from Native American tribes can be seen in this light, even if occurring only recently, and even if contests over money are at the root of increased expulsions overall.

Mexicans and West Indians each appealed to whites for recognition as different from the U.S. blacks to which they were/are often being compared. Both groups sought to increase their racial status by erasing ethnic differences between themselves and whites at the top of the racial hierarchy, or by creating and lauding ethnic differences between themselves and the persons at the bottom of the racial hierarchy.

Each group makes clear efforts to distance themselves from black Americans, and in the cases of Native Americans and Mexicans, their own blackness. Each of these groups has chosen to deny or distance themselves from the ethnic group that is believed to be the main occupier of the category "black" in the United States, that is, black Americans, also known as African Americans. It should be clear by now that U.S.-style blackness is something quite heinous, given that nearly every group identified as having an ethnic project has used African Americans as the baseline for what is racially dreadful, and against which every other ethnic group is supposedly superior. The next chapter examines this ethnic group and its own struggles for racial uplift.

Yet, these groups cannot be said to have succeeded in their ethnic projects, and indeed, these projects are ongoing and struggling. Perhaps the reason for their inability to succeed is that each of these groups threatened the racial status quo, whereas the successful ones have not. Perhaps these ethnic projects do not succeed because these are the very first groups incorporated. The racial hierarchy was created with their incorporation into the racial bottom in the U.S. land-grab that created the nation, and perhaps it took some time for the lessons of the ethnic project to be perfected, as was the case for the Euromigrants who arrived after them.

Still, Native Americans, Mexicans, and West Indians all used their agency in ways that can be marked as ethnic projects. While they did many of the things that the ethnic groups with more successful ethnic projects (described in chapter 4) did, these ethnic projects are clearly still struggling. Perhaps one reason these groups fight for ethnic recognition is that both groups had enormous difficulty buying into the U.S. racial politiculture. One requirement of a successful ethnic project is to never threaten the status quo even as you seek to create better socioeconomic conditions for your group. Perhaps this is part of the creation of the "noble savage" idea in the heads of U.S. intellectuals.

Surely they are sadly preposterous in thinking (as Chief Joseph's famous and possibly fabricated speech is supposed to suggest) that all men could possibly be created equal.

Indians certainly did not accept their position as "red" and work to move forward from there; they sought recognition, first, as the nations they were before the European colonizers appeared and began their conquest missions, and later, as equal members of the new North American society. Both of these quests were thwarted and denied. These quests, if successful, would have over-turned or at least markedly changed the existing racial hierarchy, removing an entire category (Indian, mixed, brown) from its low state and bringing it up to a high status.

Mexicans had a different sense of race altogether, and initially perhaps also actively sought to change the U.S. racial paradigm. At the very least Mexicans lived in accordance with the Latin American view of race allowing for admix-tures of many kinds and the incorporation of peoples in many more than just two racial categories. Surely, this was the goal of the Association of Multi-Ethnic Americans and its spokesperson, Carlos A. Fernandez, who said as much in 1999 when petitioning the House Subcommittee on the Census for the abil-ity to move away from singular racial identification.[127] Fernandez successfully lobbied to have the race question changed on the 2000 and 2010 Census ques-tionnaires, and the reconstructed question now allows us all to fill out answers to identify with as many races as we would like. Whether Mexicans succeed in getting North Americans to be as open and fluid in understanding race, and the possibilities for all admixtures of races, at times other than when they fill out the Census questionnaire remains to be seen.

Untitled cartoon by Melvin Tapley showing "Spanish-Americans" and the "Foreign-Born" succeeding on the back of a black individual labeled "US Folks" and accompanying the editorial "Nothing New" (October 23, 1971). Reprinted with permission from the *New York Amsterdam News*.

CHAPTER 6

AFRICAN AMERICANS
AND THE FAILED
ETHNIC PROJECT

We have fed you all for a thousand years—
For that was our doom you know,
From the days when you chained us in your fields
To the strike of a week ago
You have taken our lives, and our babies and wives,
And we're told it's your legal share;
But if blood be the price of your lawful wealth,
Good God! We have bought it fair.

Unknown Proletarian

The thing that has made the so-called Negro in America fail, more
than any other thing, is your, my, lack of knowledge concerning
history. We know less about history than anything else.

Malcolm X

The working title for this chapter was "Failed Ethnic Projects," an indication of
the certainty I had that I would discuss several historical cases that never nudged
their way out of the bottom racial category in which they were placed.[1] But studying the evidence and writing these histories has shown me that there's only one
group that clearly has "failed." That is, if we are to define failure as the inability
of an ethnic group to make sufficient changes in the ethnic lore about them—
if that group is unable to garner a degree of racial uplift or a place in popular

and scientific thought—then the African American ethnic project is a failure. This chapter chronicles some of African Americans' attempts at racial uplift, and my conclusion speculates on the reasons that these efforts ultimately failed.

WHO ARE AFRICAN AMERICANS?

When Africans first came to the land that is now the United States of America, they were free. Moreover, at the time there were no such things as "black people," nor were there "whites"; no store was placed in racial segregation. In fact, miscegenation occurred during the colonial period wherever (those we now would call) white and black persons—free or slave—would meet.

A year before the *Mayflower* landed in Massachusetts, another key event occurred. A crew of Dutch sailors raided a Spanish warship and abducted twenty ethnic Ndongans (from present-day Angola), then landed in Jamestown and traded the Africans for food.[2] Thus began the enslavement of Africans in North America. More than ten million men, women, and children suffered in 27,000 expeditions between the fifteenth and eighteenth centuries. They were survivors of the "Middle Passage," crossing the Atlantic chained in the hulls of slavers' ships. Millions more are said to have died in what is known as the *Maafa*, an era likened to the black Holocaust (*Maafa* is Kiswahili for "disaster").[3] The conditions of their forced labor began as a temporary state of indentured servitude, but soon they became lifelong chattel, a rank applied to those newly defined as "black." At the time of the United States' independence, the new Constitution offered the states a formula: one black person equaled three-fifths of a white person's worth. By then whites, blacks, and slaves existed as part of the body politic, but only whites counted as full human participants. By 1790 (the year of the first U.S. Census), black Americans comprised one-fifth of the U.S. population; 92 percent of them were enslaved.[4]

Miscegenation has occurred in all times and places wherever persons of presumably different races have met on the globe. Perhaps this predilection for mixing is why race-conscious U.S. legislators felt the need to make laws to prevent its occurrence. The first known interracial liaisons were between whites who were indentured servants and blacks who were both enslaved and free in colonial Maryland and Virginia, and these relationships came under increasingly negative public scrutiny. "White males and females were both involved

in the mixing, and both whites and blacks, males and females alike, were punished by whipping or public humiliation when interracial sexual contacts were
detected. Strong public condemnation failed to prevent illicit contacts from
becoming widespread, however, and in some cases intermarriage occurred."[5]

Just as blackness is based on a socially constructed idea, so are the rules that
decide who is black. At first, children born of these mixes in the "upper South"
had uncertain status until colonial Virginia outlawed miscegenation in 1662.
This law also declared that children of enslaved mothers were slaves regardless
of the father's status. After 1681 Virginia ruled that the white mother of a mixed
child "had to pay a fine of five years of servitude, and the child was [to be] sold
as an indentured servant until the age of thirty. The white parent, male or female, was to be banished from the colony within three months of the mixed
child's birth."[6] These are the beginnings of the "one-drop rule"—a rule of hypodescent that defines as "African American" any person with a "black" ancestor
(no matter how distant) who provided a damning single drop of "black" blood
to all descendants. This rule was applied to the offspring of blacks and lower-
class whites in the upper South.[7] In the lower South, black racial categorization
worked quite differently. There, white fathers of black children were often men
of means, and Southern society was loath to declare these children "black."
Louisiana and South Carolina—where free mulattoes outnumbered free "unmixed" blacks—at one time recognized separate racial statuses for those who
were mixes of black and white, making them a third class between black and
white, a station augmented by their role in aiding whites to control the large
number of black slaves.[8] Although in 1717 South Carolina instituted punishments for whites (both male and female) involved in interracial pregnancies,
the state refused to apply the one-drop rule to free mulattoes until the 1850s and
the state's first miscegenation law did not appear until 1865 (the year all black
slaves were manumitted). It was only in 1915 that the rule took on nationwide
relevance. Still, mulattoes had their own racial category in the U.S. Censuses
beginning in 1850 and continuing through 1930. Institutionalization of the
one-drop rule caused the number of African Americans in the United States
to swell, as the category "black" came to include births from those of African
descent and persons of any other race.

The year 1808 marked the end of the trade in slaves (but not the end of
black enslavement) in the United States. From 1808 until 1965, the number

of Africans in America increased only by birth and no longer by migration/ importation. Thus, most of the African Americans alive today have no real knowledge of Africa. It is only by making an assumption about one's ancestry that blacks born in America can claim to have ties to a country on the African continent.

Blacks in the United States do not all descend from enslaved Africans brought to the mainland United States. Beginning in the mid-1960s, blacks came to the United States from the Caribbean (in large numbers), from the African continent (in smaller numbers), and from South America. These immigration trends continued up until the year 2000, when one in twenty black persons in the United States was an immigrant. (Black migration is normally cited in history books as the result of instituting a nonracist migration law that replaced the national quota system. This is not quite true—the 1965 U.S. immigration law that replaced quotas were not expected to allow anyone into the country but white ethnics.[9])

The black race has experienced a lightening in appearance over the course of U.S. history. This is due to factors such as miscegenation—which has always occurred between those who are black and white as well as those who are brown and red—and the rule of hypodescent, which counts as "black" anyone with known black ancestry no matter how light their skin. At least three-fourths of all U.S. blacks in the United States were racially mixed by 1918, according to estimates by the U.S. Census Bureau. At the time (and until 1960) information about race was gathered by census enumerators who were given explicit instructions on how to determine the race of the person being interviewed and the race of the respondent's family.[10] No one was able to self-report their race, and many mixed-race people appear to be white, so the census estimates are likely quite conservative. For the 1940 Census (when mulattoes no longer had their own racial category delimited on the census form), census takers were given the instruction that "a person of mixed white and Negro blood should be returned as Negro, no matter how small a percentage of Negro blood. Both black and mulatto persons are to be returned as Negroes, without distinction."[11] As Jim Crow repression, separation, segregation, humiliation, and violation increased for black and mixed-race persons in the United States, so did "passing." Mixed-race persons who looked white enough lived as white, which meant abandoning their kin and loved ones of darker complexions. At the same time, Jim Crow increased and strengthened the alliances between mulattoes and blacks. Before this time, in some places, mulattoes had achieved a somewhat higher racial status.

Ira Berlin marks four migration streams that together dispersed African Americans throughout the United States. The first transported Africans to the Americas during the seventeenth and eighteenth centuries, continuing until the international trade in slaves stopped supplying Africans to the United States in 1808. In a second stream, another million slaves were transferred involuntarily from the Atlantic states into plantations in the South. The third migration occurred when a combination of sociodemographic changes, including the closing of U.S. immigration options to Europeans and the mechanization of agricultural harvesting, finally unshackled free but immobile blacks from plantation labor. As a result, six million blacks moved into Northern cities. Further complicating the ethnic group known as "African American" is recent international migration, which saw a large influx of immigrants "of color" (including black persons) after 1965. Now, one in twenty black persons in America is an immigrant; and one in ten is a child of an immigrant.[12]

Thus, the answer to the question "Who are African Americans?" is quite complex. For generations African Americans have borne children with Europeans and Native Americans to the extent that it is wrongheaded to think there is any such thing as "pure" black in North America.[13] Today, between one-fourth and one-fifth of genes among American blacks come from white ancestors (the amount varies by region), and around 1 to 5 percent of white Americans have genes from black ancestors.[14] Surely miscegenation must not be rare enough, for antimiscegenation amendments to the U.S. Constitution were proposed in 1871, 1912, and 1928.[15] Of the 48 U.S. states at the time, 30 had laws against black-white intermarriage between 1887 and 1948 (when the Supreme Court finally began striking down rather than upholding states' rights on the matter), and only 13 states had repealed their laws by the time of the *Loving v. Virginia* case that made all such states' laws unconstitutional.[16] Alabama was the last to remove its law from the books in 2000.[17] Jack Forbes explains that "modern European and North American [societies'] tendency to be obsessed with 'black-white' relations (to the near exclusion of multi-ethnic and time-space, comparative perspectives) has led to significant distortions in the use of color and 'racial' terms."[18] He warns us that to read American history as having replaced

Native peoples with Africans and Europeans is erroneous in the extreme. He says instead that both "African and Native American *survivors*" have peopled North America and the Caribbean.[19]

NAMING AFRICAN AMERICANS

Establishing a community of displaced Africans was an enormously arduous endeavor. The conditions of Africans' enslavement disallowed the formation of institutions, communities, and families that would enable them to advance a group identity.[20] The most racially dominant parts of U.S. society repeatedly deny the existence of any legitimate and worthy history for Africans in America, but African people are not without culture.[21] True, it was virtually impossible for Africans who survived enslavement to restore the national cultural heritage each held before their march to the sea and the Middle Passage. As a people who had their original ethnicities stolen and who were given a race instead as a poor replacement, they (like Jews) had no nationality that could be placed on the leftmost side of the hyphenated term that held "American" on the right. But they survived, fought their condition, and became a people by organizing for that fight. For blacks, then, deriving a name for their group had socially significant repercussions and required more contentious negotiation than did the naming process for other ethnic and immigrant groups.

Blacks during the Revolutionary War era, who participated in the creation of the newly forming United States of America, convened to discuss and decide upon the matter of what to call themselves. They settled upon the name "Negro-Americans."[22] The decision came from a desire to be associated more with the nation in which they lived, not the one from which they came or from which the European colonizers had come. As was the case with other, later debates about what to call themselves, not all blacks agreed with the decision. Many preferred instead to embrace "Africa" in their name—as did the founders of the African Methodist Episcopal Church (AME Church). The church was established in the late 1700s in response to racist encounters that blacks suffered when participating in mixed-race Protestant congregations and also to Christian theology with antiblack interpretations.[23] Marcus Garvey (1887–1940) used the term "Negro" in naming his Universal Negro Improvement Association, although at various times he used other terms such as "black," "African," and "African-American."[24]

In the 1930s and 1940s, the term "Brown America" was used with pride.[25] It first came into use as a nod to world champion boxer Joe Louis's (1914–1981) fame as the "Brown Bomber" but also indicated the widespread acceptance of the one-drop rule and its rejection by white North America of anyone with an admixture of African ancestry. At this time, there is evidence that although many mixed-race persons could pass as white, they chose not to do so, and indeed most mulattoes rejected close association with whites as well.[26]

"Colored" was the dominant term used in the mid- to late nineteenth century. The label was accepted by both whites and blacks because it was more inclusive, representing blacks that had two black parents as well as those of mixed racial ancestry. Some also understood it to include other nonwhites, including Asians.[27] The term "Negro" (used alone, replacing "Negro-American") again gained acceptance in the late nineteenth century as part of a movement led by black intellectuals and other leaders, including William Edward Burghardt Du Bois (1868–1963) and Booker T. Washington (1856–1915). There is some indication that "Negro" was favored by Civil War–era freedmen, while "colored" was more popular among those freed before the war. "Negro" was seen as a stronger term, but later it became closely associated with common racial epithets. "Colored" predominated until the 1920s, when avant-garde black New Yorkers popularized the term "Negro." Soon capitalization of the term was standardized (e.g., the *New York Times* capitalized it in 1930), and it gained greater acceptance, becoming firmly entrenched by the 1950s.[28]

In the 1960s, "black" was promoted as a preferred term because of its supposed association with racial pride and power. The Nation of Islam, and Malcolm X (1925–1965) in particular, repudiated the term "Negro." X's 1960 speech asked, "If you call yourself 'white,' why should I not call myself 'black'? . . . If Frenchmen are of France and Germans are of Germany, where is 'Negroland'? I'll tell you: it's in the mind of the white man!"[29] The term "black" was initially favored by political radicals and activists, and it later gained acceptance precisely because of its activist image; it also served as a balance for the term "white." But in the early 1960s it was also understood to be derogatory, and some continued to favor the use of "Negro." Older persons would continue to call themselves "Negro," but young people were influenced by Stokely Carmichael's 1966 call for "Black Power." Advocates for Black Power saw it as signifying needed separation, self-empowerment, and pride (as opposed to condoning assimilation, seeking acceptance, and holding shame for one's own blackness). Two years later, the song "Say It Loud—I'm Black and I'm Proud" by James Brown became a top ten hit. That year the black community's renowned magazine *Ebony* had begun to use the term "black" (and "Afro-American," although only sporadically) instead of "Negro." In 1968 only 6 percent of blacks called themselves "black" and 69 percent called themselves "Negro"; it took another six years before the majority would use "black."[30] It is true that, prior to the 1960s, many took offense to being called "black." The call to embrace the term, iconic in the "Black is Beautiful" movement, didn't manage to erase the light-skinned preferences in the black community.[31] What had been "Negro History Week" became known as "Black History Month."

But just as "Negro" came to be accepted in a preceding era, "black" was later also accepted, and it was the favored term from the 1970s until the late 1980s. "In the late 1970s, leaders of organizations of white ethnic groups such as Irish-Americans, Italian-Americans and Slavic-Americans pressured the government to change the census form by adding a question that would allow them to identify their potential members—the third and later generations."[32] This pressure from white "ethnic" groups caused the Census Bureau to modify its 1980 questionnaire to include a question about ancestry. Until then, the Census only asked about the racial group to which one belonged. The year 1980 was also the year the *Harvard Encyclopedia of American Ethnic Groups* was published as the culmination of eight years and $14 million worth of research on American ethnicity undertaken by the U.S. government–financed Ethnic Heritage Studies Program Act of 1972.[33] According to this tome, both "black" and "white" were ethnic groups, as were ninety-six other groups, 70 percent of them of European descent.[34]

And last, we come to the advent of the term "African American," a variant of the term "Afro-American" that Malcolm X seems to have embraced in the last months of his life.[35] "Of the combination American names, only the African American is as negative as positive, an accusatory reminder of past wrongs and pending debts."[36] As with the other name changes, there was not universal agreement. Many who advocated for the name "African American" hoped that using this term would deemphasize race and emphasize ethnicity. Others, like the National Association for the Advancement of Colored People (NAACP) under executive director Benjamin Hooks, did not embrace the change. Despite

Jesse Jackson's campaign that included visits to the editorial boards of several major newspapers, neither the *Washington Post* nor the *New York Times* (at least the national desks) were quick to adopt the change to "African American," but African American media outlets *Jet, Ebony,* the *Chicago Daily Defender,* and New York's *Amsterdam News* far more readily accepted it.[37]

The use of the term "African American" was first promoted in 1988 by Ramona H. Edelin, president of the National Urban Coalition, at a meeting of black leaders in Chicago, although the Reverend Jesse Jackson is given credit for leading the drive for wide acceptance of the term. It was meant to give blacks an ethnic reference, just as "every ethnic group in this country has a reference to some historical culture base."[38] The term "African American" denotes a heritage, an origin, and a present, and it is meant to imply equality with other hyphenated Americans. At this historical juncture, the project of distancing oneself from what is purely "race" means once again embracing Africa in a quest for inclusion as one of the many hyphenated Americans. Black Americans have at various times popularized cultural symbols rooted in the African continent, such as use of the Swahili language; African-inspired fashion, including the dashiki and widespread use of kente cloth or the kente-cloth pattern style; and holiday celebrations of Kwanzaa.

Ethnicity seeks to displace nature and biology (which is associated with race) and to put "culture" in its place. The move to the term "African American," then, is perhaps less a look "back" to Africa (since few can trace their ancestors to particular countries or tribal nations there) and more a reach toward an ethnic identity that is rooted in something other than race. Yet other terms have been in use at other times, and they have since fallen into disuse. "Mulatto" (and "quadroon," "octoroon," etc.), "colored," "black," African (with and without the "-American" appellation; also with a corrupted spelling, "Afrikan"), "Negro," and "Afro-American" have all been used at different times and with varied senses of pride. And just as a movement worked to resuscitate "black" and rescue it from denigration by infusing it with self-worth, so is there a movement to do the same with "nigga." Each move to make a name change has meant rebooting the ethnic system with regard to this community.

Why name and rename one's group, over and over again? Renaming processes and debates signal a desire for a paradigm shift in the thinking about the ways that African Americans/black/Afrikans/Afro-Americans/coloreds/Brown

Americans/Negroes are thought of—a desire to remove oneself from the category in the lowest position in the racial hierarchy and establish an ethnicity that quests for belonging in the American polity even while acknowledging painful pasts. This quest began in the Revolutionary War era and continues today. Du Bois wrote almost a hundred years ago: "If Men despise Negroes, they will not despise them less if Negroes are called 'colored' or 'Afro-Americans.'"[39] Kenneth Clark, whose research on racial stereotyping and its negative effect on the nation's children helped win the *Brown v. Board of Education* case, "when asked in 1995 'what is the best thing blacks should call themselves?' answered 'white.'"[40]

No other group has such a fraught history of naming themselves. Each iteration seems an effort to distance the group from their racialized name or (as is the case with "black") to embrace the negative aspects of racialization in order to upturn it and create in its place a race-based pride. In each case, however, the new ethnic name becomes racialized, made synonymous with the racial category, just as (in the most recent naming iteration) "African American" has become equivalent with "black." Indeed, it was not very many years ago that I was at a meeting of the Population Association of America listening to a fellow demographer deliver his talk. He was reviewing his PowerPoint slides listing numbers from his analysis of patterns of immigration to the United States. On the screen was a data table, a line of which read "African American immigrants," and the scholar went on to say the phrase aloud. In my shock I wondered aloud who "African American immigrants" were supposed to be, and from where these African American immigrants were supposed to have come. Aren't African Americans supposed to be from among us in the United States? Social scientists, government officials, and media agents all use "black" and "African American" as if they synonymously represent the racial category. And, seemingly, in their minds, so it is.[41]

In part, this perpetual process of making a new ethnic name indistinguishable from any other racial term describing the group can be read as society's insistence on erasing ethnicity for those who are racially black. Think of the race question on the U.S. Census. Races are listed with radial dots in the column of answers; and ethnicities are the terms separated by commas after each radial dot. To answer that one is white, there is only one choice: "white." But in case you're confused, the ethnicities that are accepted among whites are also listed. So "white" as the catchall term suggests that those persons who call themselves by any of several ethnic labels are instructed to identify as one people. Other groups similarly get the chance to identify as an ethnic. For example, if one is Asian, the 2010 Census question asks the respondent to mark a single circle if you are "Other Asian" (i.e., not Asian-Indian), and in that case one should "Print [your] race, for example, Hmong, Laotian, Thai, Pakistani, Cambodian, and so on." Black persons have no great list and no nation-based ethnic heritages from which to choose; the choices available to them are simply "Black, African Am, or Negro."

The history of the black American naming effort reflects an undeniable attempt to change the ethnic group's racial status. The Black Power movement is an ethnic project that sought to leave the category of "black" and the black American place in it intact but to change the politiculture about their ethnic group. The changes in the terms "Negro American," "Afro-American," and "African American" perhaps can be characterized as attempts to change the racial category to which the group is associated, leaving blackness behind, or perhaps changing the place of the group in the racial hierarchy by creating for them a status equal to other hyphenated or compound Americans. A group undertakes a political act when exchanging one name for another.[42] We may debate which part of the racial paradigm these efforts attempt to change, but what is sure is that these name-changing campaigns are struggles to better the black American place within the U.S. racial structure. No other ethnoracial group undertook this many iterations of concerted national action in a renaming effort. Perhaps this is because no other group has been continually relegated to the bottom place in the racial hierarchy requiring a momentous public relations effort of this sort. That the group works to change this over and over again is proof of their quest for racial uplift, and it remains an integral part of black Americans' ethnic project.

BLACK SOLDIERS

In some ways, African American history illustrates a tension between two opposites. On one side is an effort to participate in the polity in every way, perhaps in an effort to once-and-for-all prove the worth of the group as valid constituents. The second effort is one that gives up on this fight for inclusion and finds it nearly preposterous to continue efforts to join the American mainstream. The history of blacks' service as soldiers straddles both sides of this debate.

We may begin with the struggle for freedom from colonizing Britain, thinking of Crispus Attucks (1722–1770), a black man who led an uprising against Boston's British customs house and remembered as one of the first to die in the Boston Massacre. Both enslaved and free black men fought at Lexington, Concord, and Bunker Hill in the battles that started the war between England and her North American colonies. Black men fought on both sides—20,000 African Americans served with the British, 5,000 with the Continental Army.[43] The British Crown had more success with black recruitment as they promised freedom to fighters. George Washington (1732–1799) suspended black recruitment when he took over the Continental Army and only reinstituted it in 1778 when his troops had shrunk in number to 18,000. Both whites and blacks took the opportunity of war to run away; others ran from enslavement.[44] Altogether, about 100,000 black persons escaped, died, or were killed in the conflict. One writer called the American Revolution "African Americans [*sic*] largest slave revolt."[45]

Some soldiers, like Colonel Tye (1753–1780) and Boston King (ca. 1760–1802), would gain fame from their bravery and dedication.[46] Tye was a highly respected soldier who led a group of twenty-four black Loyalists called the "Black Brigade" and also a "'motley crew' of black and white refugees known as 'cow-boys.'"[47] Boston King, born in South Carolina, the son of a kidnapped African, despaired at the British loss. He made his way to New York, the last port to be evacuated by the British Army.

[P]eace was restored between America and Great Britain, which diffused universal joy among all parties, except us, who had escaped from slavery, and taken refuge in the English army; for a report prevailed at New-York, that all the slaves, in number 2000, were to be delivered up to their masters, altho' some of them had been three or four years among the English. This dreadful rumour filled us all with inexpressible anguish and terror, especially when we saw our old masters coming from Virginia, North-Carolina, and other parts, and seizing upon their slaves in the streets of New-York, or even dragging them out of their beds. Many of the slaves had very cruel masters, so that the thoughts of returning home with them embittered life to us. For some days we lost our appetite for food, and sleep departed from our eyes.[48]

The end of the war was a catastrophe for the enslaved. King negotiated with the British for freedom for black fighters in New York who enlisted before the 1782 treaty was signed and for whom a "Book of Negroes" was compiled; those 3,000 named were given certificates of freedom and allowed to board ships to Nova Scotia, but all others were to be returned to their masters. Historian Margaret Washington explains that "there are incredible letters written by southerners [about] Africans after the siege of Charleston, swimming out to boats, and the British hacking away at their arms with cutlasses to keep them from following them. So it was a very tragic situation. And of the many thousands of Africans who left the plantations, not many of them actually got their freedom."[49]

African Americans have served the United States in every war since, and as before they sometimes served for other nations. Black men offered to fight in the Union Army when Civil War brewed, and they formed their own militias, but Commander-in-Chief Abraham Lincoln said that the war was not about slavery and did not need their services. Just as happened under Washington, Lincoln's administration changed its decision when more than a year later manpower to fight was insufficient to wage war. The July 1862 Militia Act paved the legal way for black enlistment, but Lincoln still hoped to put in place his plans to repatriate blacks to Haiti, Central America, or Africa so as to not have to recognize their membership in the polity. Lincoln and his associates did not abandon this repatriation plan until 1864.[50]

African Americans were famously known as the "Buffalo Soldiers"—so named because their wooly hair resembled the coat of the buffalo[51] or perhaps because their main duty was to war with Native Americans.[52] Buffalo Soldiers were treated poorly by the government hiring them and also by the settlers they were hired to protect.[53] They fought in many of the most difficult battles waged against Native Americans, were employed in the search for Pancho Villa (1878–1923), fought in the Victorio War on the U.S./Mexico border, and held back labor protests in El Paso and Arizona; many were "struck by the incongruous sight of Negroes being a chief guardian of their oppressors."[54] The killing of Negroes in Mexico helped the soldiers rationalize the Buffalo Soldiers' planned invasion during the Mexican revolution.[55]

In the United States, whites who feared putting guns in the hands of blacks again succeeded in lessening the role of black troops. Black men made up about 10 percent of navy recruits in the 1880s and 90s, 3 percent by 1906, and 1.6 percent by 1930.[56] Whites born in the United States made up only half of the troops in the years leading up to and during Mexico's revolution and World War I, increasingly avoiding military service. European immigrants were enlisted instead, and dependence on their military might during times of conflict was reason enough to open up the assimilation route to whiteness.[57]

No similar route to high racial status was afforded the mass of black soldiers. The situation persists even today, when it is people of color who are on the front lines. A 1989 Congressional Budget Office Study reported:

Blacks and other minorities continue to be overrepresented among recruits, although to a lesser extent than at the beginning of the decade. The wealthier areas of the country contribute proportionately fewer recruits than do areas of middle and lower-middle incomes. The latter finding does not hold true for black recruits, however; they come disproportionately from areas with above average black family incomes. Early reenlistment decisions tend to reinforce the overall patterns, and to offset the contrary pattern among blacks, leading to career forces with greater concentrations of racial minorities and of people from lower-income areas than is true for recruits.[58]

Recruiters are aided by the government's sanction of recruiter access to schools in low-income neighborhoods.[59] Having military recruiters on campuses clearly increases the enlistment rate, regardless of race.[60] Moreover, African Americans reenlist at alarming rates. *USA Today* reported that reenlistments in 2005 reached a high far beyond military forecasters' expectations, and this had been the case for several of the preceding years.[61] In fact, "despite a rising tide of combat deaths and the prospect of deployments to Iraq and Afghanistan for years to come, Americans continue to volunteer for duty and are re-enlisting at record rates."[62] The armed forces seem to offer first jobs for many of the nation's young blacks who seek but do not find jobs. Unemployment rates for black men are double the rates for white men; and for black youth, about double the rates for white youth.[63] At the start of 2012, unemployment in the United States was reported to have fallen, but not for black people.[64] Could the fact that white employers fail to hire black people for the jobs to which they apply, and that 60 percent of the reenlisters received cash bonuses, have something to do with this?[65]

BLACK WORKERS

In the fifty years before World War I, a complex web of laws rooted black Americans in the Southern states. Blacks were mobile within the South, but they were unable to move North to take advantage of the increasing occupational opportunities left open when the doors to European immigration were closed.[66] Whites worked to exert control over blacks in all aspects of life, not just mobility, and this prevented black access to available jobs.

Michael Honey heard oral histories recounting the lifetimes of black workers who toiled in Tennessee.[67] Honey's respondents told endless stories of workplace segregation and black struggles against their fellow workers' prejudice and discrimination.

As workers told me over and over, whites didn't want blacks to have "white" jobs, and in one near-riotous confrontation over this issue that this group remembered, workers, black and white alike, carried pistols to the union hall. Somewhat to my surprise, these black workers remembered their past not with bitterness, but with a sense of humor and a feeling of ultimate triumph. For these former farmhands going through what seemed to me to be the disaster of proletarianization, life had improved. They worked harder than I can imagine, but not as hard as they had worked for the farm.[68]

They had lifted themselves up from sharecropping, survived Jim Crow–era racism, managed in the end to join unions, and had at the time of their retirements wages ten times that of when they began. But they never grasped the brass ring: the distinction of having toiled at "white" work and having their racial status raised as a result. This is the prize that would have brought them a status recognizable by others, who would have had to look beyond skin color and other markers of blackness to see men and women of great societal value.

It took relatively few years in the first half of the twentieth century to witness black workers being transformed from a rural force, concentrated in agricultural work in the Southern part of the United States, to a group offering their labor to factories in Northern cities. When the nation closed the doors to European immigration (due to racism against Southern and Eastern Europeans), opportunities were finally made available to blacks.[69] They were even then unwanted compared to the less than desirable whites employed in Northern industries, but at the same time not so hated that industrialists would rather close their factories and bank accounts than hire American black workers.

These historical workplace triumphs are hardly the end of the struggle for African Americans. Stephen Steinberg warns that we may be witnessing a new round of black worker dislocation comparable to the one that black laborers in the United States suffered at the turn of the twentieth century.[70] In 1900 black immigrants numbered between 20,000 and 84,000, making up approximately 1 percent of the black population in the United States; at mid-century it was up to 25 percent (114,000 black foreign-born persons). The numbers steadily increased, and now about 35 percent of blacks in the United States are foreign-born.[71] The post-1965 influx of immigration came at the exact time that African American workers were poised to make gains in the labor market: Title VII had been passed, affirmative action was deracializing the labor market, blacks had been concentrated in urban areas, and declining birth rates favored black hiring. But this time, when new immigrants flooded in, the doors were not slammed shut—instead, advocates of the "free market" championed the influx, basing their cheerleading on faulty research. There is much direct evidence that employers prefer new immigrants of color to America's native-born black workers.[72]

Antiblack racism continues to dominate labor relations, even where no immigrants are involved, and even where black and white candidates have long stood together as members of the exact same communities. Deirdre Royster combed Baltimore's neighborhoods and discovered that black men who attended school with greater regularity and graduated, and were far from choosy about jobs, still weren't rewarded with employment.[73] She reports that whites who attended the same schools, under the same teachers, and studied for the same trades used networks that aided white youth but withheld aid from black youth. Young whites' connections aided them in getting more jobs with higher status positions, that paid better wages, and they suffered both fewer/shorter periods of unemployment than blacks did. Even when young black men were employed, the networks simply did not aid them. It was not a matter of not having connections, for both blacks and whites were in the same classes and connected with the very same teachers; but these teachers gave white students material assistance that was withheld from black students. Still, whites generally believe that blacks who succeed use unfair advantages (quotas masked as affirmative action) to benefit in ways that create "reverse racism." Rather than a declining significance of race, Royster seems to find that race matters more than education, motivation, and desperation from preceding periods of unemployment; indeed, race shapes both the opportunity structure and racialized thinking of succeeding generations of both whites and blacks.

We in the United States of America repeatedly have had the opportunity to remedy the poor social and economic incorporation of our black folk, paving the way to inclusion and equality, and each time we have failed to choose the path toward racism's elimination. One of the earliest post-manumission opportunities appeared during the time of so-called Reconstruction, when policymakers were setting the course for reintegration of the formerly enslaved African American population. Instead of reestablishing their status as full citizens, we chose to encourage with federal policy the restoration of their slavelike condition.[74] Beginning in the mid-1960s and throughout the 1970s, we had another opportunity for black reincorporation. The movement for civil rights brought legislation supporting equal status and employment to African Americans, and social pressure caused affirmative action policy to actually bring about increased black integration in the labor market. Throughout both these periods, employers showed a marked preference for the immigrant. It is the key to the "mystery" behind why blacks did not migrate to northern U.S. cities after the Civil War, and it explains why the mid-twentieth-century movement for civil rights was not followed by black incorporation.

Steinberg presents many pieces of evidence to support this view. For one, when immigration was cut off after World War I, black persons flowed to cities to take advantage of opportunities finally open to them. Conversely, the top entry points for immigration are also areas of high black concentration and high rates of black un- and underemployment. Note also that scholars whose research involves direct conversation with employers find that they voice preferences for immigrants over blacks. Although employers explain that blacks are less reliable, less efficient, and have antagonistic attitudes, Steinberg says that these same scholars neither scrutinize these comments nor test them empirically to see if they have basis in truth. He posits that these comments are more likely rationalizations that mask antiblack racism, for when an entire ethnoracial group is excluded for the presumed behaviors of some, that is indeed racism.

In reviewing some of the scholarship explaining immigrant success over black American citizens seeking to contribute to the labor market, Steinberg makes special note of the euphemistic phrases used to explain every disparity without using the term "racism": ethnic economies (which violate Title VII of the 1964 Civil Rights Act via racial exclusion), network hiring (a discriminatory hiring mechanism that even absolves employers of charges of racism because they don't directly recruit), and social capital (which blacks are said to lack, thereby "causing" their own failure to be hired).

So powerful are these reified labor market "forces" in sifting workers along different occupational trajectories that, according to Waldinger and Lichter, "relatively few African-American workers are even *trying* to compete with immigrants in the latter's industrial and occupational concentrations." This is their explanation of why, several decades after the passage of Title VII, blacks in Los Angeles constitute 2 percent of the workforce in furniture manufacturing, 4 percent in eating and drinking establishments, 5 percent in printing, 7 percent in hotels, 13 percent in department stores, and 17 percent in hospitals (note that these are aggregate figures that obscure racial stratifications within these occupational domains). Small wonder that, after the Rodney King verdict, rampaging mobs vented their rage on immigrant-owned businesses. Small wonder that since the 1990s there has been a "reverse migration" of tens of thousands of Los Angeles blacks to various parts of the South. Indeed, nothing better epitomizes the extent to which African-American destiny is linked to immigration. Just as the cutoff of European immigration by the First World War provided a catalyst for the first major migration to cities in the North and West, the resumption of mass immigration after 1965 has led to the first reverse migration back to the South.[75]

The racial division of labor began when black labor was imported from Africa in a heinous transport system that meant three died for each breathing laborer delivered to the Americas and the category "black" was created to justify their degraded state. That ancient partnering of racial categorization and division of labor to create a caste-like state persists and continues to shape the lives of twenty-first-century black workers. Now, as we have so many times in the past, we have the chance to incorporate American-born black workers, but in the current iteration of black racialization we denigrate domestic (free) black workers and place them beneath foreign workers. This racial devaluation of black labor is "in the United States the essence of racial oppression" and the key to the backlash against affirmative action, which has the possibilities of redressing systematic denial of equality of access to work.[76] But we do not take that opportunity. Instead writers on the left and right of the political spectrum have served to perpetuate the mythology of the undependable and inefficient black worker who has little work ethic.[77] Black workers finally fought their way into unionized factory work and past the workplace barriers supported by Jim Crow legislation. As the United States begins deindustrialization, and moves factory production overseas, denigrated work becomes redefined as the labor of poor people of color undeserving of a living wage—but in lands far away enough that we can choose not to see their plight.[78]

BLACK CULTURE

John Herik Clarke famously noted, "The Europeans not only colonialized most of the world, they began to colonialize information about the world and its people. In order to do this, they had to forget, or pretend to forget, all they had previously known about the Africans."[79] Because of their history of displacement from the African continent, black people in the United States were repeatedly described as having no culture—or scholars helpfully explained that whatever culture African Americans did have was seriously deficient. African Americans worked hard in another part of their ethnic project to prove that their culture was just fine, perhaps even worthy of note.

In the 1920s the Black (or Harlem) Renaissance was part of a movement to influence the world's vision of black culture as lacking or, worse, nonexistent. The goal was to create something neither African nor white, but instead to draw upon both black and white to create something black and American.[80] The movement involved writers, composers, musicians, poets, dancers, and others, and involved mixed-race (mulatto) leadership—for "Renaissance leaders exalted all colors in the black community," which became known all over the world.[81]

Even the now dampened controversy about the variants of English used by African descendants in the Americas is one that seems to speak to the group's cultural worth. A great deal of scholarship questioned the origins and contemporary significance of what's variously known as "Black English," "African American Vernacular English" (or AAVE), or "Ebonics." Stuart Davis logically suggests that the conclusions to which one comes with regard to these controversies has to do with one's racial biases.[82] Davis's study of the unpublished writings of Francis Lieber (1798?–1872), the originator and editor of the first *Encyclopedia Americana,* shows that the nonracist Lieber demonstrates (in writings about the origins of the words *done* and *till*) that persons of African origin both borrowed words from and loaned words (of African- and creole-language origin) to whites, but his thinking was not widespread. For most scholars, antiblack racism made the question of the value and origin of "black English" not worth pondering.[83] Any widely accepted demonstration that the language of African and African-descended persons had patterns and words common to those with whom they had shared communities and nations before manumission would indeed be a testament to their cultural equality, for it would show that they had retained a culture even while subject to centuries of unimaginable human degradation. That little effort was made to uncover this information, and that little was made of the findings that showed the language equality to be valid, is evidence supporting the deliberate, if not intentional, differential valuing of blacks' "ethnic" culture in order to lend support to a racial (and therefore "lesser") cultural commentary.[84]

Black culture has long been marked as deficient relative to other cultures.[85] In nearly all of the other case studies discussed in this book (whether European, Asian, Hispanic, or indigenous in ancestry), ethnic groups at one time or another created ethnic projects that marked themselves in opposition to blacks. They were aided by intellectuals (some in their group, some outside of it) who contributed to sociological and public policy debates focused on deficiencies in black culture. Arguably the most important group targeted as deficient is the "underclass," defined first by Gunnar Myrdal to be a "class of unemployed, unemployables, and underemployed who are more and more hopelessly set apart from the nation at large and do not share in its life, its ambitions and its achievements."[86] While Myrdal emphasized social structure in creating the underclass, the term has—with the help of conservative journalists, psychologists, and economists—come to signify the way deficit culture marks the problematic position of black persons in the U.S. economy and society.[87] The transformation of "underclass" is similar to that of the "culture of poverty," a phrase coined by Oscar Lewis to explain how structural marginalization will create and perpetuate adverse conditions of life among the chronically poor; soon enough the term was taken by conservative writers to describe the behavioral and cultural problems of the poor as if those stood apart from the condition of poverty itself.[88]

As deficient as black urban culture is supposed to be, a lot of money is to be made from it. Author Naomi Klein's explanation for how this works is worth quoting in depth.

Over the past decade, young black men in American inner cities have been the market most aggressively mined by the brandmasters as a source of borrowed "meaning" and identity. . . . The truth is that the "got to be cool" rhetoric of the global brands is, more often than not, an indirect way of saying "got to be black." . . . cool hunting simply means black-culture hunting.

. . . Since [the single] "My Adidas" [was a hit in 1986], nothing in inner-city branding has been left up to chance. Major record labels like BMG now hire "street crews" of urban black youth to talk up hip-hop albums in their communities and to go out on guerrilla-style postering and sticker missions. The L.A.-based Steven Rifkind Company bills itself as a marketing firm "specializing in building word-of-mouth in urban areas and inner cities." Rifkind is CEO of the rap label Loud Records, and companies like Nike pay him hundreds of thousands of dollars to find out how to make their brands cool with trend-setting black youth.

So focused is Nike on borrowing style, attitude and imagery from black urban youth that the company has its own word for the practice: *bro-ing*. That's when Nike marketers and designers bring their prototypes to inner-city neighborhoods in New York, Philadelphia or Chicago and say, "Hey, bro, check out the shoes," to gauge the reaction to new styles and to build up a buzz. In an interview with journalist Josh Feit, Nike designer Aaron Cooper described his bro-ing conversation in Harlem: "We go to the playground, and dump the shoes out. It's unbelievable. The kids go nuts. That's when you realize the importance of Nike. Having kids tell you Nike is the number one thing in their life—number two is their girlfriend." Nike has even succeeded in branding the basketball courts where it goes bro-ing through its philanthropic wing, P.L.A.Y. (Participate in the Lives of Youth). P.L.A.Y. sponsors inner-city sports programs in exchange for high swoosh visibility including giant swooshes at the center of resurfaced urban basketball courts. In tonier parts of the city, that kind of thing would be called an ad and the space would come at a price, but on this side of the tracks, Nike pays nothing, and files the cost under charity.

. . . Like so much of cool hunting, [Tommy] Hilfiger's [similar] marketing journey feeds off the alienation at the heart of America's race relations: selling white youth on their fetishization of black style, and black youth on their fetishization of white wealth.[89]

What is clear is that the erasure of the black differential that would come with human equality would render the black racial category meaningless. If African Americans were no longer racially segregated, sharing in neighborhoods and all ranks in white-collar workplaces, they would likely no longer be thought to have a separate style and culture from which others can borrow or steal to make wealth that they pocket without sharing any of it with the

style and culture's creators. In a very real way, it pays to foster significant economic and social differences between American whites and blacks that can be
transformed and fed to a consumerist public as cultural and ethnic difference.

Although throughout this book I have made the point all along that ethnicity and race are continually negotiated, I must state it very clearly here: black
people in the United States are not a homogeneous monolith. Even within the
construction of the black ethnic project there is negotiation among subsets of
the group of disparate peoples lumped together in the category "black." Unfortunately for black people, who do not control the intellectual discourse about
themselves (in the way that Jews did, for example), these negotiations get played
out in social science research and in literature meant for popular consumption. Thus, unlike with groups that control the discourse about them, African
Americans are unable to present a positive front about who their people are.
With African Americans, even those who progress face some denigration—indeed, some of the most popular scholarship, public policy, and popular writings are those that denigrate African Americans or seem to prove their cultural
shortcomings.

Elijah Anderson, for example, is known for his work on the life in black
communities out-of-doors. His books, with titles like *Code of the Streets*, *A Place
on the Corner*, and *Streetwise*, offer a refrain of the ways that black culture is
played out among the "underclass" of society. Anderson's *Code of the Streets* describes his findings on the existence of two sides of the black community, one
flank of "decent" people and the other flank of those who are "street." William
Julius Wilson's *The Declining Significance of Race* and *When Work Disappears*
are others in this vein. While Wilson was a proponent of the structural (as opposed to cultural) view of the source of problems with the underclass, he did
proffer statements about the problems of black middle-class abandonment of
the underclass. (White people who move to metropolitan-area suburbs face
no comparable scrutiny for "abandoning" poor whites.) As counterweights
to these ideas, writers like Mary Patillo and Kesha Moore have written convincingly about how questionable it was to believe that the black middle class
had somehow moved away from "other" black people who didn't "make it"
in American society. Patillo explained that there are instead "dense networks
across the lines of legitimacy" where residents of black middle-class neighborhoods have to make compromises with the urban poor to which they remain

connected by family ties and also the more seamy side of their communities.[90] Moore's work describes moves that middle-class blacks make to purposefully gentrify downtrodden black communities as they move into poorer areas and buy property—to be clear, in making their home-buying choices they are making determined efforts to improve black communities for all, not just seeking cheap real estate.[91]

The black middle class itself is just holding onto their marginally higher status, particularly as the nation's economy fails, leaving black Americans un- and underemployed at many times the rates faced by white Americans. And surely many outside of the black middle class are seeking to join it. As the black male youth unemployment rate in the United States hovers between 39 and 47 percent—meaning that of 100 young black men, nearly half are seeking work and are unable to find it—comparable rates for white males are about half that, at 22 percent.[92] (Young blacks in England are facing the same difficulties finding employment, perhaps offering evidence that cultural deficiency is unlikely to be the problem, as no shared culture would plague such different communities who reside an ocean apart.[93]) Remember that the unemployment rate counts these young men because they are actually seeking work and not finding it; these numbers don't include those who have given up altogether. Nor do these data include those incarcerated, since they cannot be counted among those who would wish for a job and not get it. These data further distort the racial picture in the United States, perhaps to the degree that it makes our racial problems look better.[94] If all these young male jobseekers never land a first job, could they be expected to get a second, much less build a career? Of course, these statistics can be read in another way—perhaps young black male jobseekers are hoping against hope that they might still be able to "make it," even if the reality of being in the black race seems more like there "ain't no way."[95]

Thus, American descendants of formerly enslaved Africans recreate a common ancestry despite the facts that their ancestors were unable to pass on their cultural practices to their descendants and that these descendants do not know from which countries their ancestors came. These Negro-Americans/Coloreds/ Brown Americans/Blacks/Afro-Americans/African-Americans worked—through the Harlem Renaissance, the Black Power Movement, and Afrocentricity—to create a culture for themselves that would be recognized as valid. They created this for themselves much like the Kwanzaa celebration rituals that were created by African Studies Professor Maulana Ron Karenga. None of the African peoples celebrate Kwanzaa, yet it is widely accepted in the United States as a celebration for African Americans who desire a cultural identity that connects them with the African continent.[96]

THE STRUGGLE FOR LEGAL EQUALITY

One of the most cited markers in the history of the racial devaluation of black folks is the verdict handed down in the *Plessy v. Ferguson* case, which rejected Homer Plessy's argument made on behalf of a New Orleans organization for civil rights. Plessy made with them a plan (carried out with the cooperation of the porters). A very white-looking black man, Plessy would be arrested for attempting to board a coach reserved for whites, file suit arguing of the unfairness of the situation (given that his whiteness was "not discernable"), and the justices would have to see the absurdity of maintaining segregation when its victims don't even appear black to the eye of the average American. Of course, the plan went awry, for the Supreme Court ruled against him in 1896. The logic of the ruling was tortuous: if Plessy thought there was a problem with the separation of the races, it could only be because colored people "choose" to think of themselves as inferior, for separation does not mean inequality. Moreover, the ruling argued that only a white man could be harmed by this arrest, because the white man was entitled to ride where he liked, and if Plessy were white he could sue to have that right protected. Further, since Plessy is a black man, he could not possibly be harmed by the action of removing him from the rail car because he was deprived of no property that he deserved. In this convoluted way was white privilege protected.[97] Black people in the United States continually fought for racial equality with activism outside and inside America's courtrooms. In similar fashion, Rosa Parks was not the first black woman to refuse to leave the section of the bus reserved for white passengers, for other such bus rides had been orchestrated and rehearsed ahead of the famous ride she undertook. Moreover, Parks was no old lady simply too tired that day to agree to move; rather, she was long involved in militant antiracist activism before she took the action that started a large-scale boycott.[98]

Lighter-skinned blacks, and mulattoes, have long been role models and taken leadership positions in the black community. Along with Homer Plessy, we may cite also James Augustine Healy, the first black bishop; Walter White, NAACP president from 1931 to 1955 (estimated to be 1/64 black); A. Philip Randolph (predominantly white); and 19 of the 20 black congressmen and 2 black senators elected to office during Reconstruction.[99] Even Martin Luther King Jr. was known to have an Irish grandmother and Indian ancestry.[100] That those of mixed-race and light-skinned led rights movements is a testament to the fact that blackness in America is not so much about phenotype as it is about racial denigration.

The symbol touted as the first crack in the edifice of Jim Crow segregation is the pro-equality judgment that concluded the case *Brown v. Board of Education*. The case remains an important one (symbolically, but no longer as legal precedent) because it shows the promise of what the law can be at its best. However, this too is one case among many. In the legal battle for education, the first challenge to segregated public education met the courts more than 100 years earlier—in the 1849 case *Roberts v. City of Boston*. Kansas alone saw 11 *Brown*-like cases appear in their courts in those 100 years.[101] Derrick Bell, an admitted beneficiary of the rights won by *Brown v. Board of Education*, which hearkened an end to unequal and segregated education, laments in his book *Silent Covenants* that the judgment in the *Brown* case actually won our nation very little in terms of equality. "The Constitution is said to be America's civil religion. If *Brown*'s revised reading of the Constitution were fully enforced in the public schools across the country, it would serve eventually to eliminate racial discrimination in all aspects of life."[102] But, of course, that did not happen, and Bell offers to explain why. First, Bell argues, the *Brown* decision resulted only from a convergence of interests at the time, and not because of a real desire to ensure quality educations for black youth. It was a marker of a swing of the political pendulum, one that quickly moved toward its opposite pole (if *Brown II* is used as the marker of the retrenchment).[103]

We are well past Jim Crow, true, but we've by no means reached equality—not even the equality in education that seemed to be promised in the victory of *Brown v. Board of Education*.[104] Black Americans led a movement for civil rights for all, but they still have not had recognition in courts in their efforts to be paid reparations from the white-owned businesses that became wealthy under the slave trade. Reparations were a matter of public discourse in the 1960s, as well as the late 1980s and early 1990s, which saw renewed demands for reparations for the horrors and economic losses suffered by the United States in the time and the aftermath of the enslavement and trade of Africans. In the ethnic project model it is probably no surprise that these requests fall on deaf ears. To be awarded reparations is to receive an acknowledgment of wrongdoing and dishonor, which would move us perilously closer as a nation to conceding equality. (Some Indian tribes have been paid for the land grab committed against them, and there are cases still pending; but it also seems that their ethnic projects at this stage of history are clearly not completed.) The reality of contemporary racial politics is obscured by simple ideas (i.e., that we are past Jim Crow and now have blacks both in the middle class and in public political life) on which we hang the belief that we're in a time that is "postracial."[105]

THE FAILED ETHNIC PROJECT

If African Americans' ethnic project could be marked as "failed," it is certainly not for lack of trying. To be clear, black is the category in the United States that anchors the racial hierarchy at the bottom, and "African American" is the name of the ethnic group of black Americans. Generally speaking, the group is unable to successfully detach itself from the denigrated category "black" or change the politiculture that defines the meaning of blackness. The group has made innumerable attempts to do so, and together these attempts are what may be considered their ethnic project.

African Americans used many of the same strategies other ethnic groups used to achieve racial uplift. But one crucial project element evident in the preceding case studies was impossible for blacks in the United States to achieve. Blacks were unable to favorably and convincingly contrast their own group with a more denigrated group—for blacks in the United States seemingly are the group that one should denigrate to achieve racial uplift.

Besides having great difficulty finding a comparison group that has less value on a racial scale than themselves, African Americans have another, perhaps more serious problem with their ethnic project. An assessment of the Black American Ethnic Project would have to note that the project's goal was seeking human equality. This breaks the cardinal rule of ethnic projects—to succeed in the race game, a group cannot question the status quo of a racial hierarchy. Seeking civil rights for all is tantamount to suggesting we discard the chest of drawers that holds the racial drawers in a hierarchy. Rights cannot be for all in a society that functions under a clear racial paradigm, for the very purpose of race is to create social, economic, and political hierarchy reinforced by the social, economic, and political rules of the racial politiculture. To determine that those at the bottom of the U.S. racial paradigm are equal to those at the top is to eliminate the racial paradigm altogether.

The dominant element made a very simple counterpoint to black American efforts at renaming—each time blacks came up with a new name for themselves, each time they sought to separate their ethnicity from their race, the new name was simply used by the dominant society as a synonym for "black." For evidence, one need only look at the modern U.S. Census. In 2010, one possible answer to the race question read: "Black, African Am., or Negro." Except for having eliminated the choice "mulatto," this set of answers has not changed. It matters not to the census takers what any black American calls herself—for Nigerian, Jamaican, Kenyan, Ghanaian, Haitian, and so on are not choices for the "black." She is instructed to fill in the same radial button as anyone in any of these groups who labels himself or herself differently.

Black persons also sought to obtain equal access to North American schools and workplaces. It is clear that still in the twenty-first century blacks in the United States do not have equally equipped schools. Education is one of the few public goods funded by property taxes—none of our nation's military forces, prisons, or highways are funded in this way. This funding scheme, along with residential segregation by race and unequal access to the riches of the labor market, together all ensure that those racialized as black will not ever receive equal education.

Others have made gains in their ethnic projects when they denigrate black Americans; what race remains for the black American to denigrate in order to get ahead in the racial game? From which racialized ethnics should black Americans segregate to avoid interpersonal relations with their inferiors? Even those West Indians who escape black neighborhoods by being the first to enter white neighborhoods and integrate them are soon back where they started, as white flight begins when black native-born persons seeking relief from segregation move in. Fleeing whites are running too fast to see ethnic differentiation among their new black neighbors.[106] Black ethnics are unable to successfully self-segregate the way other ethnic groups have.

And for most ethnic groups, the stereotype of gender reversals gets switched around when their racial status rises, mainly because they compare themselves on gendered terms to other more-denigrated ethnic groups. To whom could black American women be compared to be proven more feminine, better mothers, and better partners in the home and community? And it seems that no amount of fighting abusive employers, from enslavement through Jim Crow and up until now; no amount of suffering from incarceration, police brutality, and murder; and no amount of "gangsta rap" seems to be enough to make the black man masculine enough for racial uplift.

But I offer that the most important reason that the Black American Ethnic Project fails is simple: it would be far too costly. The main text of this chapter discussed the benefits that supposedly deficient black culture provides to American commerce. But there is more. Black support for the military-industrial complex is immeasurable, partly because dollar signs are not easily placed on human life.

Black lives also support the prison-industrial complex. According to the Justice Department, fully 10 percent of the African American male population aged 25 to 29 was incarcerated in 2003; these are rates at great multiples over any other group, and an increase of over five times the rate of young black male incarceration of twenty years ago.[107] Having already reached the milestone of having the world's largest imprisoned population, we doubled the prison population since 1990, and in July 2003 exceeded two million people incarcerated in the United States.[108] In 1980 four times as many young black men were in college as imprisoned; in 2000 there were nearly 200,000 more African American men in prison than in college.[109] More African Americans are imprisoned now than were enslaved in 1850, ten years before the Civil War began.[110] The stigma of incarceration follows one all through life, negatively affecting future employment (for prison records must be declared to employers before hiring, and lying about an offense is grounds for firing); one's right to vote (several states remove voting rights from ex-convicts); and public benefits, housing, and jury service (through discriminatory practices that are legal).[111] The United States still practices the death penalty, and the majority of persons put to death in the United States are black men. Our society is not five times more dangerous than it was twenty years ago, but our prison-industrial complex (at five times the size that it was twenty years ago) hires many more times the people it ever did. Once again (as we did when blackness was created in the United States) we as a nation find ourselves with an economy with very few whites with great wealth at the top, and a great number of whites of lesser means employed as policemen, jailers, and enforcers to keep those made fictively and racially black at work and at bay. We also skew our own knowledge of our society—with our surveys focused on how households behave, our statistics ignore the millions of persons incarcerated; perhaps that makes us think things are better in the United States than they could possibly be.[112]

Finally, there is the medical-industrial complex that also benefited and continues to benefit from black denigration. Rebecca Skloot wrote in great detail about the ways medical staff in 1951 harvested cancerous cells from patient Henrietta Lacks and used them in medical research that has so far been published in more than 60,000 scientific articles. Doctors not only failed to compensate Ms. Lacks for the "gift," but experimented with them *without her knowledge*, and the experimentation continues to this day.[113] Harriet Washington mentions Ms. Lack's story on just one page of her nearly 500-page book that chronicles the long history of medical experimentation on black people in the United States, which she reports began on plantations that used black men's, women's, and children's involuntary labor and apparently hasn't yet ended.[114]

It can hardly be estimated what it would cost the U.S. economy to end the systematic recreation of the category "black" and destroy its conjoined-twin of extreme racial denigration. It would involve releasing prisoners, many of whom entered the system because of U.S. drug policy fashioned under the War on Drugs that created crimes where there had been none before. It would require informing and paying black patients for their participation in research and experimentation. It would require refraining from marketing and selling pharmaceutical drugs on the basis of race. It would require equally hiring black people (not just offer "opportunities" for hiring), especially black youth, which would bring them their first steps into a lifetime of employment. It would require replacing black people in military service (either by instituting a draft that nets all ethnicities and races equally, or by paying servicepersons and their families for the costs of lives lost). And it would require finding a new funding structure for schools so that disparate education by race is a thing of the past. And it would mean the end of a segregationist-fueled culture that makes big money for those who make wealth selling products iconically "black."

Perhaps those who carry the torch of the most current efforts in the Black Ethnic Project are those who believe in "postracial" society and have used the "postracial" adjective to describe black men in public life who find themselves well-liked by "whites." Among their members one might list Barack Obama (once senator, then president of the United States, who in one article was referred to as "the Tiger Woods of politics" before Mr. Woods's own personal and very public scandals[115]), Corey Booker (mayor of Newark as of this writing), Governor Deval Patrick of Massachusetts (from whom Obama in early 2008 was accused of having plagiarized in one of his campaign speeches), and Adrian Fenty (mayor of Washington, D.C.).[116] There are probably some black women in this group of popular figures—Oprah Winfrey certainly leads them. But being black, well-liked, and given white or near-white status is a rare combination in the U.S. racial politiculture, certainly not common enough to say that postracialism is the reality for most African Americans.

The parts of the African American experience recounted here mark persistent, sometimes violent struggles for their recognition as human beings. The goal of this chapter was not to provide a comprehensive history of blacks in the United States, but only to chronicle aspects of the black experience that could be considered consistent with a black ethnic project and the racialization that required such a project to be launched. The repeated requests for respect and equal valuation of their flesh, blood, emotions, and families are all familiar strains in these struggling ethnic projects. The category "black" seems to have a dual meaning. Blackness makes for value in terms of black labor (for surely black labor is what transformed the United States from Third World status to an economic giant with a booming agricultural economy),[117] and the bodies required to make the prison-industrial complex.[118] But blackness must be reified and devalued in order to keep black wages low and white wages high(er); black property values low and white property values high; black incarceration rates high and white incarceration rates low. The racial paradigm in the United States evolved in ways that kept the political peace by expanding the ethnic groups that could be classified as hierarchically at the top, and conversely it requires reifying a hierarchical bottom over which the higher (sometimes only marginally higher) groups may lord.[119]

Of course, one result of the civil rights movement in the United States is that it is no longer fashionable to be outwardly and verbally antiblack. (Hence, the rise of the idea of "color-blind racism"—that Americans in today's "postracial" society cannot see race although they still hold racist ideas.) But the problem of African Americans is not found in the measure of virulence of antiblack vitriol. The problem of African Americans is their placement in the bottom racial category, for there they are the foundation to the entire racial paradigm. Black Americans can never really win their struggles if the integrity of the racial paradigm is to endure. Any group seeking higher status makes their first move by stepping atop the bottom-most rung. A ladder with no bottom rung cannot be climbed. The entire system of ethnic projects in specific, and race as a system in general, both work to ensure that "black" remains the bottom rung of the ladder that all others in society are told they can and should climb. All such racialized struggles—including the struggles of African Americans— oblige us all to keep busy serving up one another as grist for the racial mill while we ignore cross-racial and cross-ethnic coalitions that have the promise of securing better lives for more of us. If history is our teacher, this story ends with no "happily ever after."

Untitled cartoon by Signe Wilkinson. Used with the permission of Signe Wilkinson, the Washington Post Writers Group, and the Cartoonist Group. All rights reserved.

THE FUTURE OF
U.S. ETHNORACISM

They know too much, we have all seen too much. . . . The tragedy
[of racism] is not mine, or at least not mine alone, it is yours, sons
and daughters of Plymouth Rock, and Ellis Island, it is yours,
children of Africa, it is the tragedy of both my wife's six-year-old
cousin and his white first grade classmates [who refused to play with
him because of his dark, unblemished skin], so that you need not
guess at what troubles me, it's on the nightly news for all to see, and
that if we could acknowledge at least that much then the tragic cycle
begins to break down.

Barack Hussein Obama, *Dreams from My Father*

SIGNPOSTS SAY WE'RE NOT "POSTRACIAL" YET

Perhaps it is fitting to begin the final chapter of this book with a quote about
Barack Obama's own reflections on U.S. race and ethnic relations.[1] After all,
the U.S. president is a symbol of the United States of America, much like the
Statue of Liberty (which I discussed at the start of the first chapter of this book).

Obama has serious heterogeneous cred in this personal sense: "brothers, sisters, nieces,
nephews, uncles and cousins, of every race and every hue, scattered across three continents." European, African, Asian. Serious practicing Christian and educated in his
formative years in a liberal Indonesian Muslim school (to the extent that some would
teabag him as actually Muslim); haole and islander, gringo and bro, a surfer kid and
'ball savvy'; half immigrant and half heartlander (but which half exactly?); east coaster

and west, ivy leaguer and Midwesterner, community organizer and constitutional lawyer; Chicago politician and upstanding US Senator. In his own words, a mutt, a mon-
grel. The quintessential American, though unlike many unabashed and unashamed
about his resonant mestizaje.[2]

Obama has had a globalized upbringing, and he is of mixed (racial and national) parentage, yet we still say he's racially "black." We will continue to say
this even though we must be aware of all the phenotypic, scientific, and political gyrations—and the blindness to miscegenation—required to say what
an "African American" is. Wherever persons of particular countries of origin
congregate in sufficiently large numbers, ethnicities become linked to certain
phenotypes. In the United States, Barack Obama may be a hybrid, but he is
seen as black. This, and the fact that he sits in the land's highest seat, is perhaps
the reason why there are death threats against him, amounting to about thirty
per day, or four hundred times those faced by his predecessor.[3] In the United
States, ethnicity and race are so related that a racially black person identifying
himself as German, for example, will be treated as if his or her listeners had
misheard. That is why when one says the word "Italian" in this country, we
think of someone who looks like Danny Aiello and not Giancarlo Esposito;
"African American" conjures up images of Halle Berry and not Charlize Theron;
and "British" makes you think of Judi Dench and not Thandie Newton. Even
the U.S. president is as constrained in his ethnic options as any other "black"
man. Thus, because he is black, he is an African American.[4]

   I have had the experience of foreign-born students in my classes speaking
out and saying to me, "Yes! You Americans have such a rigid system of race!
It's all you think about!" I even had a European student say to me this year,
"I wasn't white until I came here!" My own husband tells me that (especially
when I straighten my hair) I would barely be considered black in Austria where
he is from, and certainly my mother would not at all qualify. I am not lauding other systems of race—they're all heinous—but simply noting the extreme
rigidity of the racial system in the United States.

   How can this be, if we're presumably in a "postracial" society? How can this
be, when our own civil rights movement is a historical beacon to the world?
How can this be, when we elected a black man as president of the United States
of America? Perhaps this is part of the problem! What makes Barack Obama
a "black man"? Why isn't he the first (acknowledged) mulatto president or the

first mixed-race president? He's the first *black president* because the penurious one-drop rule persists in our "postracial" society and so his black ancestor is openly noted. Our racial categories are as strong as ever, and so our politicul-ture racializes as "black" a Kansan–Kenyan ethnic who was raised in Indonesia and Hawaii. If a dark-skinned Kenyan is present at an embryo's conception, we apply the racial label to the child that embryo becomes, and normally we do not question ethnicity at all, except perhaps to ask whether one actually quali-fies as an American. Racism, as Alexander Saxton writes, is "fundamentally a theory of history. It is a theory of who is who, of who belongs and who does not, of who deserves what and who is capable of what. . . . Racial categories themselves—their vicissitudes and the contests over them—reflect the compet-ing notions of history, peoplehood, and collective destiny by which power has been organized and contested on the American Scene."[5]

The belief that races exist persists across nations and generations. We have had for over a hundred years the proof that the mythology about the existence of race and racial difference is patently false. So how is it that racial think-ing will not die? Like a socioeconomic vampire, it lives eternally to suck the lifeblood out of generations of young people who would otherwise know that human beings are equal, and understand that if humans seem otherwise it is only because we decide to treat them unequally. Ethnic projects and the inter-group struggles they foster recur generation after generation, and throughout we fail to recognize the way these efforts perpetuate racism and racial thinking.

Every semester, whenever I have the chance, I teach my students that race is a social construction. Always, when we get to the point in my course where I have convinced them that there is neither a biological nor a genetic basis for racial differences among us, I pose a question: "So, can we now just skip the rest of the semester and go out and live our lives as if race does not exist? After all, since we made up racial categories out of whole cloth, can't we just decide to unmake them and start treating each other as human equals?" Depending on the energy in the class at the time, either the group would burst out laughing or there would be an awkward silence, as if the idea of living without racial divi-sions was totally imponderable. Life in the U.S.A. without race is perpetually thought to be absurd—and I am certain it is not because all my students are racists. Some (not all) students of color offered that they felt very comfortable in their racial group and wouldn't want to give that up. But almost everyone was perplexed as to why none of them really wanted to let it go. These young people—many of whom I suspect voted for Obama and made his presidency possible—cannot imagine U.S. society without race.

Why do we hold onto race so strongly, even after learning that it's a wholly mythical concept? What is it we're holding onto anyway? After experiencing such reactions a few times, I wanted to be able to tell my undergraduate students more about why we hold onto the idea of race. I wanted to give them a sociological answer, not one that was psychological, about identity. This book is the best answer I have as to why race is still around haunting us when we should have stopped believing in that hollow ghost of an idea so long ago. We in the United States seem to have a grave inability to promote our universal humanity over our perceived ethnoracial differences. The histories presented in this book also suggest that we are not averse to using ethnoracial thinking to better our socioeconomic station relative to others. This is the gist of the ethnic project, or at least how it has been carried out by its race-thinking proponents. History is our story, our collective story. In the power-seekers' version of our forebears' storyline, self-preservation and group uplift are linked to race in a way that cannot imagine the embrace of humanity common to all. Still, I say that it is everyone's choice to decide whether race will dominate the ethnic uplift stories we tell our inheritors, or instead, whether we teach them to form cross-ethnic coalitions and embrace their fellow human.

LESSONS FROM ETHNIC PROJECTS

In this volume, I have revisited U.S. ethnic history to present new theory about how people were racially and ethnically incorporated into North American society. The goal is to add a greater sense of dynamics to what is normally seen as a rigid racial system. Dynamics are evident in the racial paradigm's changing component parts, which include racial categories, racial hierarchies, and racial politicultures. Dynamics do not happen magically or without impetus, however. Change only happens because *people* make it happen. The ethnic project shows how actors pressure the racial paradigm to change, especially when the players in the system become conscious of their social agency and use it to manipulate their position relative to others.

This book began with an explanation of the ethnic project and its relationship to race in the United States. I thought it useful as a first step to explain and define race and ethnicity in, and give a theory-based template for, a generic *racial paradigm*. The concept of "race" is a social construction, surely, a racial fiction that is used to rank humans according to their valuation on a scale that mixes bits of folk wisdom, biological pseudoscience, stereotypes about ethnic and racial cultures, and mythology about the meaning behind phenotypes. Yet, it remains a force that systematically shapes human interactions, to the point that it almost wholly determines the quality of life for individuals, groups, and nations worldwide. To provide a mechanism by which these life-shaping systematic effects could be measured, I offered a blueprint indicating two main components and subcomponents of a racial paradigm. *Racial categories and hierarchies* are the templates used to classify and value human beings. *Racial politicultures* drive the logic that makes the racial templates seem commonplace and commonsensical. These politicultures also contain the system of rewards and punishments given to human actors according to their rank, and they organize systems of enforcement to ensure conformity and sanction from those who violate the paradigm's rules. I have further defined a few other terms for the sake of clarity. *Racialization* is the process by which a race is applied to a given subgroup of the population, ethnic groups included. *Racism* makes racialization possible: it is the explanans (the antecedent and causal condition) for both racialization and the differential socioeconomic outcomes that ethnic groups receive as the result of their being racialized. I also demonstrated how this template may be used to study a racial paradigm by applying it to the case of the United States of America.

In the chapters that followed my goal was manifold. I sought to demonstrate that ethnic groups form ethnic projects to play a high-stakes game of "king of the hill" with their lives and the lives of others with whom they share families, neighborhoods, towns and cities, and a nation. In seeking to change their own status within the racial hierarchy, these ethnic projects would only manipulate certain segments of the racial paradigm. They may seek to change the category into which they are placed, but not the fact that such categories exist; they may seek to change the politiculture about them, but generally choose not to fight in cross-racial and transethnic coalitions to destroy the existing racist politiculture. Ethnic projects seek to manipulate parts of the paradigm but question neither the validity of a racial paradigm as a whole nor the value in maintaining a racial paradigm over the course of a nation's history. As such, ethnic projects both sustain and shore up the U.S. racial paradigm, reinforcing the racism and racial structures that brought their people so much grief. By supporting ethnic projects, we may be proponents of racial thinking without having to claim overt racist orientations toward our fellow humans. We too often have thought of racial incorporation as a top-down process. Here, the historical evidence allows us to see racial agency through the lens of ethnic action. The theory of ethnic projects shows that we can see exactly how ethnicity and race are social constructions by looking at the actions of those who construct them. People tend to respond to incorporation and do their best to shape the experience to their benefit. If a group is unable or unequipped to respond well at the time they are first incorporated, they do not immediately surrender; they struggle with their racialization until they succeed in increasing their racial status and improving their well-being in a system that delivers privilege and demerits according to race.

I have used the adjectives "successful," "struggling," and "failing" as tropes to signal an ethnic group's ability to gain recognition for their worth sufficient to be rewarded with racial uplift. The point to be reiterated here is that ethnic systems of human interaction do not stand apart from racial systems. Even though ethnicity is theorized to be the basis of a self-asserting identity and culture that recalls a group's heritage, ethnicity is also a social construction. In ethnic systems some heritages are lauded and others are deemphasized. Ethnicity itself is created within a racial context, and it is the ruling class that creates the system of racial categories, hierarchies, and politiculture. Ethnic projects succeed to the point at which dominant whites are willing to concede some resources and privilege to the group petitioning for increased racial status.

Why did the whites in power decide at various times to broaden the definition of who was to be deemed racially desirable? Surely, it was only white people who created the segregationist and unequal racial policies of the New Deal and GI Bill. Nonwhites had no power or interest in creating or implementing such programs and policies, and indeed they even protested against the unfairness. The only reason that makes sense is the same one that created whiteness in the first place. Faced with the prospect of fighting a group of poor or disenfranchised whites who might unite with poor and disenfranchised blacks, whites with wealth and power decided to allow status increases over the bottom rank—but not enough to threaten the status quo of the socioeconomic hierarchy. So, Jews, Irish, and Italians were able to rise, become part of the newly formed ethnic white suburban middle class, and even become prominent in finance and politics. But still, a glass ceiling has been noted for these formerly not-quite-white ethnics, for the ranking of whites in that uppermost category of the U.S. racial hierarchy is still an ongoing practice. The word "assimilation," while battered by critiques from lesser-known but more politically progressive academics than those who laud the process, still stands as useful to many famous contemporary scholars of migration literature. While many embrace the melting pot, that pot does not embrace us all in return. Ethnic assimilation halts at the color line that marks the hierarchical binary amid the jumble of ethnoracial categories.

Social structures, of course, impinge on the ability of a group to control their own ethnic social construction. Defining the name of one's own group, navigating the rules governing group membership, and creating and allowing for the evolution or staying power of the group's culture are all achieved in a dance with the dominant forces. Ethnicity is manipulated within a racial context. For example, group membership in Native American tribes is decided by blood quantum, and the existence of the group itself is regulated by a process of recognition carried out by the U.S. federal government. Both blood quantum and federal recognition are criteria invented by forces *outside* of the group itself to regulate that very group via the racial system, but these criteria are also used by the group to define themselves and exclude members according to the needs of the tribal leadership. For Native Americans the prospect of petitioning for ethnoracial uplift, while better than it has been in many decades, is at this historical juncture somewhat limited. We group these nations in pan-ethnic categories like "Native American" perhaps because we acknowledge that their ethnic projects are so weak that they are unable to garner recognition as individual peoples with the individual names of their own groups (even names like "Creeks" and "Nez Percé" are bastardizations that don't come close to the names that these people once called themselves).

Of course, I have offered only a selected ethnic history of the United States. There is no way that I could have retold the stories of all ethnic groups to be incorporated into the United States of America. Certainly I have left out some groups that one might think important to know about. For example, persons from the Indian subcontinent are an interesting case; they are thought to be Caucasian, but many in the subpopulation are dark in skin color. In what ways would they be incorporated? Are they more like the Italian case, that is, thought to be white but denigrated nonetheless? Or will their experience be more like another group that starts with far less privilege? Dominicans and Puerto Ricans have a different history than the Mexicans to whom they are often compared—what would their ethnic projects look like? These are questions I do not tackle in this endeavor for I lack sufficient time, page space, and energy to deal with them all properly; but these stories are hardly irrelevant. The cases I do present pose sufficient evidence that supports a set of conclusions about the relationship between race and ethnicity in the United States, and the way that incorporation and agency operate with the introduction of new ethnic groups (i.e., "minorities" and immigrants) to uplift one's own group and denigrate (black) others.

When we hear the term "ethnic conflict," the United States is not the first place we think of. People in the United States fail to comprehend the impact of ethnic conflict on their own society and nation. But I did not discover carefully hidden secrets by searching for the signs of ethnic conflict while toiling in the musty archives of library backrooms rifling for difficult-to-find historical tidbits. These histories are all in plain view, and I learned by reading books found at any ubiquitous American franchise bookstore. My best answer to the question as to why knowledge about U.S. ethnic conflict remains largely unknown is that people from the United States tend not to know their own history and fail to investigate beyond the folklore they are told. This is especially true of the early-twenty-first-century moment we have labeled "postracial." Postracialism "erases the very histories producing the formations of racial power and privilege, burying them alive, but out of recognizable reach, thus wiping away the very conditions out of which guilt could arise. No guilt because nothing recognizable to be guilty about."[6] What we want from that moment is evidence that racial change has already occurred and there is nothing racial about which to concern ourselves.

While the racial system and the racial paradigms appear static and rigid at any given point in time, they constantly change and evolve according to the work of actors on the social stage. It's never a simple matter of "society" from on high sending down edicts that people live by without resistance. It is not the case that a person is simply matched to an ethnicity by their place of birth or that of their parents; nor is it true that a person's characteristics are simply compared to characteristics in a list of racial categories and that the definition they most fit is the race they are defined as forevermore. Paradigms must be developed over time by finding advocates who promote or contest positions and then audiences to accept the logic (or lack thereof) behind the paradigm that prevails. Thus, while they are extremely difficult to change, paradigms do shift, especially if they have to accommodate situations that threaten their dominant status. We create the paradigms, and when they shift, we shift them. It is only when people fight against racialization that they question the logic and perhaps even the value of embracing the racial paradigm.

People, as social actors, contest all kinds of conditions when they are not comfortable. So, people on the bottom—the "have-nots"—will use their agency to protest their condition. The "haves" struggle too, sometimes to ensure their position at the top, and sometimes because they are unhappy with their share of the goodies. Each ethnic group discussed in this book has been variously inserted into the racial hierarchy, and none were passive about that placement.

Herbert Blumer, back in 1958, explained that race is neither about biological essentialism, nor about phenotypes, but rather is about ranking oneself and others in a relational sense that establishes group positions.[7] And surely, in these ethnic projects, groups that defined themselves or were defined as ethnicities did relational work. That work continues. Zulema Valdez noted that the Latino/Hispanic ethnic entrepreneurs she studied didn't self-describe with pan-ethnic terms (like "Hispanic" or "Latino"), but instead they used those terms as racial labels and only to describe other ethnics from whom they could distance themselves.[8] Our politiculture has evolved to the point where we now think we know a Muslim or an Arab when we see one (and perhaps believe they are interchangeable); we think we know what terrorists look like (and apparently they don't look like Timothy McVeigh, the Oklahoma City bomber, or James Holmes, the Denver movie-theater assassin). Perhaps these nonwhite persons deemed likely terrorists will become the new racial nadir, but their racialization is not yet complete. As of now, racial uplift in the United States is still achieved by standing on the backs of blacks.

Toni Morrison's prognostication (quoted at the start of chapter 1)—that moving into "mainstream America always means buying into the notion that black Americans are the real aliens"—is surely on the mark if ethnic groups achieve racial uplift by distancing themselves from African Americans with whom they once worked, lived, and loved. She is right to say that every ethnic group seems to succeed by using race talk, particularly that which removes them from the lower racial categories to a higher place in the racial hierarchy, and creates anew or manipulates the current politiculture so that the lore about the newly uplifted group focuses on their deservedness and on their superiority to those who are deemed black.

WHERE DO WE GO FROM HERE?

We behave as if race is fixed (that is, we think we know what categories exist, and who is in them—and if we don't know, we ask the offending unclassifiable person, "what are you?"), but the categories are constantly changing. The ethnicity marketing campaign teaches North Americans to doubt that racism is much of a problem—it points to individual persons of African American ethnicity who are making social strides in these so-called postracial times of Barack Obama and his political ilk. Many scholars have noted that, to the contrary, racism is far from eradicated, and they track a changing racial ethnic group that they say we'd be mistaken to prematurely label as significantly diminished. They note that in the long term, history will indeed note a lessened frequency to racial violence, but that racial violence still exists. While a single black man can reach one of the world's highest offices, most of the people believed to share his racial position struggle to survive at the lowest strata of the world's economy. What's more, attempts to subvert the racial status quo—by, for example, making appeals to the equality of man—are met with social ostracization or economic chastisement. Whether the appellant is from a higher status group or a lower status group, arguments that all races are "human" are generally met with pity, punishment, or altogether ignored. Therein lies the perniciousness of ethnicity and of North Americans' belief that their nations are free of ethnic conflict. If ethnic difference were merely a matter of diffferent ways of cooking rice, perhaps North Americans would be correct. But ethnic difference mythologized to shore up human hierarchy is objectionable, and it's dangerous.

We are fooled into believing that ethnicity is different from race because ethnicity is believed to be nonhierarchical, more malleable, more openly ac-

cepted, and rooted in culture. But those beliefs are exactly what makes ethnicity highly vulnerable to campaigns that may involve all sorts of marketing,
including public display and items for cultural consumption (books, movies,
journalism). And marketing is certainly vulnerable to racialization. A group
can "sell" its ethnicity to others in ways that are difficult, if not impossible, to
do with racial identities and identifiers (especially as these are suspected to be
rooted in our genetic makeup).

In truth, ethnicity was born of race. In *The Shadow of Race: Jews, Latinos, and
Immigrant Politics in the United States*, Victoria Hattam explains that nineteenth-
century racial thought lumped together race, nation, and culture in one big
heritable stew. When these ideas were all separated (and ethnicity was declared a
healthy new twentieth-century baby emergent from this very crowded nineteenth-
century racial womb), ethnicity was not quite synonymous with immigration,
but throw in the groups that were acquired with the nation's geographic and
economic expansion and it came close. These other groups all became ethnics,
while the only group left in the racial basket were African Americans. American
sociology even declined to include African Americans in early comparative social
science; whites were the normative category, but for some scholars,

blacks . . . did not fit with either the native or foreign-born and should not be col-
lapsed in with the "foreign element." . . . [For example, in 1894 Columbia University
Professor of Political Economics Richmond Mayo-Smith explained that] he excluded
"the colored" from his discussion as they were "not so much alien" as they were "a peculiar element, separated from the rest of the community by an ineradicable mark."[9]

It seems not to come to mind that Mayo-Smith and others actually helped to
create that very mark by failing to include blacks in their social analysis. Cultural pluralists, Hattam reminds us, were never willing to really deconstruct
race as a category but rather used it to anchor ethnicity—as a way of justifying
the ethnic analyses they were making. When black Americans are included, the
norm is that they are vilified. If not vilified, they could be lauded for showing that in everyday life they actually practice civil behavior, to the surprise
of everyone concerned. Scholars reify the very category of race, and the very
nature of racism, in their own practice of social science.[10]

While race is understood as a pernicious and reliable predictor of what
one's life is in all probability going to be like, ethnicity is marketed to us as

relatively harmless—at least in the way it is represented in the United States. North Americans remain quite uneducated about the dangers that can arise when ethnicity is invoked. Most people who know about or live in places where ethnic wars take place know better. Perhaps if people in the United States become aware of the ways ethnicity and race intertwine, more caution can guide their thinking about the value of promoting ethnic differences. The racial dangers of ethnic self-promotion and stereotyping do not disappear just because we cloak them in the language of ethnic and cultural difference. Earlier I likened the racial hierarchy to a chest of drawers, and argued that ethnic groups are the drawers' contents which may move up (in status) and sometimes down.[11] If we unknowingly use ethnic relations to shore up the racial hierarchy, then we continually cause ethnic conflict. It shouldn't be news, but perhaps it is, that we have been doing this throughout the United States' history. Perhaps the modern and technologically global world we live in marks the time that we immigrant and immigrant-descended people of the United States cease looking at difference, and finally embrace our common humanity instead.

Charles W. Mills wrote a very important book that opened my eyes to the workings of the persons in the upper echelons of the Western racial paradigm. In *The Racial Contract* he argued quite successfully that whites in the West are parties to a "meta-agreement" overseeing the conduct of all social interactions and exchanges between persons (i.e., contracts) stating that whites will assume political, moral, and epistemological control over everything and relegate to nonwhites a permanent state of inferiority and disadvantage.

The general purpose of the Contract is always the differential privileging of whites as a group with respect to the nonwhites as a group, the exploitation of their bodies, land, and resources, and the denial of equal opportunities to them. All whites are *beneficiaries* of the Contract, though some whites are not *signatories* to it. It will be obvious, therefore, that the Racial Contract is not a contract to which the nonwhite subset of humans can be a genuinely consenting party (though, depending again on the circumstances, it may sometimes be politic to pretend that this is the case).[12]

Mills's analysis outlines how those at the top of the hierarchy interact with one another. Whites create a racial binary of whites and nonwhites, and undergo contractual relations according to which side of that binary the other party falls. Even mixed-race people tend to fall on one or the other side of the binary, either embracing racial priviledge or acknowledging its elusiveness.[13]

I offer that the theory of the ethnic project outlines what the nonwhites who fail to take on antiracist struggles do under a racial contract. These nonwhites choose to adjust the racial binary, creating and reinforcing a color-line shift between blacks and nonblacks. These nonwhites (or former nonwhites) who act on ethnic projects support the racial contract even as they cannot be direct signatories to it. Of course, neither all whites nor all nonwhites comply with human hierarchy—and some are certainly antiracist—but the ethnic projects analyzed in this book surely are of a unique type, particularly those ethnic projects that contain an antiblack element, for these projects show themselves to be complicit or in agreement with the process of ranking humans, with the expression of stereotypical thought about themselves and their fellow countrymen and -women, and with the idea of hoarding privileges. By making ethnic projects, they indicate to the signatories of the racial contract that they are willing to connive, and (according to this book's reading of history) those in the upper echelons reward paradigm sympathizers for their complicity.

Racism and the race science that shored it up could have been a temporary blot on the human condition. We have discarded many other dangerous "science-based" fabrications that shaped human thinking and behavior, like bloodletting available via one's local barbershop, or the various tortures and executions approved as tests for witchery. When we learned a better way, we let go of these ideas. Race has been with us for almost five centuries, begun with a preposterous mix of science and folk wisdom not so unlike the one we use today. We have known better for over a hundred years, yet we are still reluctant to let it go.

In fact, it almost seems there are factions in U.S. (and European) society that embrace it all the harder. Recently, in the presidential election campaigns carried out between the two major U.S. political parties, one party put forward a leader that campaigned either with "Keep America America!" or "Keep America American!"—the latter a phrase made popular by the first Imperial Wizard of the Ku Klux Klan.[14] In Alabama, funds are being used to both restore and expand upon a monument to that same Imperial Wizard.[15] And the Internet is being used with great success to recruit newbies to the world of hate, allowing them to access hate and consort with other haters from the comfort of their own homes.[16] But I do not suggest that leadership is solely to blame. I sat that anyone who stands for, or fails to distance themselves from hate are complicit in reenergizing our racial morass. Those who buy into the hype about what those "illegals" are doing to our nation, or the indolent who "don't pay taxes," are shoring up racist thought if they believe there are cogent links between these categories of paperwork and persons of certain racial and ethnic character.

Am I saying that phenotype does not matter? I know it does not explain everything there is to know about contemporary racism. Many groups other than today's African Americans were considered "black" but they still made it out of that bottom racial category. If phenotype mattered, then would the "black" phenotype be allowed to change enough to release them? And let's also look at this from the other side: widespread acceptance of the rule of hypodescent made it possible to include very-white-looking people tainted only with one-drop on the "black" side of the color line dividing North Americans. Further, South Asians are phenotypically dark but are neither considered "black" nor are they considered socioeconomic equivalents of African Americans. The social significance of phenotype is wildly malleable, and it changes to meet the social and economic requirements of time and space. Phenotype is just one shifting aspect of an ever-adaptable racial paradigm.

Isn't racial slavery to blame for this? Perhaps, but then again, perhaps not. True, racial slavery was a blight upon the earth, as is all enslavement (to which we have a global problem numbering in the millions of slaves and trillions of dollars). But Europeans were enslaved, and Indians were enslaved too, so racial slavery cannot completely explain the differential outcomes for all these groups. Moreover, racial slavery ended 150 years ago, and we've known for 100 years that race is a lie; yet we are still acting as if black people exist, as if they constitute a class of humans that we should avoid, corral in separate neighborhoods and occupations, or jail.

Watching racialized American politics and socioeconomic life unfold, I am reminded of the 1995 novel *Blindness* by Nobel Prize–winning author Jose Saramago. In it, an epidemic blindness afflicts one human after another, and the ways human beings respond shows that only exceptional ones avoid taking many opportunities to get the better of their fellow man, if not abuse him altogether. Indeed, in Saramago's *Blindness,* circumstances permit the worst of human iniquity and miscreancy to emerge, and emerge it does. At every point, the horror of what humans can do to each other is apparent, as is the horror of what happens to all when the depraved few take their chance at what wrongdoing they can get away with. The few who stand on the side of morality and human equality hardly have a chance, but stand they do, to survive to the end, but ever so barely do they make it through. It turns out the blindness they suffer is only temporary. But the world and the humans upon it are nearly destroyed before they learn that there was another way, and that this blight on the planet can and will pass; in the end the survivors inherit an obliterated land and a civilization in tatters. In my mind, this blindness parallels the scourge race has been upon our planet. Race was a mere idea, but racial thinking has evolved to engulf us all. It could have been a blip in our human existence, only a temporary blindness, yet it has instead been a plague that has inspired the worst of human behavior: imperialism, colonialism, kidnapping, pillaging, enslavement, torture, rape, lynching, random murder, neocolonialism, mass imprisonment, and needless chronic inequity in nutrition, health, education, employment, and well-being—not to mention the mind-boggling loss of life that all these enterprises have caused. We could have done better. We still can. But sometimes when I read the news, and occasionally in the middle of a sleepless night, I fear that we never will.

But, as Evelyn Hammonds eloquently said, "Race is a human invention. We created it, we have used it in ways that have been in many, many respects quite negative and quite harmful. And we can think ourselves out of it. We made it, we can unmake it."[17] I cannot use that clichéd phrase, "we are at a crossroads," because we are not. We have always had before us the chance to unmake race. We simply have not chosen to do it. Of course the task is enormous, but so is the potential for the human race if we eliminate this blight on the economies and societies and souls of all people.

I am reminded of another fictional story, *The Lottery*, written by Shirley Jackson and published in 1948. In the story, villagers prepare for their annual lottery, and while they note that other villages have dropped the ritual, they consider the thought of doing the same a folly; they draw names, and they all gather to stone (presumably to death) the "winner." The parallels to racial thinking are striking. One character says, "There's always been a Lottery," as if this is an explanation for why the villagers have held on so long to a horrid ritual that began with the very first villagers in the settlement. Everyone in the village is polite—they chat with one another amicably, but never discuss the question of the lottery itself. The ritual is carried out in a way that ensures no single person can be blamed for the lottery's method of extinguishing life. A scapegoat is made to suffer horribly for what is thought to be the good of the community; no one speaks out against it even though it is clear that some must have their doubts. Finally, each villager participates in the heinous act—even children are encouraged to join in. Of course, the difference between this fictional story and American racial life is that in the story the victim is chosen at random; in a racialized society, there is not an equal chance for all, and the most denigrated racial clan is the group from which the victims are constantly served up.

Many of us were taught about race and ethnicity (or, more specifically, our racial structure) in the same way we learned our first language. We got our ideas from hearing people talk with us, including our parents; from our peers in schools and on our playgrounds we picked up new ways of using the words and ideas we learned. We even learned new words and ideas altogether. We heard all that chatter, but were not allowed to comment—it is still quite unpopular to discuss race in mixed social circles. For example, in his book *White Like Me*, Tim Wise explains that when he became an antiracist, willing to discuss racism openly, friends and family would ask him, "What happened to you?" as if by learning what happened to him they could protect themselves from becoming like him.

But we must talk about it. We who know the fallacy of race have to speak up. We who see race in the language of ethnicity, culture, and nationhood, and know it to be noxious and not benign, must speak up and speak loudly enough to be heard over the wagging tongues of the race makers. We know that standing for race is almost always siding with powers who win more than we ever could when we regrettably, but yet again, vote against our own interests. We must be willing to stand apart. We can do better and we must do better. Our future depends upon it.

NOTES

FRONT MATTER

The epigraph introducing the book is from Ronald Takaki, *A Larger Memory: A History of Our Diversity, with Voices* (New York: Back Bay Books, 1998), 4–5.

CHAPTER ONE

1. The epigraph at the opening of this chapter is from Ian F. Haney López, *Racism on Trial: The Chicano Fight for Justice* (Cambridge, MA: Belknap Press of Harvard University Press, 2003). The words attributed to Lady Liberty come from the sonnet "The New Colossus," written in 1883 by poet Emma Lazarus and etched in bronze at the base of the statue. It reads:

> Not like the brazen giant of Greek fame,
> With conquering limbs astride from land to land;
> Here at our sea-washed, sunset gates shall stand
> A mighty woman with a torch, whose flame
> Is the imprisoned lightning, and her name
> Mother of Exiles. From her beacon-hand
> Glows world-wide welcome; her mild eyes command
> The air-bridged harbor that twin cities frame.
> "Keep, ancient lands, your storied pomp!" cries she
> With silent lips. "Give me your tired, your poor,
> Your huddled masses yearning to breathe free,
> The wretched refuse of your teeming shore.
> Send these, the homeless, tempest-tost to me,
> I lift my lamp beside the golden door!"

2. The number of existing continents varies between one and seven depending upon the geographical convention to which one adheres. For example, while Lady Liberty's spires

signify seven continents, the rings of the Olympic Games symbol reference the five-continent model. Sometimes America is one continent, and sometimes it is divided into North and South; sometimes Eurasia is one continent, and sometimes it is divided into Europe and Asia; sometimes Antarctica counts, and sometimes it does not. In most minds the Americas include North America, South America, and Central America, yet persons from the United States identify themselves as "Americans" in a monopolistic way that uses the term exclusively to describe them, as if the others within the continent cannot be so named.

3. The "bootstrap" idea can be attributed to Horatio Alger, a nineteenth-century novelist who wrote about 130 stories about people overcoming extraordinary circumstances by living in morally right ways and working hard. In truth, the characters in his novels who met with economic and social success did so by way of wealthy benefactors, much like Daddy Warbucks's benevolence to Little Orphan Annie.

4. The text of APAi's Oath No. One is: "I hereby denounce Roman Catholicism. I hereby denounce the Pope, sitting at Rome or elsewhere. I denounce his priests and emissaries and the diabolical work of the Roman Catholic church, and hereby pledge myself to the cause of Protestantism to the end that there may be no interference with the discharge of the duties of citizenship, and I solemnly bind myself to protect at all times, and with all the means in my power, the good name of the order and its members, so help me God. Amen." Further, Oath No. Four reads, "I do most solemnly promise and swear that I will always, to the utmost of my ability, labor, plead and wage a continuous warfare against ignorance and fanaticism; that I will use my utmost power to strike the shackles and chains of blind obedience to the Roman Catholic Church from the hampered and bound consciences of a priest-ridden and church-oppressed people; that I will never allow any one, a member of the Roman Catholic Church, to become a member of this order, I knowing him to be such; that I will use my influence to promote the interest of all Protestants everywhere in the world that I may be; that I will not employ a Roman Catholic in any A.P.A. city if I can procure the services of a Protestant." See William D. P. Bliss, ed., "American Protective Association," in *The New Encyclopedia of Social Reform, including All Social-Reform Movements and Activities, and the Economic, Industrial, and Sociological Facts and Statistics of All Countries and All Social Subjects* (New York: Funk & Wagnalls, 1908), 38.

5. Stephen Steinberg, *Ethnic Myth: Race, Ethnicity, and Class in America,* 3d ed. (Boston: Beacon Press, [1981, 1989] 2001).

6. Vilna Bashi and Antonio McDaniel, "A Theory of Immigration and Racial Stratification," *Journal of Black Studies* 27, no. 5 (May 1997): 668–682.

7. Mary Waters, *Ethnic Options: Choosing Identities in America* (Berkeley: University of California Press, 1990), 2.

8. This book expands upon ideas I first wrote about in two articles that theorized about the ways race and ethnicity intertwined in American society. See Bashi and McDaniel, "Theory of Immigration and Racial Stratification"; and Vilna Bashi, "Racial Categories Matter because Racial Hierarchies Matter: A Commentary," *Ethnic and Racial Studies* 21, no. 8 (September 1998): 959–968. I explained that certain ethnic groups were associated with particular racial groupings, and that an individual's choice to first identify themselves with an ethnic label does not indicate an inability to identify racially. In fact, I suggested that racial and ethnic identities are indeed far from being separate, for the choice of ethnic label is not so much about one's self-image as it is about the place one is accorded in the larger hierarchical framework where race and ethnic group labels are constructed. Moreover, in the conclusion to my first book, *Survival of the Knitted: Immigrant Social Networks in a Stratified World* (Stanford, CA: Stanford University Press, 2007), I showed that immigrants who

work together to help one another actually help to construct themselves as an ethnic group in the eyes of the employers, realtors, and neighbors with whom they share workplaces and communities. Of course, immigrants are not the only ones who have networks or who work to their groups' collective good.

9. Audrey Smedley, *Race in North America: Origin and Evolution of a Worldview*, 3d ed. (Boulder, CO: Westview Press, 2007).

10. The word "ethnoracial" was used by Karen Brodkin in *How the Jews Became White Folks: And What That Has to Say about Race in America* (New Brunswick, NJ: Rutgers University Press, 1998). She used the combined term to explain that in her book the words "'race' and 'ethnicity' [are used] more or less interchangeably" (189n1). In *The Ethnic Project* I don't use the words interchangeably, but the term "ethnoracial" is useful to suggest those contexts and historical moments in which ethnicity is highly racialized, i.e., when/where the salience of race makes visible the actions, intentions, and messages of ethnic agents.

11. This is an argument I first made in my 1998 article "Racial Categories Matter."

12. See Bashi and McDaniel, "Theory of Immigration and Racial Stratification."

13. Steinberg, *Ethnic Myth*.

14. Toni Morrison, "On the Backs of Blacks," *Time*, December 2, 1993, 57.

15. Since its inception, the Department of Homeland Security has had five hearings on Muslim radicalization but none on right-wing terrorism, despite the fact that the right wing in the United States has committed six times more "murderous attacks" than Muslim radicals. (While more deaths may be attributed to Muslims in attacks in the twenty years between 1990 and 2010, 99.2% of all those deaths in the period happened with one event, the attack on 9/11/2001.) See "The Benefits of Hindsight: The Need for More Monitoring of Domestic Terrorism," *The Economist*, August 18, 2012, *http://www.economist.com/node/21560566*, accessed November 1, 2012.

16. See Barry Moreno, *The Statue of Liberty Encyclopedia* (New York: New Line Books, 2005); the 1985 documentary *The Statue of Liberty*, directed by Ken Burns for Florentine Films; and the Public Broadcasting Service website about the film, *http://www.pbs.org/ken burns/statueofliberty*, accessed October 1, 2012.

17. See "African Burial Ground: Revisit the Past to Build the Future," at *http://www .africanburialground.gov*, or the National Park Service's site "African Burial Ground" at *www .nps.gov/agbg*, both accessed August 1, 2012.

CHAPTER TWO

1. See The Online Etymology Dictionary, *http://www.etymonline.com/index.php?term=ethnic*, and the Merriam-Webster Dictionary Online, *http://www.merriam-webster.com/dictionary/ ethnic*, both accessed January 10, 2012.

2. Donna R. Gabaccia, "Race, Nation, Hyphen: Italian-Americans and American Multiculturalism in Comparative Perspective," in *Are Italians White?*, ed. Jennifer Guglielmo and Salvatore Salerno (New York: Routledge, 2003), chap. 3, 44–59.

3. Ibid., 56.

4. Nathan Glazer and Daniel Patrick Moynihan, *Ethnicity: Theory and Experience* (Cambridge, MA: Harvard University Press), 1975, 1.

5. Ronald Cohen, 1978, "Ethnicity: Problem and Focus in Anthropology," *Annual Review of Anthropology* 7: 379–403.

6. Steinberg, *Ethnic Myth*.

7. Richard Schermerhorn, *Comparative Ethnic Relations: A Framework for Theory and Research* (New York: Random House, 1970), 12.

8. Juan Flores, *The Diaspora Strikes Back: Caribeño Tales of Turning and Learning* (New York: Routledge, 2008).

9. Richard Shermerhorn, "Toward a General Theory of Minority Groups," *Pychon* 25 (1964): 238–264.

10. Theodore Allen writes that the way racialization works is "[to destroy] the original forms of social identity among the subject population, and then [exclude] the members of that population from admittance into the forms of social identity normal to the colonizing power" and subsequently "to deny, disregard, delegitimate previous or potential social distinctions that may have existed among the oppressed group, or that might tend to emerge in the normal course of development of a class society" (Theodore Allen, "Summary of *Invention of the White Race*," 1998, par. 34, *http://clogic.eserver.org/1-2/allen.html*, accessed June 30, 2011). The definition of racialization provided here also relies on Michael Banton's 1997 articulation of the concept; for this see Rohit Barot and John Bird, "Racialization: The Genealogy and Critique of a Concept," *Ethnic and Racial Studies* 24, no. 4 (July 2001): 601–618.

11. Michael Cremo and Richard Thompson, in *Hidden History of the Human Race* (Los Angeles: Bhaktivedanta, 1999), show that falsehoods in anthropology and archeology continue to push the idea that (racial) divisions among humans exist and persist until today.

12. Surely class and gender are stratifying systems also widely acknowledged as social constructions, but no one asks whether, as figments of our collective imagination, they carry sufficient weight for us to continue to devote resources to studying them. Perhaps no one does this because it is clear that these are all real in the sense that we stake people's lives and life chances on the ways they fit or are excluded from particular categories within each of these systems. Race—at least in North America—certainly defines one's quality of life and therefore, in my opinion, needs to be discussed and studied, in order to combat its effects on our human societies.

13. At *http://www.pbs.org/race/000_General/000_00-Home.htm*, accessed January 10, 2012, the companion site for the film series *Race, The Power of an Illusion*, there is a page entitled "Ten Things Everyone Should Know about Race." In brief (omitting the site's explanations) these are: 1. Race is a modern idea. 2. Race has no genetic basis. 3. Human subspecies don't exist. 4. Skin color really is only skin deep. 5. Most variation is within, not between, "races." 6. Slavery predates race. 7. Race and freedom evolved together. 8. Race justified social inequalities as natural. 9. Race isn't biological, but racism is still real. 10. Colorblindness will not end racism. Contrast these ideas with those of Vincent Sarich, professor emeritus of anthropology at the University of California at Berkeley, and Frank Miele, senior editor of *Skeptic* magazine, who remarkably disagree with each of these ten points (remarkable given that the first eight points are based on fact). In their book *Race: The Reality of Human Differences* (Boulder, CO: Westview Press, 2005), they write, "we present the evidence we believe refutes the first eight points and explain why we reject points nine and ten, not only for economic but ethical reasons as well" (ix). Sarich and Miele oppose the social constructionist position altogether, believing it is being used to justify "public policies based on racial privileges," and suggest further that race is indeed "a valid biological concept" (ibid.).

14. Each of these writers have used their public and scholarly writing to downplay the impact of race in shaping a person's life in the United States. See, e.g., Thomas Sowell's "Three Black Histories," in *Essays and Data on American Ethnic Groups*, ed. Thomas Sowell (N.p.: Urban Institute, 1978), 7–64; William Julius Wilson's *The Declining Significance of Race* (Chicago: University of Chicago Press, 1980); and Dinesh D'Souza's *The End of Racism: Principles for a Multiracial Society* (New York: Free Press, 1996). George Lipsitz, Ian F. Haney Lopez, and Tim Wise have used their writings to dispute perspectives like these. See George

Lipsitz's *The Possessive Investment in Whiteness* (Philadelphia: Temple University Press, 1998); Ian F. Haney Lopez's "The Social Construction of Race: Some Observations on Illusion, Fabrication, and Choice," *Harvard Civil Rights–Civil Liberties Law Review*, vol. 29 (Winter 1994): 1–62; reprinted as chap. 16 in *Critical Race Theory: The Cutting Edge*, ed. Richard Delgado and Jean Stefanic (Philadelphia: Temple University Press, 2000), 163–175; Tim Wise's *White Like Me: Reflections on Race from a Privileged Son* (New York: Soft Skull Press, 2007); or Wise's *Dear White America: Letter to a New Minority* (San Francisco: City Lights, 2012).

15. Alan Goodman, "Two Questions about Race," in the April 20, 2005 *Is Race "Real"? SSRC Web Forum* (New York: Social Science Research Council, 2005), found at *http://race andgenomics.ssrc.org/Goodman/pf/*, accessed January 22, 2007.

16. Charles W. Mills, *The Racial Contract* (Ithaca, NY: Cornell University Press, 1999).

17. If you seek good works tracing the history of the falsehood that is race, or understanding the fallacious nature of the science that presumably backs it, you might read the writings of Audrey Smedley, *Race in North America*, 2007; and James King, *The Biology of Race*, rev. ed., (Berkeley: University of California Press, 1981).

18. Smedley, *Race in North America*, 15.

19. Steinberg, *Ethnic Myth*, 263.

20. Thomas Kuhn, in his book *The Structure of Scientific Revolutions* (Chicago: University of Chicago Press, 1970), explains: "Normal science, the activity in which most scientists inevitably spend almost all their time, is predicated on the assumption that the scientific community knows what the world is like. Much of the success of the enterprise [of science] derives from the [scientific] community's willingness to defend that assumption, if necessary at considerable cost. Normal science, for example, often suppresses fundamental novelties because they are necessarily subversive of its basic commitments" (5). Racial knowledge is this kind of science.

21. In *Race in North America* Smedley called these ideas "folk wisdom" and chronicled their development, including Thomas Jefferson's call for scientific methods to (dis)prove nascent U.S. racial ideologies.

22. Bashi, *Survival of the Knitted*, esp. chap. 7.

23. See Smedley, *Race in North America*; and Stephen Jay Gould, *The Mismeasure of Man* (New York: W. W. Norton, 1996).

24. Armand Marie Leroi, "A Family Tree in Every Gene," *New York Times*, March 14, 2005, A23.

25. George M. Frederickson, *White Supremacy: A Comparative Study of American and South African History* (London: Oxford University Press, 1982).

26. Karen Farquharson, "Racial Categories in Three Nations: Australia, South Africa, and the United States," conference paper presented at the 2007 Joint Meetings of the Australian Sociological Association (TASA) and the Sociological Association of Aotearoa New Zealand (SAANZ), December 4–7, 2007, *http://www.tasa.org.au/conferences/conferencepapers07/papers/276.pdf*, accessed September 10, 2012.

27. It is very difficult to make a concise statement about racialization in Brazil. In the entry on "Brazilian Racial Formations" (*Online Encyclopedia http://encyclopedia.jrank.org/ articles/pages/6027/Brazilian-Racial-Formations.html*, accessed August 19, 2010), the complex race-color-class/education/money scheme upon which Brazilians base their understandings of race is explained. In "Racial Classifications in Latin America," you may see why government census–imposed categories don't really work in Brazil since here the author lists the 134 self-reported color-based classifications found in the Brazilian Institute of Geography and Statistics' 1976 survey (accessed August 19, 2010 at *http://www.zonalatina.com/Zldata55.htm*).

Livio Sansone explains that the Brazilian census uses 5 categories, but people he interviewed in one site made reference to 26 separate categories, and in a different region, they referred to a quite different list of 26; he warns that others have suggested that Brazil has 3 languages of race: official institutional categorization (the source of the 3 or 5 categories that have been variously used in Brazil's censuses), the language used to discuss the romantic foundational myths about the origins of Brazil, and the language the people use in their everyday inter-actions. See Livio Sansone, *Blackness without Ethnicity: Constructing Race in Brazil* (New York: Palgrave Macmillan, 2003), esp. 22. See also Edward Telles, "Racial Ambiguities among the Brazilian Population," *Ethnic and Racial Studies* 25, no. 3 (May 2002): 415–441.

28. Frank Dikkster, ed., *The Construction of Racial Identity in China and Japan* (Hong Kong: Hong Kong University Press, 1997); and Pyong Gap Min, "A Comparison of the Ko-rean Minorities in China and Japan," *International Migration Review* 26, no. 1 (1992): 4–21.

29. The ironies are explained in Gould's 1994 article "The Geometer of Race," pub-lished in *Discover Magazine* (*http://discovermagazine.com/1994/nov/thegeometerofrac441*, ac-cessed August 22, 2012). Suffice it to say in this note that Blumenbach did not invest much in the superiority and inferiority of races. He simply used the one white skull he possessed to surmise that whites had white skulls and darker-skinned folk must have darker bones. Thus, if one knows anything about color theory, white cannot be made from mixing other colors—but brown can be made from the mixing of many colors. So, white must be the unmixed origin, for it cannot come from the mixing of any other color. Thus, it comes at the pyramidal top, yet other colors may be mixed with it to get the darker skin/bone colors of the pyramid's lower layers.

30. Other examples of processes of category creation are manifest in Winthrop Jordan's writings about the meaning of "blackness"; F. James Davis's explanation of how categories are organized to give to mixed-race persons higher or lower status than that of their parents; or Thandeka's study of how one learns to be white in America. See Winthrop Jordan, *White over Black: American Attitudes toward the Negro, 1500–1812* (Chapel Hill: University of North Carolina Press, 1968); F. James Davis, *Who Is Black? One Nation's Definition*, 10th anniversary ed. (University Park: Pennslyvania State University Press, 2001), esp. chap. 5; and Thandeka, *Learning to Be White: Money, Race, and God in America* (New York: Continuum, 2000).

31. Thandeka, *Learning to Be White*.

32. Davis, *Who Is Black?*, 2001.

33. Noel Ignatiev, *How the Irish Became White* (Oxford: Routledge, 1996); Brodkin, *How the Jews Became White Folks*.

34. See Reynolds Farley's "Identifying with Multiple Races: A Social Movement That Suc-ceeded but Failed?" Population Studies Center Research Report 01-491, University of Michigan (n.d., *http://www.psc.isr.umich.edu/pubs/pdf/rr01-491.pdf*); P. J. Aspinall, "The Conceptuali-sation and Categorisation of Mixed Race/Ethnicity in Britain and North America: Identity Options and the Role of the State," *International Journal of Intercultural Relations* 27, no. 3 (May 2003): 269–296; Tim Padgett, "Still Black or White: Why the Census Misreads Hispan-ics," *Time.com U.S.*, March 29, 2012, *http://www.time.com/time/nation/article/0,8599,1975883,00.html*, accessed September 3, 2012; Hope Yen, "Census Bureau Proposes Changes: Hispanics as Distinct Category and End Use of Term 'Negro,'" *Huffington Post*, August 12, 2012, *http://www.huffingtonpost.com/2012/08/09/census-bureau-changes-race-hispanics-negro_n_1760467.html?ncid=edlinkusaolp00000003*; and also Lornet Turnbull, "Latinos May Get Own Race Category on Census Form," *Seattle Times*, August 30, 2012; all accessed September 3, 2012.

35. George Lipsitz, *The Possessive Investment in Whiteness: How White People Profit from Identity Politics* (Philadelphia: Temple University Press, 1998).

36. See, for example, Walter Benn Michaels, "The Trouble with Diversity," *American Prospect*, August 13, 2006, *http://www.prospect.org/cs/articles?articleId=11864*, accessed October 29, 2010; see also Yehudi O. Webster, *The Racialization of America* (New York: Palgrave Macmillan, 1993).

37. For a body of work on racial hierarchical distinctions look to the following tomes, which teach how the segregation of labor and neighbor help to create hierarchy among racial categories by keeping them separate and unequal in residences, labor markets, and interpersonal relationships: Douglas Massey and Nancy Denton, *American Apartheid: Segregation and the Making of the Underclass* (Cambridge, MA: Harvard University Press, 1993); Neil MacMaster, *Racism in Europe: 1870–2000* (Basingstoke, UK: Palgrave Macmillan, 2001); Dierdre A. Royster, *Race and the Invisible Hand: How White Networks Exclude Black Men from Blue-Collar Jobs* (Berkeley: University of California Press, 2003); Cheryl I. Harris, "Whiteness as Property," *Harvard Law Review* 106, no. 8 (1993): 1709–1795, 1710–1712; Evelyn Nakano Glenn, *Unequal Freedom: How Race and Gender Shaped American Citizenship and Labor* (Cambridge, MA: Harvard University Press, 2004); as well as the aforementioned works by Stephen Steinberg, *Ethnic Myth* (2001), Ian Haney Lopez, *White by Law* (1997), and Audrey Smedley, *Race in North America* (2007).

38. Critiques and commentaries on color-blindness are offered by Patricia Williams, *Seeing a Color-Blind Future: The Paradox of Race* (New York: Farrar Straus & Giroux, 1998); Eduardo Bonilla-Silva, *Racism without Racists: Color-Blind Racism and the Persistence of Inequality in the United States* (Lanham, MD: Rowman & Littlefield, 2003); and Tim Wise, *Colorblind: The Rise of Post-Racial Politics and the Retreat from Racial Equity* (San Francisco: City Lights, 2010).

39. This list is not exhaustive, of course; there are many other works that can be included here.

40. When Michael Omi and Howard Winant in their book *Racial Formation in the United States: From the 1960s to the 1990s*, 2nd ed. (New York: Routledge, 1994) explain that we have moved from a racial dictatorship under Jim Crow to racial hegemony marked by the post–civil rights era, they are describing a change in the racial politiculture.

41. Cheryl I. Harris, "Plessy," in *The Social Construction of Race and Ethnicity in the United States*, ed. Joan Ferrante and Prince Brown (New York: Prentice-Hall, 2000), 351–354.

42. Ian F. Haney López, *White by Law*.

43. In *Making Race and Nation* (Cambridge, UK, and New York: Cambridge University Press, 1998), Anthony Marx presents the thesis that races are political tools used by groups vying for political power, and are the basis for coalition making or exclusion from the political process. Michael Omi and Howard Winant made the argument earlier, but differently, in their book *Racial Formation in the United States*.

44. Thandeka, *Learning to Be White*.

45. See the accounts with citations at BlackPast.org, "Howard Beach Incident (1986)," *http://www.blackpast.org/?q=aah/howard-beach-incident-1986*; the *Houston Chronicle*, "White Supremacist Executed for Jasper Dragging Death," September 21, 2011, *http://www.chron.com/life/article/White-supremacist-executed-for-Jasper-dragging-2182561.php*; BBC News, January 3, 2012, "The Timeline," *http://www.bbc.co.uk/news/uk-16283806*, and November 14, 2011, "Merkel Says German 'Neo-Nazi' Murders Shameful," *http://www.bbc.co.uk/news/world-europe-15727841*; CNN.com, July 6, 1988, "Three Whites Indicted in Dragging Death of Black Man in Texas," *http://edition.cnn.com/US/9807/06/dragging.death.02/*; Huffington Post, November 14, 2011, "National Socialist Underground: Far-Right Terror Group Shocks Germany," *http://www.huffingtonpost.com/2011/11/14/national-socialist-undergound-terror-group_n_1092308.html*; and

David Edwards, July 31, 2012, "Florida Man Charged with Hate Crime Says He "Only Shot a Nigger," *TheBackStory.com*, *http://www.rawstory.com/rs/2012/07/31/florida-man-charged-with -hate-crime-says-he-only-shot-a-nigger/*, all accessed September 1, 2012.

46. Bob Egelko, "Hate Crime Charges Dropped in Tahoe Beating," *San Francisco Chronicle*, July 31, 2008, *http://www.sfgate.com/bayarea/article/Hate-crime-charges-dropped-in -Tahoe-beating-3201839.php*, accessed September 1, 2012.

47. Mills, *Racial Contract*.

48. See Smedley, *Race in North America*; and France Winddance Twine, *Racism in a Racial Democracy* (Piscataway, NJ: Rutgers University Press, 1997).

49. Barbara J. Flagg, *Was Blind, But Now I See: White Race Consciousness and the Law* (New York: New York University Press, 1998).

50. See Omi and Winant, *Racial Formations*; and also Howard Winant, *Racial Conditions: Politics, Theory, Comparisons* (Minneapolis: University of Minnesota Press, 1994).

51. And why should "New Yorker" not be an ethnicity? We have our own accents, clothing style—all black is the signature I think—and a culture that includes waiting in the street and not on the corner if we are trying to walk across, and not waiting for the stoplight to change to green before we start walking. I'm being only slightly facetious here—if ethnicity can lump together peoples of different origins and tongues in new destinations, and if they may be accepted as one people in the racial paradigm, either New Yorkers can be an ethnic group, or the fallaciousness of ethnic groupings is evident by this example.

52. Grouping all "black" people together may mean as little as nothing except they have nonwhite skin. *The Mis-adventures of Awkward Black Girl* (*www.awkwardblackgirl.com*) is a comedic web series rich in showing the diversity within blackness and may make this point far better or at least funnier than I can.

CHAPTER THREE

1. The epigraphs at the opening of the chapter are from Toni Morrison, "On the Backs of Blacks," *Time*, December 2, 1993, 57; and Peter Nabokov, ed., *Native American Testimony: A Chronicle of Indian-White Relations from Prophecy to the Present, 1492–1992*, with a foreword by Vine Deloria Jr. (New York: Viking Penguin, 1991, [1978]), 184.

2. Amy Chua, *World on Fire: How Exporting Free Market Democracy Breeds Ethnic Hatred and Global Instability*, 2nd ed. (New York: Anchor, 2004), 190.

3. Brodkin, *How the Jews Became White Folks*, is just one of many authors to state this.

4. Smedley, *Race in North America*.

5. Ibid.

6. Ibid.; and Allen, *Invention of the White Race*, 1:1994.

7. "Their ideologies about individualism and accumulating property guided their assault on foreign lands and their treatment of the indigenous peoples of the New World. These ideologies also helped to determine the kind of slavery that evolved in North America. Possessive individualism and the near sacredness of property and property rights in seventeenth-century English culture facilitated the transformation of Africans into slave property and their concomitant demotion to nonhuman forms of being" (Smedley, *Race in North America*, 52).

8. Ibid., 59.

9. Ibid., 55–56.

10. Ibid., 63–64.

11. Ibid., 63.

12. Theodore W. Allen, *Invention of the White Race*, see par. 28.

13. Smedley, *Race in North America*, 77.

14. Ibid., 77, 89.

15. Michael A. Gomez, *Reversing Sail: A History of the African Diaspora*, Series: New Approaches to African History (Cambridge: Cambridge University Press, 2004).

16. Anthony S. Parent Jr., *Foul Means: The Formation of a Slave Society in Virginia* (Chapel Hill: University of North Carolina Press, 2003), 109.

17. Ibid.,116.

18. Max Weber, *The Protestant Ethic and the Spirit of Capitalism* (New York: Charles Scribner's Sons), 1958. The quotations come from the introduction by Anthony Giddens in this same text, 3, 4.

19. "The possibility of adventure and profit attracted men and women away from familiar forms of social control, away from family, kinspeople, employers, patrons, friends, and clients, into interactions with alien merchants, adventurers, pirates, sailors, and other strangers. The frequent anonymity of these new interactions underscored the need for a familiar identity to which others could relate. With growing competition and protonationalistic conflicts among the various nations of Europe, the English, like other Europeans, often found it critical to establish political and/or commercial alliances predicated on religious affiliation. Thus, whether one was Catholic, Protestant, or some variant thereof was often the key not only to the identity of others but also to how they were to be treated" (Smedley, *Race in North America*, 66).

20. The Spanish developed mechanisms for issuing "certificates of Limpieza de Sangre" and "elaborate tests for finding social genealogical connections" to prove one's purity, as in free of Jewish or Moorish heritage (Smedley, *Race in North America*, 69). Thus did blood become the site where—in North American thinking—racial character resides.

21. See Smedley, *Race in North America*; Davis, *Who Is Black?*; and Tomás Almaguer, *Racial Fault Lines: The Historical Origins of White Supremacy in California* (Berkeley: University of California Press, 2008).

22. Virginia Dominguez, *White by Definition: Social Classification in Creole Louisiana* (New Brunswick, NJ: Rutgers University Press, 1986), 30.

23. "Miscegenation" has roots in the Latin words *miscére*, meaning "mix," and *genus*, meaning "race."

24. Dominguez, *White by Definition*, 33–34.

25. This quote comes from the jacket of Allen 1994, *Invention of the White Race.*

26. Ibid.; and Theodore Allen, *The Invention of the White Race: Volume Two, The Origin of Racial Oppression in Anglo-America* (London: Verso, 1997).

27. Nell Irvin Painter, *Creating Black Americans: African-American History and Its Meanings, 1619 to the Present* (New York: Oxford University Press, 2007). Painter details how slavery helped construct whiteness. She explains that Europeans enslaved one another before this time with no remarkable connotations that the term "white slavery" later had. In fact, "it is said that Dublin was Europe's largest slave market during the eleventh century" and "in Ireland, a female slave represented a unit of currency, like a dollar or a euro"; *odalisques* and other images of beautiful white slave women (notably often in harems) are a cornerstone of European art (34, 36). White slave systems were in place until the sixteenth century until the advent of sugar slavery showed itself to be productive on the African and South American coasts. Racial slavery was an invention for a later time.

28. Stephen Jay Gould, *The Mismeasure of Man* (New York: W. W. Norton, 1996); California Newsreel, 2003, "Interview with Stephen Jay Gould," Public Broadcasting System, for the film *"Race, the Power of an Illusion,"* "Background Readings," accessed at *http://www.pbs.org/race/000_About/002_04-background-01-09.htm* on July 15, 2011; the quote is from Painter, *Creating Black Americans*, 1.

29. Jefferson's logic would show that Africans and their descendants in the Americas were naturally deserving of enslavement (i.e., by default, not Americans). Smith did not agree but thought both Southern Americans and Southern Europeans to be as "savage" as native North Americans.

30. Painter, *Creating Black Americans*.

31. Parent, *Foul Means*; Allen, "Summary of the Argument of *The Invention of the White Race* (Part Two)," *Cultural Logic* 1, no. 2 (Spring 1998), *http://clogic.eserver.org/1-2/allen2.html*, accessed June 30, 2011; and Allen, *Invention of the White Race*.

32. Parent, *Foul Means*, 107.

33. Allen, *Invention of the White Race*, par. 107.

34. Ibid., 56, 57.

35. Ibid., par. 108.

36. Ibid., 265–266.

37. Ibid., par. 112.

38. Parent, *Foul Means*, 121.

39. Davis, *Who Is Black?*.

40. Natalie Angier, "Do Races Differ? Not Really, DNA Shows," *New York Times*, August 22, 2000. Also available at *http://www.nytimes.com/library/national/science/082200sci -genetics-race.html*, accessed September 1, 2012.

41. Smedley, *Race in North America*.

42. Gould, "Geometer of Race"; Smedley, *Race in North America*.

43. Between 1993 and 1997, the U.S. government's Office of Management and Budget (OMB) reviewed the government standards for collecting and reporting data on race and ethnicity, and released an October 30, 1997 *Federal Register* entry (see *http://www.whitehouse .gov/omb/fedreg_1997standards*, accessed September 22, 2010) noting revisions guiding government uniformity on these matters. "The revised standards will have five minimum categories for data on race: American Indian or Alaska Native, Asian, Black or African American, Native Hawaiian or Other Pacific Islander, and White. There will be two categories for data on ethnicity: 'Hispanic or Latino' and 'Not Hispanic or Latino.'" See also David A. Hollinger, "Group Preferences, Cultural Diversity, and Social Democracy: Notes Toward a Theory of Affirmative Action," *Representations* 55, Special Issue: Race and Representation: Affirmative Action (Summer 1996): 31–40.

44. Brodkin, *How the Jews Became White Folks*.

45. The image may be viewed at *http://museum.msu.edu/exhibitions/virtual/Immigration andcaricature/7572-107.html*, accessed December 15, 2012. It depicts 17 small sketches of the head of George Washington (and one additional head, Theodore Roosevelt's) drawn with the supposed facial features of different ethnic groups. The groups included were Chinese, Negro, Irish, Italian, Russian, German, French, Spanish, Boer, Indian, Swede, Greek, Turk, Alaskan, Hawaiian, Russian Jew, Jap [*sic*], and (this one Roosevelt) Filipino.

46. Reading this, some might wonder at the coincidence that Allen says here what Marxists have said about race all along—that it is part of a "divide and conquer strategy" that (merchant and planter) capitalists used to realign classes. On this, Allen (himself a Marxist scholar) would certainly agree, but there are two caveats to this agreement. First, Allen doesn't pose it as a theory of history—he writes two volumes presenting historical evidence that this is in fact the case. Second, Allen would not agree at all that this means that race is a subordinate matter to class. In fact, I think he provides evidence to the contrary. He writes his two-volume set *The Invention of the White Race* noting that whiteness (a racial state of being and behaviors meant to obscure protections of privileges and wealth,

and not black enslavement, a class position justified by race) is the peculiar institution that most needs explaining. He counters (in Allen, *Invention of the White Race*) the prevailing thought that there weren't enough poor whites to matter when the idea of white supremacy was created—and argues instead that class differentiation would be quite enough in that case, and race would be redundant and less than utile. Instead, he argues that race is *necessary* precisely because there are far too many poor whites at the time that planters need to protect their interests and privileges, and something must be given them so that they accept the unequal status quo. Race is the thing given to them. Said in other words, Allen devotes his life's work to understanding the invention and evolution of racialized thinking and the race that promulgated it because he believed that to be (to borrow from Du Bois's words) the problem of the twentieth, and even now, the twenty-first, centuries.

47. David Brooks, "The Triumph of Hope over Self-Interest," *New York Times*, January 12, 2003, *http://www.nytimes.com/2003/01/12/opinion/the-triumph-of-hope-over-self-interest .html?pagewanted=all&src=pm*, accessed June 1, 2012.

48. Allen, Summary of *Invention of the White Race*, par. 87.

49. Ibid.

50. R. M. Schneiderman, "Why Do Americans Still Hate Welfare?" *New York Times*, December 10, 2008, *http://economix.blogs.nytimes.com/2008/12/10/why-do-americans-still-hate -welfare/*, accessed September 9, 2012.

51. Martin Gillens, *Why Americans Hate Welfare: Race, Media, and the Politics of Anti-poverty Policy*, Studies in Communication, Media, and Public Opinion (Chicago: University of Chicago Press, 2000).

52. Paul Krugman writes: "Cornell University's Suzanne Mettler points out that many beneficiaries of government programs seem confused about their own place in the system. She tells us that 44 percent of Social Security recipients, 43 percent of those receiving unemployment benefits, and 40 percent of those on Medicare say that they 'have not used a government program.'" See Paul Krugman, "Moochers against Welfare," *New York Times*, February 16, 2012, accessed September 7, 2012. Presumably, then, voters imagine that pledges to slash government spending mean cutting programs for the idle poor, not things they themselves count on. And this is a confusion politicians deliberately encourage.

53. Rickie Solinger, *Beggars and Choosers: How the Politics of Choice Shapes Adoption, Abortion, and Welfare in the United States* (New York: Hill & Wang, 2002); Frances Fox Piven and Richard Cloward, *Regulating the Poor: The Functions of Public Welfare* (New York: Vintage, 1993).

54. As examples, see Thandeka, *Learning to Be White*; Lipsitz, *Possessive Investment in Whiteness*; Wise, *White Like Me*; and Lillian Smith, *Killers of the Dream* (New York: W. W. Norton, 1994).

55. Thandeka, *Learning to Be White*; Wise, *White Like Me*.

56. John Hartigan, *Odd Tribes: Toward a Cultural Analysis of White People* (Durham, NC: Duke University Press, 2005), 59.

57. Ibid., 89.

58. Ibid., 107.

59. Hammonds says this in the film "The Difference Between Us," part one in the 2003 trilogy *Race: The Power of an Illusion*, produced by California Newsreel, distributed by the Public Broadcasting System. A transcript can be found at *http://www.pbs.org/race/000_ About/002_04-about-01.htm* (accessed September 27, 2010).

60. Nonwhites may see racism as systematic, and are likely more aware of sociological concepts like institutional racism, even if they do not use the same words for it. See Joe P.

Feagin and Melvin R. Sikes, *Living with Racism: The Black Middle-Class Experience* (New York: Beacon Press, 1995).

61. Herbert Blumer, "Race Prejudice as a Sense of Group Position," *Pacific Sociological Review* 1, no. 1 (Spring 1958): 3–7. Reprinted in 2007 in *Rethinking the Color Line: Readings in Race and Ethnicity*, 3rd ed., ed. Charles A. Gallagher (New York: McGraw-Hill, 2007), 169–175. The quote is from the reprint, 169.

62. Ibid., 173.

63. Bonilla-Silva, *Racism without Racists*, makes reference to: (1) Jim Sidanius et al., "It's Not Affirmative Action, It's the Blacks," in *Racialized Politics*, ed. David O. Sears, Jim Sidanius, and Lawrence Bobo (Chicago: University of Chicago Press, 2000), 191–235; (2) Lawrence D. Bobo, James A. Kluegel, and Ryan Smith, "Laissez-Faire Racism: The Crystallization of a Kinder, Gentler, Antiblack Ideology," in *Racial Attitudes in the 1990s: Continuity and Change*, ed. Steven A. Tuch and Jack K. Martin (Westport, CT: Prager, 1997), 15–44; (3) Mary R. Jackman, *The Velvet Glove: Paternalism and Conflict in Gender, Class, and Race Relations* (Berkeley: University of California Press, 1994).

CHAPTER FOUR

1. The epigraph that opens this chapter is from David Roediger's introduction to *Black on White: Black Writers on What It Means to Be White* (New York: Random House Digital, 2010), 19; and Roediger cites Ralph Ellison's *Going to the Territory* (New York: Random House, 1970), 111.

2. Mary C. Waters and Tomás R. Jiménez, "Assessing Immigrant Assimilation: New Empirical and Theoretical Challenges," *Annual Review of Sociology* 31 (2005): 105–125.

3. The thirteen colonies were named the Connecticut Colony, the Delaware Colony, the Province of Georgia, the Province of Maryland, the Province of Massachusetts Bay, the Province of New Hampshire, the Province of New York, the Province of New Jersey, the Province of North Carolina, the Province of Pennsylvania, the Colony of Rhode Island and Providence Plantations, the Province of South Carolina, and the Colony of Virginia.

4. Steinberg, *Ethnic Myth*, 8–9.

5. Ibid., 11.

6. Allen, *Invention of the White Race*, 16, 18.

7. Brodkin, *How the Jews Became White Folks*.

8. Ibid.

9. Ibid., 54.

10. Allen, Summary of *Invention of the White Race*, par. 27.

11. Ibid.

12. Smedley, *Race in North America*, 60, 61.

13. Allen, Summary of *Invention of the White Race*, par. 27.

14. Painter, *Creating African Americans*, 134.

15. Ignatiev, *How the Irish Became White*, 139.

16. Ibid.

17. Ibid., 40–41.

18. Ibid., 41.

19. David Roediger, *Working Toward Whiteness: How America's Immigrants Became White: The Strange Journey from Ellis Island to the Suburbs* (New York: Basic Books, 2005); and Thandeka, *Learning to Be White*.

20. Brodkin, *How the Jews Became White Folks*, 64.

21. Ignatiev, *How the Irish Became White*, 111.

22. David R. Roediger, *The Wages of Whiteness: Race and the Making of the American Working Class* (New York: Verso, 2007), 141.

23. Ibid, 140.

24. Ibid., 154.

25. Ibid., 134.

26. Ibid., 136.

27. See Christine Stansell, *City of Women: Sex and Class in New York: 1789–1860* (Urbana and Chicago: University of Illinois Press, 1987); and also Steinberg, *Ethnic Myth*.

28. Steinberg, *Ethnic Myth*.

29. Kerby A. Miller, *Emigrants and Exiles: Ireland and the Irish Exodus to North America* (New York and Oxford: Oxford University Press, 1985), 497–498.

30. Ibid.

31. Ibid., 508, 509.

32. Dan Caldwell, "The Negroization of the Chinese Stereotype in California," *Southern California Quarterly* 53 (June 1971): 123–132; 125.

33. Terry E. Boswell, "A Split Labor Market Analysis of Discrimination against Chinese Immigrants, 1850–1882," *American Sociological Review* 51, no. 3 (June 1986): 352–371.; see 358, where Boswell is quoting other sources.

34. Luther W. Spoehr, "Sambo and the Heathen Chinee: Californians' Racial Stereotypes in the Late 1870s," *Pacific Historical Review* 42, no. 2 (May 1973): 185–204; quoting Stuart Creighton Miller's *The Unwelcome Immigrant: The American Image of the Chinese, 1785–1882* (Berkeley: University of California Press), 1969, 11.

35. The quote is from Spoehr, "Sambo and the Heathen Chinee," 1973, 191, 192. To be fair, Spoehr might be annoyed with my use of his work here. This is because, unlike me, Spoehr distinguishes between two types of racism: *racial naturalism* (racism based on a group's biological inferiority) and *racial nationalism* (racism based on a belief in cultural inferiority), and argues that the anti-Chinese racist words I'm citing here constitute a case of racial nationalism, while antiblack racism is a different case, i.e., racial naturalism. Spoehr also argues that there was a far broader consensus denigrating the black man, and that anti-Chinese sentiment was less widely held and more varied. As Spoehr (193–194) shows, there were some who disagreed with the Senate Committee's final report, and even some who argued that the Chinese were far inferior to whites but still superior to blacks. But Spoehr notes in his conclusion that the ideas of Chinese cultural inferiority approached the consensus on the inferiority of blacks both in culture and biology. And seeing no evidence that the hearings and the report itself were overtaken by a minority opinion or concluded outside of the consensus-garnering process, then I suggest that this account of the sentiment of the day should withstand a simple scruitiny—i.e., I ask that the words be read for the racist thoughts they offer, although I offer that we scruitinize them here in a way that Spoehr would question, i.e., undifferentiated with regard to how they fit racism's possible types.

36. Ibid., 202, citing the Committee Report, 1051.

37. Ibid., 197, citing the Committee Report, 289.

38. Boswell, "A Split Labor Market Analysis."

39. George Kraus, "Chinese Laborers and the Construction of the Central Pacific," *Utah Historical Quarterly* 37, no. 1 (Winter 1969): 41–57.

40. Boswell, "A Split Labor Market Analysis," 362.

41. Claire Jean Kim, "The Racial Triangulation of Asian Americans," *Politics & Society* 27, no. 1 (March 1999): 105–138. The quote is from 111.

42. Ronald Takaki, *Strangers from a Different Shore: A History of Asian Americans* (Boston: Little, Brown, 1989), 217.

43. Ibid., 219.

44. Lopez, *White by Law*, 51–52.

45. Luther Spoehr, "Sambo and the Heathen Chinee," argues that this demographic fact means that we may usefully take Californian's sentiment about the Chinese in the 1870s as representative of the nation as a whole. Claire Jean Kim ("The Racial Triangulation of Asian Americans," 111) says, too, that "the mass media explosion and emergence of the penny press that the official race talk during this period filtered both outward across regional lines and downward to the level of colloquial discussion" so that thought racializing the Chinese was "increasingly a national phenomenon" with some regional variation.

46. Boswell, "A Split Labor Market Analysis," 365.

47. Ibid.

48. Charles Reagan Wilson, "Mississippi History Now: An online publication of the Mississippi Historical Society," found at *http://mshistorynow.mdah.state.ms.us/articles/86/mississippi-chinese-an-ethnic-people-in-a-biracial-society*, accessed December 1, 2012.

49. James W. Loewen, *The Mississippi Chinese*, 2nd ed. (Prospect Heights, IL: Waveland Press, 1988 [1971]), viii.

50. Kim, "The Racial Triangulation of Asian Americans," 11, quoting a journalist whose words are given in Eric Foner, *Reconstruction: America's Unfinished Revolution, 1863–1877* (New York: Harper & Row, 1999), 419.

51. Ibid., 30–31.

52. Ibid., 61, emphasis his.

53. Susan Dente Ross and Paul Martin Lester, *Images That Injure: Pictoral Stereotypes in the Media*, 3rd ed. (Santa Barbara, CA: Praeger, 2011), 144n7.

54. Loewen, *The Mississippi Chinese*, says that blacks and Chinese in the Delta were seen as equated—and perhaps the evidence in their intermarriage gives his argument increased validity (see especially 225n8). It may be useful to note here that scholars debate whether whites believed the Chinese to be as racially inferior as blacks or whether they believed the Chinese to be a group intermediate between white and black. Most of the debate about this seems to be focused on the Chinese in California—except for Kim, "The Racial Triangulation of Asian Americans," who follows the Chinese from California to the South and describes a complex "triangulation" where blacks are below the Chinese but at least are not foreigners. I neither comment on nor do I intend to contribute to this ranking debate. My purpose here is not to determine with any certainty the exact nature of ethnic group ranks at given points in history, but only to study cycles of racialization and group agency in response to said racialization.

55. Ibid., 65, emphasis his.

56. See "Mississippi Delta Chinese—Schooling," found at *http://mississippideltachinese.webs.com/schooling.htm*, accessed March 10, 2013.

57. I note here that I found sources where the Chinese in the Delta are written about as if Chinese racialization had never occurred. Take these words of Robert O'Brien as an example: "Wherever the Chinese have gone, especially in the southern Pacific, they have tended to go into business and become leaders in the mercantile world" (Robert W. O'Brien, "Status of Chinese in the Mississippi Delta," *Social Forces* 19, no. 3 (March 1941): 386–390; 387). O'Brien further notes that although Mississippi law confined the Chinese to the "colored race," the Chinese refused that position assigned them, and that there were not Chinese sharecroppers. It is worth noting that this sociologist's scholarship also has no mention of

Negro-Chinese intermarriage or shared occupations. Later works that interrogate racialization have given new life to the history of black-Chinese relations in the South.

58. Loewen, *The Mississippi Chinese*, 75.

59. Ibid., 135.

60. Ibid., p. 137.

61. Ibid.

62. Ibid., 71.

63. Ibid.

64. Robert Seto Quan, *Lotus Among the Magnolias: The Mississippi Chinese*, in collaboration with Julian B. Roebuck, foreword by Stanford M. Lyman (Jackson: University Press of Mississippi, 1982).

65. The term "model minority" was first applied to the Japanese in the *New York Times* article "Success Story, Japanese-American Style," published in 1966, and was applied to the Chinese in subsequent articles in other print media; see Kim, "The Racial Triangulation of Asian Americans," 119.

66. Wesley Yang, "Paper Tigers: What Happens to All the Asian-American Overachievers When the Test-Taking Ends?" *New York Magazine*, May 16, 2011, 22.

67. Ibid., 28.

68. Ibid., 29.

69. Eugenia Kaw, "'Opening' Faces: The Politics of Cosmetic Surgery and Asian American Women," in *In Our Own Words: Readings on the Psychology of Women and Gender*, ed. Mary Crawford and Rhoda Unger (New York: McGraw-Hill, 1997).

70. Ibid., 66.

71. Ibid., 55–73.

72. Ibid., 95.

73. Jerre Mangione and Ben Morreale, *La Storia: Five Centureis of the Italian American Experience* (New York: Harper Collins, 1992).

74. David A. J. Richards, *Italian American: The Racializing of an Ethnic Identity* (New York: New York University Press, 1992).

75. Thomas A. Guglielmo, "'No Color Barrier': Italians, Race, and Power in the United States," chap. 2 in *Are Italians White? How Race is Made in America*, ed. Jennifer Guglielmo and Salvatore Salerno (New York: Routledge, 2003), 29–43.

76. Steinberg, *The Ethnic Myth*, 41.

77. Mangione and Morreale, *La Storia*, 27.

78. Mangione and Morreale, *La Storia*.

78. Thomas A. Gugielmo, *White on Arrival: Italians, Race, Color, and Power in Chicago, 1890–1945* (New York: Oxford University Press, 2003).

80. Richard Brookhiser, "Others, and the WASP World They Aspired To," chap. 60 in *Critical White Studies: Looking Behind the Mirror*, ed. Richard Delgado and Jean Stefancic (Philadelphia: Temple University Press, 1997), 360–367. See also Mangione and Morreale, *La Storia*.

81. Ibid.; T. Guglielmo, "No Color Barrier," 33; T. Guglielmo, *White on Arrival*.

82. T. Guglielmo, "No Color Barrier," 40; see also Gould, "Geometer of Race."

83. Mangione and Morreale, *La Storia*.

84. Guglielmo, "No Color Barrier."

85. T. Guglielmo, *White on Arrival*.

86. Vincenza Scarpaci, "Walking the Color Line: Italian Immigrants in Rural Louisiana, 1880–1910," chap. 4 in J. Guglielmo and S. Salerno, *Are Italians White?*

87. Ibid., 63.

88. Ibid., 71.

89. Mangione and Morreale, *La Storia*, 186.

90. Louise DeSalvo, "Color: White/Complexion: Dark," chap. 1 in J. Guglielmo and S. Salerno, *Are Italians White?*; Scarpaci, "Walking the Color Line"; Richards, *Italian American*.

91. Richards, *Italian American*.

92. Matthew Frye Jacobson, *Whiteness of a Different Color: European Immigrants and the Alchemy of Race* (Cambridge, MA: Harvard Unversity Press, 1998), 56.

93. DeSalvo, "Color: White/Complexion: Dark," 22.

94. Jacobson, *Whiteness of a Different Color*, 57; emphasis his.

95. T. Guglielmo, *White on Arrival.*

96. James R. Barrett and David Roediger, "Inbetween Peoples: Race, Nationality and the 'New Immigrant' Working Class," *Journal of American Ethnic History* 16, no. 3 (Spring 1997): 3–44; the quotation is from 32.

97. Jacobson, *Whiteness of a Different Color*, 57.

98. David Roediger, "Du Bois, Race, and Italian Americans," Afterword in Guglielmo and Salerno, *Are Italians White?*, 259–263. See also Guglielmo, "No Color Barrier." The phrase "white on arrival" comes from the title of T. Guglielmo, *White on Arrival.*

99. Scarpaci, "Walking the Color Line."

100. Ibid., 75.

101. Roediger, *Working toward Whiteness*, 111–112.

102. This quotation comes from Roediger, "DuBois, Race, and Italian Americans," 261; it is quoted again in Roediger, *Wages of Whiteness*, 112. The original article is W. E. B. Du Bois, "The Inter-racial Implications of the Ethiopian Crisis: A Negro View," *Foreign Affairs* (October 1935): 82–92.

103. See Stefano Luconi, 2003, "Frank L. Rizzo and the Whitening of Italian Americans in Philadelphia," chap. 11 in Guglielmo and Salerno, *Are Italians White?*, 177–191. "Animosities between African Americans and Italian Americans broke out in Philadelphia as early as the mid-1930s, following the impact of the domestic repercussions of the Italian-Ethiopian War. While most Italians rushed to support the successful Fascist invasion and subsequent annexation of this country, black Philadelphians mobilized to prevent Italy's military and diplomatic victory in eastern Africa" (179). However, Luconi advises a read of the Philadelphia Italians' actions as a strengthening of ethic consciousness, and not an acceptance of a white self-image, which he argues was not conscious among Italians as a whole until the 1960s.

104. Roediger, *Wages of Whiteness*, 112.

105. Ibid., 112; see also 281n43.

106. Salvatore Salerno, "*I Delitti della Razza Bianca (Crimes of the White Race): Italian Anarchists' Racial Discourse as Crime*," chap. 7 in Guglielmo and Salerno, *Are Italians White?*, 111–123; 123.

107. David A. J. Richards, *Italian American: The Racializing of an Ethnic Identity* (New York: New York University Press, 1999).

108. Ibid., 119.

109. Michael Miller Topp, "'Is It Providential That There Are Foreigners Here': Whiteness and Masculinity in the Making of Italian American Syndicalist Identity," chap. 6 in Guglielmo and Salerno, *Are Italians White?*, 98–110, 100; Richards, *Italian American,* also suggests similar thinking.

110. Richard Alba, *Italian Americans: Into the Twilight of Ethnicity*, Prentice-Hall Ethnic Groups in American Life Series (New York: Prentice Hall College Division, 1985).

111. See Richards, *Italian American*—his work is an exception.

112. I critiqued how sociological scholarship studies race and ethnicity in Bashi, "Racial Categories Matter."

113. Lawrence DiStasi, ed., *Una Storia Segreta: The Secret History of Italian American Evacuation and Internment during World War II* (Berkeley, CA: Heyday, 2001), 312.

114. Ibid., xvii.

115. T. Guglielmo, "No Color Barrier," 2003b.

116. Mary J. Hickman, "Reconstructing Deconstruction 'Race': British Political Discourses about the Irish in Britain," *Ethnic and Racial Studies* 21, no. 2 (March 1998): 288–307.

117. Even people among the top 5% of all earners in the United States believe themselves to be middle class (Catherine Rampell, "Everyone Is 'Middle Class,' Right?", *New York Times*, April 27, 2001, *http://economix.blogs.nytimes.com/2011/04/27/everyone-is-middle-class-right/* on June 16, 2011). Perhaps this is because many people in the statistical middle-class cannot afford a middle-class lifestyle, while those making over $100,000 in income per year are living beyond their financial means. (See "What is Middle Class?", *The Washington Times*, November 9, 2003, accessed *http://www.washingtontimes.com/news/2003/nov/29/20031129-105855-7412r/?page=all#pagebreak*, accessed June 16, 2011). Since privilege is relative, those at the top may not feel so fortunate if they are comparing themselves to their advantaged neighbors while remaining unaware of the full distribution of power and privilege among the haves and have-nots.

118. Jennifer Guglielmo, "Introduction: White Lies, Dark Truths," chap. 6 in Guglielmo and Salerno, *Are Italians White?*, 1–16; 4.

119. Ibid., 2003.

120. Library of Congress, July 27, 2010, "From Haven to Home" exhibition, "A Century of Immigration, 1820–1924," *http://www.loc.gov/exhibits/haventohome/haven-century.html*, accessed October 8, 2012.

121. Brodkin, *How Jews Became White Folks*, 27–29.

122. Jacobson, *Whiteness of a Different Color*, 62.

123. Ibid., 63.

124. Ibid., 65. Jacobson writes: "No one has examined the racial element of the Frank case as closely as Jeffrey Melnick in his recent study of Black-Jewish relations early in the century, and there is no improving upon his analysis." See Jeffrey Melnick, "Ancestors and Relatives: The Uncanny Relationship of African-Americans and Jews," Ph.D. diss., Harvard University, 1994; now a book, *Black-Jewish Relations on Trial: Leo Frank and Jim Conley in the New South* (Jackson: University Press of Mississippi, 2000).

125. Brodkin, *How the Jews Became White Folks*, 10.

126. Library of Congress, 2010.

127. Ibid., 115.

128. Ibid., 125.

129. Ibid., 118.

130. Victoria Hattam, *In the Shadow of Race: Jews, Latinos, and Immigrant Politics in the United States* (Chicago: University of Chicago Press, 2007), 38.

131. Ibid.

132. "Irving Berlin," Encyclopedia of Composers and Songwriters, WLIW21 and Public Broadcasting System, *http://www.pbs.org/wnet/gperf/shows/songbook/multimedia/bio_berlin.html*, accessed October 8, 2012; see also the "Irving Berlin" entry of the New World Encyclopedia at *http://www.newworldencyclopedia.org/entry/Irving_Berlin*, accessed October 8, 2012.

133. Ibid., 46–47.

134. Ibid., 48.

135. Brodkin, *How the Jews Became White Folks*, 30–31.

136. Ibid., 141.

137. Ibid.

138. Ibid., 143.

139. Ibid., 152.

140. Ibid., 153.

141. Ibid., 145.

142. Ibid., 148.

143. Ibid., 148–149; an alternative but related interpretation is offered by Thandeka, *Learning to Be White*, 28–37.

144. Brodkin, *How the Jews Became White Folks*, 158. This is Brodkin's summary of Hasia Diner, *In the Almost Promised Land: American Jews and Blacks, 1915–1935* (Westport, CT: Greenwood Press, 1977).

145. Brodkin, *How the Jews Became White Folks*, 156–157.

146. Ibid.

147. Ira J. Katznelson, *When Affirmative Action Was White: An Untold History of Racial Inequality in Twentieth-Century America* (New York: W. W. Norton, 2005); Brodkin, *How the Jews Became White Folks*, 1998; Lipsitz, *Possessive Investment in Whiteness*.

148. Hattam, *In the Shadow of Race*, 68.

149. Ibid., 6.

150. Barrett and Roediger, "Inbetween Peoples," 3.

151. Richards, *Italian American*, 2–3.

CHAPTER FIVE

1. Jack D. Forbes, *Africans and Native Americans: The Language of Race and the Evolution of Red-Black Peoples* (Urbana and Chicago: University of Illinois Press, 1993), 270–271.

2. Gregory Rodríguez defines *mestizaje* as "racial and cultural synthesis." Today it is used to reference mixtures of African, Indian, and European, but the term originated in Spanish and Portuguese and referenced mixtures of indigenous and European peoples. Rodríguez quotes Alan Riding, author of *Distant Neighbors: A Portrait of the Mexicans* (New York: Vintage, 2000) as stating, "Mexico alone is truly mestizo: it is the only nation in the hemisphere where religious and political—as well as racial—mestizaje took place." See Rodríguez, *Mongrels, Bastards, Orphans, and Vagabonds: Mexican Immigration and the Future of Race in America* (New York: Pantheon, 2007), ix–xii.

3. Howard Zinn, *A People's History of the United States* (New York: HarperCollins, [1980] 2010), 11.

4. Ibid., 16.

5. Ibid., 74.

6. Alvin M. Josephy Jr., *500 Nations: An Illustrated History of North American Indians* (New York: Alfred A. Knopf, 1994), 317.

7. Ibid.

8. Herman J. Viola, *After Columbus: The Smithsonian Chronicle of the North American Indian* (Washington, DC: Smithsonian Books, 1990), 144.

9. Josephy, *500 Nations*.

10. Gloria Jahoda, *The Trail of Tears: The Story of the American Indian Removals 1813–1855* (New York: Wings, [1975] 1995), 3.

11. Ibid., 18.

12. Josephy, *500 Nations*, 322–323.

13. Jahoda, *Trail of Tears*, 39.

14. Viola, *After Columbus*, 1990; and Jahoda, *Trail of Tears*, x.

15. Jahoda, *Trail of Tears*, 1975.

16. Josephy, *500 Nations*, 1994.

17. Ibid., 327.

18. Jahoda, *Trail of Tears*.

19. Josephy, *500 Nations*.

20. Ibid., 328.

21. Katja May, *African Americans and Native Americans in the Creek and Cherokee Nations, 1830s to 1920s: Collision and Collusion* (New York: Garland, 1996), 45.

22. Josephy, *500 Nations*, 325.

23. Fay A. Yarbrough, *Race and the Cherokee Nation: Sovereignty in the Nineteenth Century* (Philadelphia: University of Pennsylvania Press, 2008), 73.

24. May, *"African Americans and Native Americans,"* 43.

25. Brian Klopotek, *Recognition Odysseys: Indigeneity, Race, and Federal Tribal Recognition Policy in Three Louisiana Indian Communities* (Durham, NC: Duke University Press, 2011).

26. Ibid., 214.

27. Elise Lemire, *"Miscegenation": Making Race in America* (Philadelphia: University of Pennsylvania Press, 2002), 47.

28. Ibid.

29. Thomas Head, "Interracial Marriage Laws, A Short Timeline History," on the site "News & Issues: Civil Liberties," About.com, *http://civilliberty.about.com/od/raceequal opportunity/tp/Interracial-Marriage-Laws-History-Timeline.htm*, accessed October 8, 2012; see also Thomas Head, "Poll: Only 40% of Mississippi Republicans Think Interracial Marriage Should Be Legal," on the site "News & Issues: Civil Liberties," About.com, *http://civilliberty .about.com/b/2011/04/07/poll-only-40-of-mississippi-republicans-think-interracial-marriage-should -be-legal.htm*, accessed October 8, 2012. The second article notes also that State Governor Haley Barbour seeks to commemorate a founding KKK leader with a state license plate. Tom Head is author of 24 books, including the recently published *Civil Liberties: A Beginner's Guide* (Oneworld, 2009), an officer in several Mississippi civil liberties organizations, and he maintains the *Mississippi Human Rights Report,* a blog dedicated to human rights and civil liberties issues in his home state.

30. Klopotek, *Recognition Odysseys*, 217, 218.

31. Ibid.

32. "Scholars and tribal members have challenged both the criteria themselves and OFA's [Office of Federal Acknowledgement] administration of them, identifying a series of significant problems: the criteria have been applied inconsistently, so that what qualified as proof of tribal existence in one case often does not in the next; the level of proof required to meet individual criteria keeps going up, and OFA does not inform tribes of this until after the fact; certain staff members have been characterized as incompetent and unqualified; there is evidence of pre-decisional bias; OFA serves as prosecutor, defense, and judge; the criteria for recognition are much more stringent than the precedents on which they claim to be based; the staff is too secretive about its sources and findings; OFA expects unrecognized tribes to have the same form as recognized tribes; the regulations rely too heavily on non-Indian observations about petitioners, observations that are bound to rigid conceptions of 'authenticity'; OFA will not accept oral history as evidence; the process favors petitioners without African ancestry; and petitions are reviewed at such a sluggish pace that decades pass before determinations are made on active petitions" (ibid., 4).

33. Ibid.

34. Viola, *After Columbus*, 274–275.

35. Evelyn Nieves, "Putting to a Vote the Question 'Who Is Cherokee?'" *New York Times*, March 3, 2007, *http://www.nytimes.com/2007/03/03/us/03cherokee.html?em&ex=117307 0800&en=59cfee51293c4781&ei=5087%0A*, accessed December 29, 2011.

36. Ibid.

37. Ibid.

38. May, *African Americans and Native Americans*, 79.

39. See the BBC article "Cherokees Eject Slave Descendants," Sunday, March 4, 2007, at *http://news.bbc.co.uk/2/hi/americas/6416735.stm*; and NowPublic's "Cherokee Nation Ejects African Members" (*http://www.nowpublic.com/cherokee_nation_ejects_african_members_0*) (both accessed December 29, 2011) for more information about the 2007 vote.

40. "Cherokee Nation Expels Descendants of Tribe's Black Slaves," HuffingtonPost.com, August 25, 2011, *http://www.huffingtonpost.com/2011/08/25/cherokee-nations-expels-d_n_936930 .html*, accessed September 23, 2012.

41. Steve Olafson, September 24, 2011, "Cherokees Vote for Chief as Freedmen Issue Settled," Reuters.com, at *http://www.reuters.com/article/2011/09/25/us-cherokee-vote-idUS-TRE78O03N20110925*, accessed September 23, 2012. The U.S. Department of Housing and Urban Development withheld a $33 million disbursement and the Bureau of Indian Affairs said it would not recognize results of an upcoming election for tribal principal chief because of the membership issue.

42. Steve Olafson, October 1, 2011, "Black Cherokee Lose Lawsuit but Tribal Citizen Issue Unsettled," Reuters.com, *http://www.reuters.com/article/2011/10/02/us-freedmen-oklahoma -idUSTRE79102D20111002*, accessed September 23, 2012.

43. Steve Olafson, October 19, 2011, "Cherokee Tribe Gets New Chief After Contentious Election," Reuters.com, *http://www.reuters.com/article/2011/10/20/us-cherokee-chief-election -idUSTRE79J09P20111020*, accessed September 23, 2012.

44. James Dao, "In California, Indian Tribes with Casino Money Cast Off Members," *New York Times*, December 12, 2011, at *http://www.nytimes.com/2011/12/13/us/california-indian -tribes-eject-thousands-of-members.html?_r=2&hp=&adxnnl=1&adxnnlx=1325189296-pOonw P9nFukxrXrppzsMoQ*, accessed December 29, 2011.

45. Marc Cooper, "Tribal Flush: Pechanga People 'Disenrolled' en Masse," *LA Weekly News*, LAWeekly.com, January 2, 2008, *http://www.laweekly.com/2008-01-03/news/tribal-flush -pechanga-people-disenrolled-en-masse/*, accessed September 24, 2012; and David E. Wilkins, "Depopulation in Indian Country, 21st Century Style," March 19, 2012, *Indian Country: Today Media Network.com, http://indiancountrytodaymedianetwork.com/ict_sbc/depopulation -in-indian-country-21st-century-style*, accessed September 24, 2012.

46. Wilkins, "Depopulation in Indian Country."

47. Cooper, "Tribal Flush."

48. Ibid.

49. Ibid., 4. Cooper writes, "In a richly detailed report, received by the Pechanga Enrollment Committee in late 2004, Johnson concludes that the 'preponderance of evidence gathered from the surviving documents leads to the conclusion that Paulina Hunter was a tribal member of Temecula and Pechanga.' When asked later by a reporter to be more specific, Johnson said there was a '90 percent' chance that Hunter was a Pechanga. In the KNBC story, he was even more emphatic: 'She's definitely Pechanga Indian, 100 percent.' The tribe, however, flatly ignored its own commissioned expert report and proceeded with the expulsion.

'They ignored whatever I did in their decision making,' Johnson told *L.A. Weekly* after the disenrollment was formalized. 'It's too bad economics and politics have been injected' into the tribal rulings.

While Johnson's probe was pushed aside, the tribe wound up basing its ruling on the written allegation of a somewhat less expert source, former tribal chairman Vincent Belasco Ibanez, who at the time was completing an eight-year prison term for sexual molestation of a minor. And while Johnson had earned a doctorate in anthropology at UC Santa Barbara and had established a 30-year history as an expert in probing Indian culture and archival records, former chairman Ibanez was known primarily for guiding nature walks focused on native plants."

50. Wilkins, "Exiling One's Kin," 2004.

51. Dao, "In California, Indian Tribes with Casino Money Cast Off Members"; Cooper, "Tribal Flush."

52. Wilkins, "Exiling One's Kin," 256.

53. Dao, "In California, Indian Tribes with Casino Money Cast Off Members."

54. Klopotek, *Recognition Odysseys*, 2011.

55. Ibid., 15.

56. Ibid., 8.

57. Francis Haines, *The Nez Percé: Tribesmen of the Columbia Plateau* (Norman: University of Oklahoma Press, 1955).

58. Ibid.; Jacqueline Fear-Segal, *White Man's Club: Schools, Race, and the Struggle of Indian Acculturation* (Lincoln: University of Nebraska Press, 2007).

59. See "Chief Joseph" from "New Perspectives on the West," Public Broadcasting System (PBS), *http://www.pbs.org/weta/thewest/people/a_c/chiefjoseph.htm* accessed on May 20, 2009.

60. Haines, *The Nez Percé*, 1995.

61. See "Archives of The West: 1874–1877; Chief Joseph Speaks, Selected Statements and Speeches by the Nez Percé Chief," from "New Perspectives on The West," online at the website for the Public Broadcasting Service, *http://www.pbs.org/weta/thewest/resources/archives/six/jospeak.htm*, accessed January 3, 2012.

62. Thomas H. Guthrie, "Good Words: Chief Joseph and the Production of Indian Speech(es), Texts, and Subjects," *Ethnohistory* 54, no. 3 (Summer 2007): 509–546.

63. Merrill D. Beal, *"I Will Fight No More Forever": Chief Joseph and the Nez Perce War* (Seattle: University of Washington Press, 1963); Elliott West, *The Last Indian War: The Nez Perce Story* (New York: Oxford University Press, 2009).

64. L. V. McWhorter was adopted by the Yakama Indian nation and is described by the Washington State University archives as a fighter for Indian rights. He documented and then published the autobiography of Yellow Wolf, a veteran of the Nez Percé war of 1877, in the 1940 book *Yellow Wolf: His Own Story*, and himself wrote *Hear Me My Chiefs: Nez Perce Legend and History*, posthumously published by McWhorter's son. See "The L.V. McWhorter Native American Artifact Collection" online at *content.wsulibs.wsu.edu/cdm-lv_mcwhorte/*, accessed on December 19, 2011.

65. Beal, "I Will Fight No More Forever," 248.

66. Guthrie, "Good Words," 531.

67. Ibid., 537.

68. Beal, "I Will Fight No More Forever," v.

69. Excerpted from the speech given at his meeting with President Rutherford Hayes, Washington, DC, 1879.

70. Jahoda, *500 Nations*.

71. Rodríguez, *Mongrels, Bastards, Orphans, and Vagabonds*, 9.

72. López, *Racism on Trial*.

73. Rodríguez, *Mongrels, Bastards, Orphans, and Vagabonds*,27–28.

74. Ibid., 28.

75. Ibid.

76. Ibid., 29–30.

77. Ibid., 24, 29.

78. Ibid.

79. Ibid., 48.

80. *Criollos* are colonial locals of Spanish descent. As such they are higher in caste than others, but not as highly ranked as the Spanish-born colonizers themselves.

81. Gerald Horne, *Black and Brown: African Americans and the Mexican Revolution, 1910–1920*, American History and Culture Series, ed. Neil Foley, Kevin Gaines, Martha Hodes, and Scott Sandage (New York: New York University Press, 2005).

82. Ibid., 14.

83. This paragraph is based on Rodríguez, *Mongrels, Bastards, Orphans, and Vagabonds*.

84. Horne, *Black and Brown*.

85. Rodríguez, *Mongrels, Bastards, Orphans, and Vagabonds*, 108.

86. Ibid.

87. Ibid., 169.

88. López, *White by Law*, 61.

89. Rodríguez, *Mongrels, Bastards, Orphans, and Vagabonds*, 169; for this language he cites Fernando V. Padilla, "Early Chicano Legal Recognition: 1846–1897," *Journal of Popular Culture* 13, no. 3 (Spring 1980): 571.

90. Neil Foley, *The White Scourge: Mexicans, Blacks, and Poor Whites in Texas Cotton Culture* (Berkeley: University of California Press); Horne, *Black and Brown*.

91. Ibid., 5.

92. Ibid., 2.

93. Rodríguez, *Mongrels, Bastards, Orphans, and Vagabonds*, 106. The Mexican-American War began in 1846 and ended in 1898.

94. Horne, *Black and Brown*, 182.

95. Carlos Kevin Blanton, "They Cannot Master Abstractions but They Can Often Be Made Efficient Workers: Race and Class in the Intelligence Testing of Mexican Americans and African Americans in Texas during the 1920s," *Social Science Quarterly* 81, no. 4 (December 2000): 1014–1026; 1023.

96. Ibid., 1014.

97. Blanton, "They Cannot Master Abstractions," 1023.

98. Jason McDonald, "From Bipartite to Tripartite Society: Demographic Change and Realignments in Ethnic Stratification in Austin, Texas, 1910–30," *Patterns of Prejudice* 29, no. 1 (2005): 1–24.

99. Foley, *The White Scourge*.

100. Rodríguez, *Mongrels, Bastards, Orphans, and Vagabonds*, 166.

101. *Instructions to Enumerators, Population and Agriculture*, Form 15-100 (Washington, DC: U.S. Department of Commerce, Bureau of the Census, 1930), 26. The instructions may be found at *http://www.census.gov/history/pdf/1930instructions.pdf*, accessed December 3, 2012.

102. Rodríguez, *Mongrels, Bastards, Orphans, and Vagabonds*, 174.

103. Ibid., 173, 174.

104. *Abridged Instructions to Enumerators: Population*, Form P-103 (Washington, DC: U.S. Department of Commerce, Bureau of the Census, 1940), 7, emphasis theirs. The instructions may be found at *http://www.census.gov/history/pdf/1940instructions.pdf*, accessed December 3, 2012.

105. McDonald, "From Bipartite to Tripartite Society."

106. Foley, *The White Scourge*, 208, 211.

107. Neil Foley, "Becoming Hispanic: Mexican Americans and Whiteness," chap. 4 in *White Privilege: Essential Readings on the Other Side of Racism*, ed. Paula S. Rothenberg (New York: Worth, 2005).

108. López, *Racism on Trial*.

109. Ibid.

110. Ibid.

111. Ibid., 11.

112. Ibid., 206.

113. Ibid.

114. Frank D. Bean and Marta Tienda, *The Hispanic Population of the United States*, Population of the United States in the 1980s: A Census Monograph Series (New York: Russell Sage, 1988), 51–52. The relevant citation reads that Bean and Tienda chose the Spanish origin question to define Hispanics in 1980, except to exclude "persons of Mexican origin who also reported their race as black and who reside outside of the five southwestern states. Evidence indicated the vast bulk of these were poorly educated blacks who mistakenly identified themselves in the Mexican origin category."

115. Neil Foley, "Becoming Hispanic: Mexican Americans and Whiteness," in *White Privilege: Essential Readings on the Other Side of Racism*, ed. Paula S. Rothenberg, 2nd ed. (New York: Worth, 2005), 55–65.

116. Forbes, *African Americans and Native Americans*, 55–56.

117. Sowell, "Three Black Histories."

118. Vilna Bashi, *Survival of the Knitted: Immigrant Social Networks in a Stratified World* (Stanford, CA: Stanford University Press, 2007).

119. Ibid.

120. Mary C. Waters, *Black Identities: West Indian Immigrant Dreams and American Realities* (Cambridge, MA: Harvard University Press, 1999).

121. Ibid., 65.

122. Ibid.

123. Ibid.

124. Bashi, *Survival of the Knitted*, 178.

125. Ibid.; Charles Tilly, *Durable Inequality* (Berkeley: University of California Press, 1999).

126. Deirdre Royster, *Race and the Invisible Hand: How White Networks Exclude Black Men from Blue-Collar Jobs*, George Gund Foundation Book in African American Studies (Berkeley: University of California Press, 2003).

127. Rodríguez, *Mongrels, Bastards, Orphans, and Vagabonds*.

CHAPTER SIX

1. The source of the first epigraph is quoted in Theodore W. Allen, *The Invention of the White Race* (London: Verso, 1997), 9. He notes that this is the concluding stanza of "We Have Fed You All for a Thousand Years," by "An Unknown Proletarian," in *IWW Songs*,

Songs of the Workers, 27th ed., 1939, Chicago, IL, 64. The second epigraph is from Malcolm X, *End of White World Supremacy: Four Speeches* (New York: Arcade, 2011), n.p.

2. Charles Johnson, Patricia Smith, and the WGBH Series Research Team, *Africans in America: America's Journey through Slavery* (New York: Harcourt, 1998), 36; and Painter, *Creating African Americans*, 23.

3. Painter, *Creating African Americans*, 23.

4. Ibid.

5. Davis, *Who Is Black?*, 33.

6. Ibid.

7. Davis *Who Is Black?*; Painter, *Creating African Americans*.

8. Davis, *Who Is Black?*

9. Vilna Bashi, "Globalized Anti-Blackness: Transnationalizing Western Immigration Law, Policy, and Practice," *Ethnic and Racial Studies* 27, no. 4 (July 2004): 584–606.

10. Enumerator instructions may be found at *http://usa.ipums.org/usa/voliii/inst1930.shtml*, the site of the Minnesota Population Center at the University of Minnesota, accessed on January 8, 2012.

11. See *http://www.census.gov/history/pdf/1930instructions.pdf*.

12. Ira Berlin, *The Making of African America: The Four Great Migrations* (New York: Penguin Books, 2010).

13. Jack D. Forbes, *Africans and Native Americans: The Language of Race and the Evolution of Red-Black Peoples*, 2nd ed. (Urbana and Chicago: University of Illinois Press, 1993); Davis, *Who Is Black?*

14. Davis, *Who Is Black?*, 21.

15. Edward Stein, "Past and Present Proposed Amendments to the United States Constitution Regarding Marriage," *Washington University Law Quarterly* 82, no. 3 (Fall 2004): 611–685.

16. Ibid.

17. Ibid.

18. Forbes, *Africans and Native Americans*, 267.

19. Ibid., 270, emphasis his.

20. Tom W. Smith, "Changing Racial Labels: From 'Colored' to 'Negro' to 'Black' to 'African American,'" *Public Opinion Quarterly* 56, no. 4 (Winter 1992): 496–514; quote from 511.

21. Berlin, *The Making of African America*.

22. John S. Butler, "Multiple Identities," *Society* 27 (May/June 1990): 8–13.

23. AMEC—African Methodist Episcopal Church, "About Us—Our History," *http://www.ame-church.com/about-us/history.php*, accessed October 6, 2012.

24. Butler, "Multiple Identities."

25. Davis, *Who Is Black?*, 59.

26. Ibid., 60.

27. Smith, "Changing Racial Labels," 497.

28. Anthony Neal, "The Naming: A Conceptualization of an African American Connotative Struggle," *Journal of Black Studies* 32, no. 1 (September 2001): 50–65; Ben L. Martin, "From Negro to Black to African American: The Power of Names and Naming," *Political Science Quarterly* 106, no. 1 (Spring 1991): 83–107.

29. C. Eric Lincoln, *Black Muslims in America* (Boston: Beacon Press, 1961), 68.

30. Martin, "From Negro to Black to African American."

31. Ibid.

32. Waters, *Black Identities*, 9.

33. Ariana Hernandez-Reguant, "Kwanzaa and the US Ethnic Mosaic," in *Representa-*

tions of Blackness and the Performance of Identities, ed. Jean Muteba Rahier (Westport, CT: Greenwood, 1999), 101–122; see 103. Hernandez-Reguant cites Stephan Thernstrom, Ann Orlov, and Oscar Handlin, eds., *The Harvard Encyclopedia of American Ethnic Groups* (Cambridge, MA: Belknap Press of Harvard University Press, 1980).

34. Ibid., 103, citing Thernstrom et al.

35. Liz Mazucci, "Going Back to Our Own: Interpreting Malcolm X's Transition from 'Black Asiatic' to 'Afro-American,'" *Souls* (Winter 2005): 66–83.

36. Martin, "From Negro to Black to African American," 92.

37. Ibid.

38. See Smith, "Changing Racial Labels."

39. Randall Kennedy, "Finding a Proper Name to Call Black Americans," *Journal of Blacks in Higher Education* 46 (Winter 2004–2005): 72–83; 76.

40. Neil Foley, "Black, White, and Brown," *Journal of Southern History* 70, no. 2 (May 2004): 343–350, quoting from James T. Patterson, *Brown v. Board of Education: A Civil Rights Milestone and Its Troubled Legacy* (New York: Oxford University Press, 2002), 210.

41. Note the (admittedly somewhat dated) findings of the Roper Organization about divergent preferences for labeling black Americans. Brad Edmonson, "What Do You Call a Dark Skinned Person?" *American Demographics* 15, no. 10 (October 1993): 9. Of racially black persons ages 18 to 39 in 1993, 38 percent preferred to call themselves "African American," yet only 16% of whites chose to use the term; 57 percent of whites use the term "black" where 42 percent overall but only 34 percent of young people cared for it. In similar fashion, 3 and 1 percent of blacks used "colored" and "Negro," but whites used the terms in proportions of 5 and 3 percent, respectively, for terms describing dark-skinned people. In the same article, Brad Edmonson (the author) said *American Demographic Magazine* uses "black" because they report government statistics, and "black" is the term used by the U.S. Census; a Census Bureau representative acknowledged inaccuracies in applying "African American" to everyone, but noted that some of the press releases use "African American" when the statistics reported may refer to people from the Caribbean or other ethnic groups; and *Emerge: Black America's Newsmagazine* editor-in-chief George Curry said the periodical uses "black," even though "African American is acceptable because it connects us to our African roots. But as a journalist, it's hard to put African American in a headline. It's just too long."

42. Martin, "From Negro to Black to African American."

43. Painter, *Creating African Americans,* 72.

44. Ibid.

45. "Blacks and the American Revolution," *http://www.coloradocollege.edu/Dept/HY/HY243Ruiz/Research/revolution.html,* accessed January 17, 2010.

46. Public Broadcasting System (PBS) site "Africans in America: The Revolutionary War," *http://www.pbs.org/wgbh/aia/part2/2narr4.html,* accessed January 17, 2010. From that site, note also this quote:

"Many thousands of African Americans who aided the British lost their freedom anyway. Many of them ended up in slavery in the Caribbean. Others, when they attempted to leave with the British, in places like Charleston and Savannah, were prevented. And there are incredible letters written by southerners of Africans after the siege of Charleston, swimming out to boats, and the British hacking away at their arms with cutlasses to keep them from following them. So it was a very tragic situation. And many of the thousands of Africans who left the plantations, not many of them actually got their freedom." (Margaret Washington, historian, on the evacuation of Charleston)

47. Public Broadcasting System, "Colonel Tye," in "Africans in America," *http://www.pbs.org/wgbh/aia/part2/2p52.html,* accessed September 30, 2012.

48. Public Broadcasting System, "Boston King," in "Africans in America," *http://www*
.pbs.org/wgbh/aia/part2/2p60.html, accessed February 5, 2010.

49. This quote from Margaret Washington, historian, on the evacuation of Charleston,
is excerpted from the Public Broadcasting System website "Africans in America," found at
http://www.pbs.org/wgbh/aia/part2/2narr4.html, and accessed February 5, 2010.

50. Painter, *Creating African Americans*; Steinberg, *Ethnic Myth*.

51. Horne, *Black and Brown*.

52. Painter, *Creating African Americans*.

53. Horne, *Black and Brown*.

54. Ibid., 93.

55. Ibid.

56. Ibid., 104.

57. Ibid.

58. Congress of the United States, Congressional Budget Office (CBO), *Social Representation in the U.S. Military*, CBO Publication #499, October 1989.

59. See Michael Moore's award-winning 2004 documentary film *Fahrenheit 9/11*.

60. Meredith Kleykamp, "College, Jobs or the Military? Enlistment during a Time of
War" (Princeton, NJ: Office of Population Research, Princeton University, 2005); available
online at *http://theop.princeton.edu/reports/forthcoming/SSQrevisionMilitary.pdf*, and accessed
January 8, 2012.

61. Dave Moniz, "Soldiers Re-enlist beyond U.S. Goal," *USA Today*, July 1, 2005, *http://
www.usatoday.com/news/nation/2005-07-17-soldiers-re-enlist_x.htm*, accessed January 8, 2012.

62. *The Virginian-Pilot*, "Military Numbers Are Rising," *Military.com's* Today
in the Military "Headlines" section, dated April 14, 2004, at *http://www.military.com/
NewsContent/0%2C13319%2CFL_numbers_041404%2C00.html?ESRC=airforce-a.nl*, accessed
January 8, 2012.

63. Bureau of Labor Statistics, "Unemployment Rates by Age, Sex, Race, and Hispanic
or Latino Ethnicity," Table E-16, *http://www.bls.gov/web/empsit/cpseed16.pdf*, accessed September 30, 2012.

64. Annalyn Censky, "Unemployment Falls . . . but Not for Blacks," *CNNMoney*, published online by CNN.com, *http://money.cnn.com/2012/01/06/news/economy/black_unemploy
ment_rate/index.htm*, accessed January 8, 2012.

65. Moniz, "Soldiers Re-enlist." (For comparison, note that Hispanics are underrepre-
sented among military recruits.) See Beth J. Asch, Christopher Buck, Jacob Alex Klerman,
Meredith Kleykamp, and David S. Loughran, *Military Enlistment of Hispanic Youth*, pre-
pared for the Office of the Secretary of Defense by the National Defense Research Institute
(Santa Monica, CA: Rand Corporation, 2009).

66. Steinberg, *Ethnic Myth*; William Cohen, *At Freedom's Edge: Black Mobility and the
Southern White Quest for Racial Control, 1861–1915* (Baton Rouge: Louisiana State University Press, 1991).

67. Michael Keith Honey, *Black Workers Remember: An Oral History of Segregation,
Unionism, and the Freedom Struggle* (Berkeley: University of California Press, 1999).

68. Ibid., 3.

69. Steinberg, *Ethnic Myth*.

70. Ibid., 3.

71. Berlin, *Making of African America*, 203–205; Gunnar Myrdal, with the assistance
of Richard Sterner and Arnold Rose, *An American Dilemma* (New York: Harper, 1944), 165.

72. Stephen Steinberg, "Immigration, African Americans, and Race Discourse," *New*

Politics 10, no. 3 (Summer 2005): 42–54.; Bashi, *Survival of the Knitted*; Roger Waldinger and Michael I. Lichter, *How the Other Half Works* (Berkeley: University of California Press, 2003).

73. Royster, *Race and the Invisible Hand*.

74. Steinberg, *Ethnic Myth*.

75. Steinberg, "Immigration, African Americans, and Race Discourse," cites (italics in original) Roger Waldinger and Michael I. Lichter, *How the Other Half Works: Immigration and the Social Organization of Labor* (Berkeley: University of California Press, 2003), 20.

76. Stephen Steinberg, "Occupational Apartheid," *The Nation*, December 9, 1991, 744–746; 744.

77. Stephen Steinberg, "The Role of Racism in the Inequality Studies of William Julius Wilson," *Journal of Blacks in Higher Education* 15 (Spring 1997): 109–117.

78. Honey, *Black Workers Remember*.

79. John Henrik Clarke, "Why Africana History?" *Black Collegian*, 1997 [1986], n.p.

80. Davis, *Who Is Black?*

81. Ibid., 59.

82. See Stuart Davis, "'Is This Negroish or Irish?' African American English, The Antebellum Writings of Francis Lieber, and the Origins Controversy," *American Speech* 78, no. 3 (Fall 2003): 285–306.

83. Ibid., 298; Davis writes in his conclusion: "But why do we not find other individuals like Lieber documenting observations on the speech of slaves? I believe that to a large extent this has to do with the prevailing racial (i.e., racist) ideologies that operated in the American South in the antebellum period. It is significant that not only do we not find academic references to slave speech, but we do not find any interest in antebellum America in the study of African languages, despite the fact that there were many native speakers of African languages in America during most of the antebellum period. This is contrasted with the academic interest in Native American languages during the same period, where one finds individuals like Henry Rowe Schoolcraft, 'the backwoods linguist,' who spoke several Native American languages and married a woman of Native American heritage. Consequently, prevailing racial ideologies made it difficult for anyone to make meaningful academic observations on the nature of slave speech, whether public or private. Nonetheless, had there been an academic interest in slave speech in antebellum America, Lieber's question, 'Is this negroish or Irish?' suggest that the origins controversy would have existed even then" (ibid.)

84. Jews made up 15 percent of the population in Vienna before World War II, and the Viennese dialect (an offshoot of Austrian dialect, which itself is an offshoot of German) adopted many words from Hebrew and Yiddish. The Viennese were anti-Semitic when they adopted these words, just as they were in later years, during the Nazi-led Holocaust. To this day the Jewish influence on the Viennese dialect is not well accepted or even well known.

85. Brodkin, *How Jews Became White Folks*.

86. Gunnar Myrdal, *Challenge to Affluence* (New York: Random House, 1963), 10.

87. Herbert Gans, "From 'Underclass' to 'Undercaste': Some Observations about the Future of the Post-Industrial Economy and Its Major Victims," in *Urban Poverty and the Underclass*, ed. Enzo Mingione (Cambridge, MA: Blackwell, 1996), 141–152; Loïc Wacquant, *Urban Outcasts: A Comparative Sociology of Advanced Marginality* (Malden, MA: Polity Press, 2008).

88. Steinberg, *Ethnic Myth*, esp. chap. 4.

89. Naomi Klein, *No Logo* (New York: Picador, 2009 [2000]), 74–76, italics are in the original.

90. Mary Patillo-McCoy, *Black Picket Fences: Privilege and Peril among the Black Middle Class* (Chicago: University of Chicago Press, 1999).

91. Kesha S. Moore, "Gentrification in Black Face?: The Return of the Black Middle Class to Urban Neighborhoods," *Urban Geography* 29, no. 8 (2008): 1–25.

92. The Bureau of Labor Statistics posts unemployment rates online at *www.bls.gov*; these data were obtained from *http://www.bls.gov/news.release/empsit.t02.htm*, and accessed September 30, 2012.

93. Ian Woods, "More Than Half of Young Black Men Jobless," *SkyNews.com, http:// news.sky.com/story/2267/more-than-half-of-young-black-men-jobless*, accessed September 30, 2012.

94. Becky Petit, *Invisible Men: Mass Incarceration and the Myth of Black Progress* (New York: Russell Sage, 2012).

95. Jay MacLeod, *Ain't No Makin' It: Aspirations and Attainment in a Low-Income Neighborhood* (Boulder, CO: Westview Press, [1987] 1995).

96. Hernandez-Reguant, "Kwanzaa and the US Ethnic Mosaic."

97. Harris, "Plessy"; and Cheryl Harris, "Whiteness as Property," *Harvard Law Review* 106, no. 8 (1993): 1710–1791.

98. Aldon D. Morris, *Origins of the Civil Rights Movement: Black Communities Organizing for Change* (New York: Free Press, 1986).

99. Davis, *Who Is Black?*

100. Ibid., 8.

101. The Brown Foundation, *"Brown v. Board of Education* Myths and Truths," at *http:// brownvboard.org/mythsandtruths*, accessed February 23, 2010.

102. Derrick Bell, *Silent Covenants: Brown v. Board of Education and the Unfulfilled Hopes for Racial Reform* (Oxford: Oxford University Press, 2004), 3.

103. "The initial court ruling rendered in 1954 that determined racial segregation in public education was unconstitutional is known as Brown I. The court implementation mandate of 'with all deliberate speed' in 1955 is known as Brown II. In 1979, three young African American attorneys in Topeka petitioned the court to reopen the original Brown case to examine whether or not the local School Board had in fact ended all vestiges of segregation in public schools. That case is known as Brown III, which resulted in Topeka Public Schools building three magnet schools to comply with the court's findings" (Brown Foundation, *"Brown v. Board of Education* Myths and Truths"). Brown II mandated that "all deliberate speed" should be used to desegregate schools, but did not specify how speedy the change needs to be, and left its implementation to local jurisdictions. Thus, many understood it to be a marker of retrenchment.

104. Stephen Steinberg, "Silent Covenants: Brown v. Board of Education and the Unfulfilled Hopes for Racial Reform," *Journal of Blacks in Higher Education* 44 (Summer 2004): 122–125.

105. Stephen Steinberg, "False Optimism on Race," *Socialism and Democracy* 17, no. 1 (Winter–Spring 2003): 13–24.

106. Bashi, *Survival of the Knitted*, 2007.

107. See data provided by Pearson Education, in their higher education database "Infoplease" found at *http://www.infoplease.com/ipa/A0881455.html*, and accessed January 8, 2012.

108. Ibid.

109. Ibid.

110. Michelle Alexander, *The New Jim Crow: Mass Incarceration in the Age of Colorblindness* (New York: New Press, 2010), 175.

111. Ibid.

112. Petit, *Invisible Men*.

113. Rebecca Skloot writes, "When I tell people the story of Henrietta Lacks and her cells, their first question is usually *Wasn't it illegal for doctors to take Henrietta's cells without*

her knowledge? Don't doctors have to tell you when they use your cells in research? The answer is no—not in 1951, and not in 2009, when this book went to press." Tissue research is not covered under the Federal Policy for the Protection of Human Subjects because the researchers don't ever know the identity of the tissue "donors" and if that's the case it's not considered research on humans. See Rebecca Skloot, *The Immortal Life of Henrietta Lacks* (New York: Crown, 2010), 315, emphasis hers.

114. Harriet A. Washington, *Medical Apartheid: The Dark History of Medical Experimentation on Black Americans from Colonial Times to the Present* (New York: Anchor, 2006).

115. Tommy Stevenson, "'Post-racial' politics?" *Tuscaloosa News*, February 24, 2000, *http://politibits.blogs.tuscaloosanews.com/10262/post-racial-politics/*, accessed August 13, 2010.

116. Daniel Henninger (Deputy Editor of the *Wall Street Journal*'s editorial page and award-winning editorial columnist who has written on "postracial" politics) would add to this list Harold Ford Jr. (who lost a Tennessee race for Senate by three votes); Michael Steele, former Lieutenant Governor of Maryland; and J. C. Watts, former congressman from Oklahoma. See Daniel Henninger, "Obama and Race," *Wall Street Journal*, February 21, 2008, A16.

117. Steinberg, *Ethnic Myth*.

118. Alexander, *The New Jim Crow*.

119. Anthony W. Marx, *Making Race and Nation: A Comparison of South Africa, the United States, and Brazil*, Cambridge Studies in Comparative Politics (Cambridge, UK: Cambridge University Press, 1998).

CHAPTER SEVEN

1. Barack Obama, *Dreams from My Father: A Story of Race and Inheritance* (New York: Crown, 2007).

2. David Theo Goldberg, "The Tale of Two Obamas," *Qualitative Sociology* 35, no. 2 (2012): 201–212. Here, I reprint Goldberg's (202) own footnote, made at this juncture in the quoted paragraph. "'Teabagging' is a reference to the Tea Party Movement in the US that emerged politically in 2009 largely to protest what its loose coalition of conservative and overwhelmingly white members criticize as the prevailing tax and spend policies dominating the US Congress. It is committed to smaller government, a literalist reading of the US Constitution, unqualified individual freedoms and the right of individuals to use guns in self defense. The movement takes its name from the Boston Tea Party that led to the American Revolution in 1776 the mantra for which was 'no taxation without representation.' 'Teabagging' characterizes the criticism members of the movement direct at any politician they detest, chiefly at President Obama, who is derided as a socialist, anti-American, and Islamic."

3. Toby Harnden, "Barack Obama faces 30 death threats a day, stretching US Secret Service," *The Daily Telegraph*, August 3, 2009, *http://www.telegraph.co.uk/news/worldnews/barackobama/5967942/Barack-Obama-faces-30-death-threats-a-day-stretching-US-Secret-Service.html*, accessed October 5, 2012.

4. Bashi, "Racial Categories Matter."

5. Jacobson, *Whiteness of a Different Color*, 6, 9.

6. Goldberg, "Tale of Two Obamas," 209.

7. Blumer, "Race Prejudice as a Sense of Group Position."

8. Zulema Valdez, *The New Entrepreneurs: How Race, Class, and Gender Shape American Enterprise* (Stanford, CA: Stanford University Press, 2011).

9. Hattam, *In the Shadow of Race*, 41.

10. Stephen Steinberg (in *Race Relations: A Critique* [Stanford, CA: Stanford Social Science, 2007]) made this point well before I ever did, and has made a career of comment-

ing on this very problem. But I won't put the onus completely on him to do all the work. I give here just one example of my own. Jennifer Lee (*Civility in the City* [Cambridge, MA: Harvard University Press, 2002]) argues in her introduction (6) that civility between urban retail merchants and black customers is commonplace "because merchants actively work to manage tensions and smooth out incidents before they escalate into racially charged anger," and in her conclusion (182), "that civility prevails in everyday life because merchants and their employees actively work to preserve it." There is little indication in the work that civility routinely can be expected in interactions with a black person, that black people routinely make efforts to maintain civil relations with racial and ethnic others, or that black people are routinely civil, period.

11. I have written similar analyses elsewhere. See Bashi and McDaniel, "A Theory of Immigration and Racial Stratification"; Bashi, "Neither Ignorance nor Bliss"; and Bashi, *Survival of the Knitted.*

12. Mills, *The Racial Contract*, 11.

13. Hephzibah Strmic-Pawl, "What Are You? Multiracial Identity and the Persistence of Racism in a 'Post-Racial Society,'" Dissertation, University of Virginia, 2012.

14. The controversy is summarized in a blog post by John Avarosis, "Did Mitt Romney adopt KKK slogan 'Keep America American?'" found at *http://americablog.com/2011/12/did -romney-adopt-kkk-slogan-keep-america-american.html*, accessed March 10, 2013.

15. See NBC News report and video segment by Samuel King, August 22, 2012, "KKK Monument Renovations Cause Controversy," found at *http://www2.nbc26.tv/news/2012/ aug/22/kkk-monument-renovations-cause-controversy-ar-4390300/*, and accessed October 1, 2012.

16. See the documentary film *Hate.com: Extremists on the Internet*, from HBO's (Home Box Office's) America Undercover series, 2000.

17. Evelynn Hammonds, Professor of History of Science and Afro-American Studies, Harvard University, spoke these words near the end of the 2003 documentary film *Race: The Power of an Illusion—Episode I: The Difference Between Us*, California Newsreel.

INDEX

ABCs of Attraction, 85–86
affirmative action, 154, 155, 156
African Americans: African languages spoken by, 213n83; vs. Afro-Caribbeans, 30, 130–33, 134; vs. Chinese, 77–79, 80–81, 85, 199n35, 200n54; civility among, 181, 215n10; culture of, 157–62, 166, 167; English spoken by, 157–58, 213n83; as ethnic group, 15, 21, 130, 135, 146, 147–48, 164, 165, 168–69; ethnic project of, 15, 139–40, 144–49, 157, 160; incarceration of, 166–67, 168; and intelligence tests, 93, 125–26; vs. Jews, 144, 160; in middle class, 160–61, 164; migration of, 142, 143, 156; naming/renaming of, 9, 144–49, 165, 211n41; racial equality advocated by, 6, 104, 164–65; and racial uplift of other ethnic groups, 5–7, 14, 15–16, 43, 73–76, 107, 134–36, 158, 164, 165, 169, 178, 179–80, 181; relations with Afro-Caribbeans, 131–32; relations with Chinese, 80, 81, 82, 101, 200nn54,57; relations with indentured servants, 140–41; relations with Irish, 72–73, 73–74, 76, 101; relations with Italians, 88, 90, 92, 101, 202n103; relations with Jews, 97–98, 101; relations with Mexicans, 105, 123, 125, 127, 129; relations with Native Americans, 104, 105, 106, 107, 111–17, 134, 143, 206n43; relations with white Texans, 124–25; during Revolutionary War, 144, 148, 150–51,

211n46; skin color of, 142–43, 162–63; as soldiers, 148, 149–52; vs. South Asians, 178, 184; unemployment among, 152, 154, 155–56, 161; work done by, 6, 152–57, 168. *See also* mixed-race persons; race; racism
African American Vernacular English (AAVE), 157–58
African Methodist Episcopal Church (AME Church), 144
Afro-Caribbeans: vs. African Americans, 30, 104, 130–33, 134; and English colonialism, 130; ethnic project of, 15, 131–33, 135; as immigrants, 8, 130–33, 142; vs. Native Americans, 104, 134; relations with African Americans, 131–32; as second-generation, 133; transnational networks among, 131, 132–33; work done by, 131, 132–33
Afrocentricity, 161
Alabama, 108, 143, 183
Alba, Richard, 91
Alger, Horatio, 12–13, 188n3
Allen, Theodore: on blackness and slavery, 55, 69–70, 71; on English colonialism in Ireland, 71; *The Invention of the White Race*, 196n46, 209n1; on race, 59, 196n46; on racialization, 190n10, 196n46; on whiteness, 53, 59, 196n46
Amalgamated Clothing Workers Union (ACWU), 94
American Demographic Magazine, 211n41

Stanford Studies in
COMPARATIVE RACE AND ETHNICITY

Published in collaboration with the Center for Comparative Studies in Race and Ethnicity, Stanford University

SERIES EDITORS
Hazel Rose Markus
Paula M.L. Moya

EDITORIAL BOARD
H. Samy Alim
Gordon Chang
Gary Segura
C. Matthew Snipp

This series publishes outstanding scholarship that focuses centrally on comparative studies of race and ethnicity. Rather than exploring the experiences and conditions of a single racial or ethnic group, this series looks across racial and ethnic groups to take a more complex, dynamic, and interactive approach to understanding these social categories.

On Making Sense: Queer Race Narratives of Intelligibility
Ernesto Javier Martínez
2012